After Campus Sexual Assault

After Campus Sexual Assault

A Guide for Parents

Susan B. Sorenson

ROWMAN & LITTLEFIELD
Lanham • Boulder • New York • London

Published by Rowman & Littlefield
An imprint of The Rowman & Littlefield Publishing Group, Inc.
4501 Forbes Boulevard, Suite 200, Lanham, Maryland 20706
www.rowman.com

6 Tinworth Street, London SE11 5AL, United Kingdom

British Library Cataloguing in Publication Information Available

Library of Congress Cataloging-in-Publication Data
Names: Sorenson, Susan B., author.
Title: After campus sexual assault : a guide for parents / Susan B. Sorenson.
Description: Lanham : Rowman & Littlefield, [2021] | Includes bibliographical references and index. | Summary: "This book looks at the real stories of college students assaulted on campus and the steps they and their families can take together to acknowledge their experience and begin healing"— Provided by publisher.
Identifiers: LCCN 2020049704 (print) | LCCN 2020049705 (ebook) | ISBN 9781538117729 (cloth) | ISBN 9781538117736 (epub)
Subjects: LCSH: Rape in universities and colleges—United States. | Women college students—Violence against—United States. | Rape victims—Services for—United States. | Parents of rape victims—United States.
Classification: LCC LB2345.3.R37 S67 2021 (print) | LCC LB2345.3.R37 (ebook) | DDC 371.7/8—dc23
LC record available at https://lccn.loc.gov/2020049704
LC ebook record available at https://lccn.loc.gov/2020049705

Contents

Acknowledgments

I am grateful to the students, parents, and university staff members whose openness made this book possible. The trust they placed in me is a gift.

Preparation of the manuscript was a solitary, but not solo, endeavor. I extend my appreciation to the many people who helped in all sorts of ways, especially:

Bill Meyers, Sarah Ricks, Janice Asher, and Tanya Jain for their astute comments on drafts of the chapters. Their suggestions improved the work in ways big and small.

Joan Parker, Suzanne Staszak-Silva, Linda Carbone, Michael Wilde, and Erica Wassall, who helped make the idea of a book into reality.

Katherine Camabreri for her wonderful photographs.

The Ortner Center on Violence and Abuse at the University of Pennsylvania, whose support allowed me to take a one-semester break from teaching in order to write.

Kas, Lori Ann, Roberta, and Sarah. Each believed in this work from its inception and provided encouragement and support at times I needed it most.

Richard and Michael, for everything.

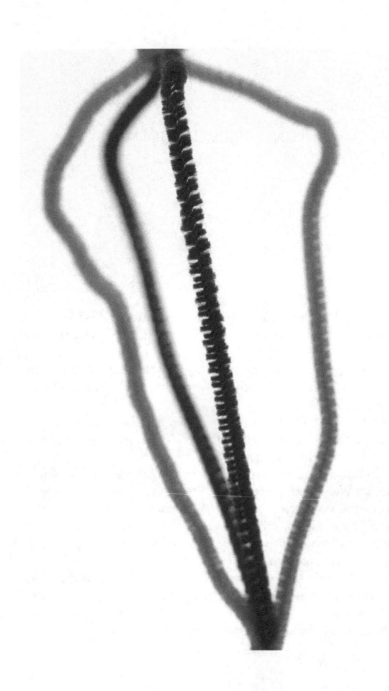

Preface

It was a perfect, cloudless August day. Interrupting her own greeting at an end-of-summer party, Connie froze and blurted out that her daughter, Angela, had just been raped on a study abroad program. "I got back last night from seeing her," Connie said. "Can we talk later?" I was shocked and worried. What exactly had happened? How badly hurt was Angela? Where was she? Connie engages others easily, and she kept it up throughout the party. I kept wondering if anyone else noticed her distracted look as she chattered away.

As the guests began to leave, we met in the shade of a floral umbrella and Connie spoke:

She called, sobbing, in the middle of the night wanting to come back. It was two guys, strangers she met at a bar that night. We got her a ticket and flew her back right away, and I flew out to meet her at her school. Now she wants to return. Going to that country has always been her dream and she's spent years learning the language. But the study abroad program isn't sure they want her back, which is really pissing her off – "I didn't do anything wrong. I'm the *victim* here." But the school wants her to stay on campus and get counseling. We don't know what to do. We've been turning ourselves inside out trying to figure out the right thing to do. We've been searching for some guidance somewhere, but there are no books or anything. There are a few blog posts, but who the hell are those people? What should we do?

As I hugged her husband goodbye, I whispered in his ear, "Connie told me about Angie. I'm really sorry." He looked so sad.

We had known each other for years and were more than acquaintances but less than share-our-secrets friends. I could count probably on one hand the number of times we had talked on the phone; email was our medium. So I waited a day or two and sent an email offering my ear and shoulder and suggesting that she might want to consider writing about her experience. (She has a popular blog and wrote a genre-busting textbook in her profession.) Whether it was something that she tucked away and never showed to anyone else, something she blogged about one day, or something more formal such as an article or book, I thought it might be useful as she struggled to figure out how to help her daughter. Her response was swift: "This is a book for you."

It was decades ago when someone first suggested that I write a book. I was part of a team involved with one of the first community-based studies of sexual assault. Funded by the National Center for the Prevention and Control of Rape, which was part of the National Institutes of Health, more than three thousand women and men were interviewed in English and Spanish in the early 1980s. I joined the team as a postdoctoral scholar at the UCLA School of Public Health. It was a groundbreaking study – one of the first to document that when a woman is sexually assaulted, it's likely to be by a man she knows – and the resulting articles were visible and highly cited. Back then I laughed off the suggestion.

Connie's statements intrigued me. How was it possible that there was "nothing out there"? I checked and also couldn't find anything written for parents faced with the sexual assault of their child during college.

I thought about it. Although I had been clinically trained and had a wide range of experience, most of my knowledge came from my public health research. And that wouldn't do. Public health focuses on prevention, populations, and policy. We were dealing with something different here – something after the fact and intensely personal. Hoping to pair the discipline of a researcher with the sensitivities of a clinician,

I had one overriding thought: Listen. And so I listened to young women who had been sexually assaulted while a student, I listened to their mothers and fathers, and I listened to campus service providers.

I wrote this book with the hope of helping young women who have been the victim of a sexual assault as they decide whether and how to tell their parents and of helping parents understand. Watching a child cope with the aftermath of a traumatic event can be heartrending. The book is filled with quotes from hundreds of pages of transcripts from my interviews with dozens of daughters, mothers, fathers, and campus staff members. Their experiences, a slice of their world at a slice of time, are best told in their own words.

Introduction

This is not a book I wanted to write. I wanted to write a book about the end of sexual violence, how views of women had changed so much that sexual assault was rare. But that's not a book anyone can write.

This probably is not a book you want to read. But you have reason to pick it up. You want to help, to understand. You will make mistakes, and maybe you've already said and done things that you consider mistakes. Keep going.

Don't feel you need to read the book in a certain order. In fact, I anticipate that you will start with the chapter that is most relevant to you and skip around after that. So some ideas will appear in more than one chapter.

To put together the book, I designed a project in which I would talk with college students who had been sexually assaulted to learn about their decisions regarding whether and what to tell others, including their parents, about the assault. For the sake of simplicity, I decided to focus on young women. Given the additional complexities of male sexual assault, a separate chapter on sons would not be sufficient. Perhaps I or someone else will write that book one day. And maybe one day I or someone else will write a book for parents of young men – it's mostly young men – who perpetrate campus sexual assault. And, of course, there are students who define themselves as being outside the male-female gender binary, whose rates of campus sexual assault are comparable to those of undergraduate women.[1] But for now, given that very little has been written for the parents of the most common victims – daughters – I wrote with them in mind.

The work first needed to be reviewed by the Institutional Review Board (known more commonly as the human subjects protection committee) at the University of Pennsylvania, where I am a professor, to be certain that it met federal research ethics standards. After submitting an application with eleven attachments, responding to their questions, and obtaining their approval, I set out at four Philadelphia-area colleges and universities to find students who had been sexually assaulted while at college. I sought students who had made decisions – even if they were "for now" decisions – about whom to talk with about the assault rather than with those whose experience was so recent that they were in the midst of deciding. If a student had told her parent(s), I asked her permission to contact them to see if they would be willing to talk with me. Flyers about the study were posted in women's bathroom stalls in widely used buildings on four campuses.

Six hours after the flyers were posted, I got the first call. Eventually I would meet with twenty young women of all shapes, sizes, colors, cultures, and classes. Scrubbed clean and carefully made up. One by one for months. Shy, gregarious, purposeful, they told a complete stranger about having been sexually assaulted. For most, the assault had been a year or so before they contacted me, but for some had been three years earlier; the most recent had been ten weeks prior. For some, I was one of many they told; for others, one of a few; and for others yet, I was the only one. Some came because "I want to help someone else," others because "I didn't know what it would be like to talk about and, well, I guess I'm here because I want to see what it's like." Whether motivated by altruism, curiosity, or seeking the safety of a stranger, they spoke of parties, lots of alcohol, guys they had just met, and long-term boyfriends. Some were monogamous, others part of the hookup scene, and others not sexually active. They were studying business, engineering, science, and the arts. They lived in residence halls, substandard housing near campus, and fancy high-rise apartments. They were Every Girl on campus.

"Girl" is their label. I am of a generation for whom "girl" was a demeaning way to refer to someone who for years has possessed the ability to produce a child. But "young woman" appears to seem foreign to current college students who identify as female; they call themselves "girls," not "young women." I don't have the sense that they are claiming the label with irony; they simply see themselves as girls. And gendered language has its limits. As one student wrote in an online discussion post in one of my recent courses:

> "woman" has a connotation of age and maturity (e.g., "You're becoming a woman"), "girl," in contrast, has a connotation of youth, "lady" has a connotation of maturity, but also status, class, and prestige, "female" has a biological, reproductive and almost reductive connotation (and denotation honestly) that makes it ineffective, "gal" has a very colloquial connotation (and I believe historically is even negative) that prevents it from being widely applied.

So I'll call them girls.

Do college students who identify as male call themselves boys? No. But they don't call themselves men either – it's "guys," a label that spans the years and sometimes the sexes. (There are a few exceptions: Harvard men have always been Harvard men.) Each of the girls who spoke with me relayed an incident involving a male, which is consistent with research findings: males are the perpetrators of 99.1 percent of the sexual assaults of undergraduate girls.[2] So the question remained of what to call them. The students who spoke with me either used the term "the guy" or called him by his name. I avoided "offender" and "assailant" given their criminal justice implications. "Harm-doer," a label that is not likely to be in the vocabulary of most parents but one some college students use in discussions these days, seems distant and abstract. After considerable deliberation, I chose "perpetrator" because it conveys the reality that the girls felt that harm had intentionally been done to them.

I typically refer to the girls as "girls who had been sexually assaulted at college." The decision to use what's called person-first language keeps the focus where I believe it belongs: on the person who has experienced a trauma. The language choice also avoids the current controversy regarding whether they should be called victims or survivors. For the record, if asked to choose, I consider persons in the immediate aftermath of a traumatic incident to be victims. As they pick up and start to put the pieces together again, as they grow in unexpected ways, they become survivors.

About half of the girls were people of color, and we can surmise that they have experienced specific stressors that make them victims and survivors in additional ways. Whether U.S.-born or immigrants or the children of immigrants, these students carried their identity into the white-majority institutions of higher education they attended. Ethnic and cultural considerations related to the assault were mentioned by some of them, often in general terms, and appear in subsequent pages as they were told to me. Perhaps such content was perceived as not relevant to their decisions about whom to talk with about the incident, or maybe it was consciously or unconsciously screened out while talking with me, a white woman. (I can recommend *Surviving the Silence: Black Women's Stories of Rape* by Charlotte Pierce-Baker and *Dear Sister: Letters from Survivors of Sexual Violence*, which was edited by Lisa Factora-Borchers.[3]) I tried to stay close to what each told me rather than make inferences or draw broad conclusions about the various groups of which they are members.

Most had told friends; telling a parent was far less common. Only three of the first ten girls who spoke with me had told a parent, so given my focus I posted different flyers to recruit those who had talked with their parents; all of the next ten had told a parent. I was keenly aware that the girls were telling me things that they hadn't told – and some planned never to tell – the adults who had devoted years of their lives to them. With varying degrees of comfort, they were living an "as if" life with their folks – "as if" the assault hadn't happened.

But when they do tell, what comes next? I decided to supplement the stories of the daughters with accounts of parents; after talking with college girls, I met with eighteen parents – eleven mothers and seven fathers. They were parents of some of the girls who had talked with me or responded to a variety of posted notices. Some came to my office, others I boarded a train or plane to talk with in a hotel meeting room or connected with via online video. I was hesitant at first to connect online, thinking it would feel too impersonal, but parents and their offspring at a distance communicate via FaceTime, WhatsApp, Zoom, and other such media so commonly these days that any initial awkwardness quickly gave way. Not surprisingly, like their daughters, they were of all shapes, sizes, and backgrounds, some with a high school education, others with graduate and professional degrees; they were of various ages and stages of life, some young and wrinkle-free, some working multiple jobs to put their kids through school, and others comfortably retired.

Given the ubiquity of campus sexual assault, a lot of students and many parents have to deal with assault and its aftermath. And few know how. Colleges and universities that receive federal dollars – with rare exception, virtually all of them – are required to provide sexual assault prevention programming. Sexual assault is a standard topic at freshman orientations across the nation, and student groups organize to address the topic through campus advocacy, trainings, performances, marches, and support groups. Special services are in place for victims at student health and campus counseling. But for parents? That's another story.

Talking about the assault and its effects brought up a lot of emotions – in the daughters, the parents, and me. Some were dry-eyed through the conversation, while others wept. Glistening eyes quietly spilling tears was not uncommon. Sometimes simply extending a box of tissues gave the person a chance to take a few breaths and gather themselves. When I remembered, I offered a few plush "pipe cleaners," like those used in crafts activities. They provided a physical outlet for some of the discomfort, and interviewees twisted them into tight balls, spirals, and hearts. Some took them when we finished, others left them behind. Images of some that were left behind are incorporated into the book.

I also listened to a variety of college administrators and service providers at the University of Pennsylvania. They included campus police officers whose primary responsibility is to respond to reports of sexual assault, a campus mental health service provider who developed coordinated individual and group services for victims and offenders, a physician at student health services, staff of the women's center that houses several of the campus activist groups addressing sexual assault, a university staff member whose sole responsibility is to initiate and coordinate emergency interventions for students in crisis, staff associated with the university's study abroad program, one of the campus chaplains, the university's sexual assault prevention coordinator, and one of the sexual violence investigative officers charged with investigating incidents reported to campus authorities and determining a resolution that is sufficiently satisfactory to both parties. My goal in obtaining their unique perspectives is to provide parents with a window into campus policies and procedures, as well as specialized services.

During my decades in academia, I have taught courses on violence (perhaps most relevant here is a course on violence in relationships), conducted scientific research and published articles in scholarly journals, and served on nonprofit boards and government agency advisory committees. I have served on faculty panels for hearings to help determine whether sexual misconduct occurred and, if so, to recommend an appropriate sanction. Sexual assault has been, in effect, part of my job description for almost thirty years. Yet I learned entirely new perspectives from the nearly fifty people who generously spoke with me about their lives and their work.

The book is organized into ten chapters. The first set of chapters provide essential context. Chapter 1, "College Today," acknowledges the excitement, anxiety, and relief daughters and parents feel when she begins college. Parents who attended college can't assume, however, that their often rosy recollections of those years will be the experience of their daughters. Some things are the same, some aren't. Chapter 2, "The Big Picture," presents the historical and social context for considering campus sexual assault. Chapter 3, "How Families Work," acknowledges that neither the girl nor the family are a blank slate; by the time they get to college, most students have dealt with other trying circumstances that have shaped who they are and how they deal with the world. It also addresses the different ways that families function and how those functions can be challenged as well as reinforced when dealing with the crisis of a sexual assault.

Chapter 4, "So What Happened?" outlines the range of experiences that comprise sexual assault; it's information that parents rarely get in detail. Chapter 5, "Giving and Getting the News," talks about girls' decisions to tell or not tell a parent and the parent's initial reactions, sometimes helpful and sometimes the source of additional stress. It also describes the definitions and labels daughters give to their experiences, a process that shapes the conversations, if any, that follow. Chapter 6, "Fathers," recognizes that fathers play an important role in their daughters' lives. Although not all did, when it came to sexual assault, it was common for fathers to stay on the sidelines. Chapter 7, "Mothers," addresses the unique role of mothers. Typically the go-to parent for emotional support, mothers often provide substantial logistical advice and action. They also provide a reference point of sorts: not surprisingly, given rates of sexual assault, some mothers had been victims too.

In chapter 8, "Campus Resources," I talk about the resources that are available to students who have been sexually assaulted and how to get help navigating them. Surprisingly few contact any campus resource at all. Knowing what's available, parents can help their daughter get what she needs. Chapter 9, "Struggling and Problem Solving," asserts that campus sexual assault is more than a single event. Daughters and parents – even those who aren't told about the incident – deal with the event and its aftermath for an extended period, often negotiating and renegotiating their relationship in the process. The chapter focuses on the immediate and intermediate aftermath. In chapter 10, "Look to Where You Want to Go," I convey some of the ways in which daughters and families begin to come to terms with what happened and their hopes for the future. It acknowledges that, like a rock in your shoe, the experience of having been sexually assaulted is always there; it might become less salient over time, but it's always there.

Each chapter contains multiple quotes from those who spoke with me. The quotes have been lightly edited for clarity. To protect their privacy, I created pseudonyms for the girls. The names are used interchangeably; for example, a quote from "Jenny" might be attributed to Jenny one time, to Jocelyn another time, and to Leah another time. I did this so that parents, if recognizing a word or phrasing that is unique to that person or family, would not be able to track their daughter's statements throughout the book. Mothers, fathers, and college service providers and support staff members are referred to by their role. They, like I, hope their experiences provide helpful guidance.

CHAPTER 1

College Today

When you're that age, you're just leaving home and you want to feel like, Oh, I have this, I'm on top of this, I'm careful, I know what's going on. . . . I mean, you get it, you hear about it, but it's weird – there's some disconnect between it and that this could actually happen to me. —Mother

I think the tendency is sort of to say, Okay, our kids have gone to college, we did our job. We just pay the tuition and good luck, shake hands, have a good life. In many ways, they need you the most during college – it's a really rough transition even in perfect circumstances. —Mother

The college application process is brutal. Devouring hours that might be spent in more leisurely pursuits, its beginning is typically considered to be fall of the junior year of high school when Preliminary Scholastic Aptitude Tests (PSATs) are administered in classrooms across the country. By then, adults' queries about classes and sports have already given way to "So where are you thinking of going to college?" and "What do you plan to do with your life?" These are daunting questions, especially for people who aren't old enough to have a driver's license. No wonder they feel pressure. Yes, some of the pressure is internal and some of it is parental, but as a society we seem to think that they should have answers – or at the very least should be contemplating answers – to these questions. The decisions about whether and where to go to college loom large for years. They occupy a huge space in the family, often the last couple of years that, barring a "boomerang" experience, a child will live at home.

Part of the college preparation process includes parents issuing warnings and imparting wisdom to their children. It's been decades since my great aunt and uncle made the six-hour drive shortly before I left for college to caution me to never leave a drink unattended because it might be "mickey-ed." What parents told me about preparing their daughters these days sounds remarkably similar. One mother said, "When she went to college I told her, 'Don't be alone. Even if you think you know the boy, don't bring him in your room alone. You just don't know. The way the dormitories are built, somebody may not hear you if you're calling for help.'" And a father sounded as if he and his wife had drilled warnings into their daughter:

> We have talked about it since she was a little, little thing. . . . We had probably 5,000 conversations with her about things you don't do. You don't accept an open container of something to drink at a college party because you don't know if someone put something into it. . . . And you don't trust the seemingly nice boy who you don't really know, who's being really nice to you and offers to walk you back alone from a party. . . . How do you, as a parent, teach your child to be a little less trusting and a little less gullible and a little less naïve? And frankly, do you want to try to teach them that, because naiveté and gullibility is delightful, it's goodness of heart, and you don't wanna just snatch that out either.

Relief vies with pride as the dominant emotion of both parents and students. We've made it! You're in! (I smiled when a father told me "[She's at] her first-choice school, she applied early decision and got in. It was like God himself reached down and gave His blessing and said, 'You may go to this wonderful institution.'") So it's perhaps understandable that students' first year of college is marked by tension release: too much partying, too little sleep. And sometimes by avoidance: inconsistent class attendance, not wanting to deal with parents. Parents, in turn, drop them off at their residence hall and return home with nostalgia for all the sports games gone by, the music performances they'll never hear again, and the late-night worrying before their child returns home that they won't be doing. On some level both parents and students think that, at last, all that is over. It's not.

Rosy Memories

Many of the parents whose daughters spoke with me had themselves gone to college. And those who hadn't gone had created their own images of what it would have been like. This section is about those memories – real, distorted, or imagined – of college days.

Sometimes we think that our kids' experience of college will be like our own. For many parents, college is where and when they felt like they grew up. They had a sense of belonging, of feeling that they were all out there discovering the world together. College felt fresh, new, and safe, and things were only going to get better:

> I remember going to college and being like, I don't know what I'm gonna major in. I think I'm gonna be a computer major. And so I tried engineering and then, I was, like, yeah, not gonna be an engineer. . . . We used to go to the football games, we used to tailgate; our daughter says nobody goes to the football games now, they don't have the time. It was known that we had to study really hard. But you studied all day and then at 10:00 you'd go out, you still would go and do things. —Mother

> One of the things that my wife and I really respected and loved about the institution is that the students, by and large, seemed to be there to learn and were intellectually curious. A good number wanted to better themselves and have a better future than their parents. There was a lot of the American dream all wrapped up into the fabric of the school and a certain amount of industriousness but in a kinda lighthearted, casual way. Kind of a mutually supportive "We're here, we're gonna do better." . . . There wasn't a lot of backbiting, there wasn't a lot of undercutting. People would get C's and be cool with it. —Father

The rose-colored glasses come off when parents start to hear from their children about college life today. They learn that the college that their daughter is in is not like the college they went to. College no longer is an ivory tower set apart from the world (if it ever was); the issues that society is struggling with are very much alive on campus. And perhaps the students coming in are different too. A mother told me that, although her daughter was enrolled at the school that she and her husband attended, "It's a very different school, a very different school from when we went there." Another parent said that times have changed: "We were all still quite youthful and full of marvel and amazement, and [the university] opened our eyes. The kids going in now, they're pretty knowledgeable. . . . [I]t's a different gestalt now."

Freshman Year

I tell students that the first year of college is largely about finding their tribe or tribes. They know how to learn, they know how to write papers and take tests, so they'll manage the introductory classes they'll take during their first year. It's the sense of belonging, of finding people they trust and who will have their back, that is important to establish. Having a cohesive friend group is an important antidote to the anxiety and confusion that are inherent in living away from home for the first time and all the changes and challenges that lie ahead. They have just left, after all, friends they probably have had for years and the watchful eyes of multiple adults.

They will find their tribes, but it takes a while, and tribes and affiliations change and grow over the years.

Everybody is trying to act cool as they figure it out. (I recall going into the women's room between every class as a first-week college freshman. I'd go into a stall, close the door, sit down without any need or intention to use the facility, and pull out a crumpled campus map to figure out how to get to my next class. Face-saving is important for all of us, right?) The people they meet and hang out with during the first weeks of school might not be people they're even talking with by the end of the semester.

The beginning of a girl's freshman year sometimes is referred to as the Red Zone – and it has nothing to do with a football team being between the twenty-yard line and the goal. The first six to twelve weeks are called the Red Zone because they are considered to be a high-risk time for sexual assault. The unfamiliar setting and booze-filled back-to-school parties pose a particular risk for first-year college girls who might have little experience with unrestricted drinking and are trying to meet people but don't yet have an established network of friends who look out for one another. One mother described it like "the demon came out her. She wouldn't come home, she wanted to be out, wouldn't have really good conversations."

A "demon" that comes out in one student becomes a problem for an unwitting roommate. In hindsight, parents were keenly aware of the challenges of the first year of college:

> Her freshman year was not good for a number of reasons. . . . She also had a whackadoodle roommate . . . and she was struggling with her grades because she was taking classes that were not a particularly good fit for her. She had some good friends, but not great friends. It was just a bit of a train wreck of a freshman year. She kept reporting back about the level of competition and the emotional strain of the students. Her mom and I asked her many times if she wanted to transfer, and she said no. . . . The assaults [*the daughter was sexually assaulted twice during her first year of college*] were a terrible part of this really sad year. —Father

> The freshman and sophomore year were pretty intense for her. Everything has always come very easily for our daughter. At college she was pre-med, and it was not coming easily for her. . . . My husband and I had met at [the same university] . . . she'd romanticized the place in a lot of ways. —Mother

Competition

The world students are navigating is different than it was a generation ago. The entire context of college is simply not the same. I recall how the recession of 2008 changed students; it wasn't just the economy that crashed, their confidence in a future that would be better than the one their parents had was shaken. Maybe they weren't going to be able to be and get more than their parents after all. They were frightened and ramped up their efforts at school. Some seemed to approach it as another hurdle. They wanted to prove to their parents and themselves that they could succeed and excel even when the U.S. and global economies were crumbling. The economy has improved substantially since then, and perhaps the sense of "not enough" has receded, but maybe not given that income inequality continues to grow. The COVID-19 pandemic, which is upon us as I write, can be expected to have similar reverberations.

Parents spoke of the increased competition both on and off campus. As one father said:

> I think, in a global economy, the level of competition is greater. There are just more people competing for what actually is a shrinking number of jobs. While we were in college, we saw international students, but I think now kids in these universities understand that they're competing with other kids around the world – the level of competition is a lot more. I think that the divide between the haves and the have-nots is growing. It's very palpable. Even young kids realize that if you fall on the wrong side of the line, you can be impoverished just like that. You get out of school and you're not in the top, best-paying jobs, you're in okay-paying jobs, and you have a serious health condition and then you're bankrupt. It's very easy to fall on the wrong side of the line. I think kids see a lot of failure and a lot of risks and a lot of worries and concerns, and they're getting it younger and younger.

The competitiveness that students experience with their peers can affect friendship patterns. It might not feel safe to turn to a roommate after being sexually assaulted if that person is applying for the same award or seeking the same job.

Grades don't matter much in college – that is, unless the student plans to apply to medical school, graduate school, or some other advanced degree program. In fact, as one recruiter told me, if, two years after graduating, a job applicant still wants to talk about their major and GPA in college, that application goes to the bottom of the pile. Employers want to know what someone can do, not what grades they got. That said, faculty hold a lot of power with grades and letters of reference, and in small schools and departments, students can be concerned that one instructor might say something that would negatively affect the perceptions of other faculty. Being a faculty member myself, I see both extremes: students who seem taken aback that their work could be considered anything other than stellar and are not hesitant to make it known as well as students who are timid and don't seem to know how to speak up for themselves.

One mother put it like this:

> The kids don't advocate for themselves. I didn't even know about the professor telling her he wouldn't let her out [for a medical appointment that would determine treatment for a serious health condition] and how he was giving her a zero if she left, until a month later when I see a zero. I said, "We're going to complain." She was like, "No, I'm not. I'm going to have that guy again. He's going to retaliate against me." They're afraid.

Moreover, grades are a metric by which students have been judged and by which they judge themselves. Dealing with the aftermath of sexual assault can disrupt previously high achievement, which can become an additional source of stress and distress.

Mental Health

Anxiety runs high. In a 2019 American College Health Association (ACHA) survey of 54,497 undergraduates at ninety-eight schools across the country, nearly two-thirds of undergraduates reported that they experienced "overwhelming anxiety" during the previous twelve months – one-third had experienced it in the previous two weeks. The anxiety negatively affected the academic performance of over half of the students who experienced it: they bombed a test, got a lower grade in a course, or dropped a course. Thus it's no surprise that students sought professional help; one-fourth of undergraduates reported that they were diagnosed with and/or treated for anxiety in the previous year. About half of those students – one-eighth of *all* students – were treated with medication or medication plus psychotherapy.[1]

Depression is common too. Nearly two-thirds of students who participated in the ACHA survey said that they had at one time felt so depressed that it was difficult to function. About half had felt that way in the previous twelve months, nearly one-fifth in the previous two weeks. More than half of those who reported being depressed in the previous year said that it negatively affected their academic work. About one in five had sought professional help and been diagnosed with or treated for depression in the previous year. More than one in ten had received medication for depression in the previous year.

The demand for mental health services has grown substantially, not just since the widespread establishment of student counseling centers beginning in the 1960s but in just the past few years. Campus mental health services are tasked with providing care for a range of concerns, from transitory problems such as adjusting to being away from home and relationship difficulties to serious psychiatric issues. Several major mental disorders are first evidenced in young adulthood, that is, the college years, and some students come to college having already had treatment in one form or another. There has been a steady increase in the number of students arriving on campus who are already on psychiatric medication.[2]

Campuses are expanding services and increasing the diversity of their staff.[3] The good news is that two-thirds of the centers report that they do not have a waitlist, but among those that do, the average wait for a first appointment is more than three weeks.[4] Parents spoke about why students use campus mental health services and the limit placed on the number of visits at some colleges:

> I get the impression kids are pretty strung out, pretty stressed. I know high school kids are really stressed compared to when we were in high school. I mean, it's just ridiculous. And it seems to carry over into the university. —Father

> The [university's counseling center is] so supportive; you can go as many times as you want to see a counselor. And the people who are a part of it are very compassionate. . . . Whereas I understand at [another university], it's ridiculous, there's a three-month waitlist to go see a counselor. . . . I've also heard that at [another university] it's terrible, there's a lifetime cap while you're a student of five visits to the counseling center. So it really does vary. If mental health is an important issue for your child, you might want to look at that when you're looking at universities. —Mother

Campus mental health services can be especially important for students who have been sexually assaulted. In addition to the anxiety and depression that many college students experience these days, they are dealing with a traumatic event. Counseling can help.

Alcohol and Other Drugs

Students come to college expecting to socialize, and many of those opportunities involve alcohol and other drugs. Some schools have a reputation of being a party school, whereas others have the opposite. Many colleges and universities acknowledge that students, regardless of minimum drinking age and the (il)legality of the drugs, will drink and use. Although some campuses prohibit alcohol and other drug use, the general sentiment among college administrators seems to be that doing so will only drive the issue underground and create a new set of problems.

Excessive drinking is pervasive on college campuses, and that isn't new. College students are more likely than their same-aged peers who are not in college to drink, to drink often, and to binge drink.[5] (Binge drinking is defined as "five or more drinks [for males] or four or more drinks [for females] on the same occasion [that is, at the same time or within a couple of hours of each other]."[6]) The 2019 ACHA survey found that while 75 percent of undergraduates have used alcohol and 40 percent have used marijuana, the use of other drugs – cocaine, amphetamines, sedatives, hallucinogens, opiates, inhalants, and "club drugs" – is low, in the single digits.[7]

A surprising number of students are seen in local emergency departments for alcohol poisoning. Many colleges and universities take a harm-reduction approach in which students are given "medical amnesty," that is, they aren't disciplined if they get themselves or a friend who is severely intoxicated to medical care. (As part of that amnesty, a university usually doesn't contact the parents. Of course, if the student is on the parents' health insurance, the parents find out about the emergency department visit when they get the bill.) The introduction of such a policy typically results in more rather than fewer students being taken to an emergency department.[8]

When asked how much they drank the last time they partied, one-third of students in the ACHA survey reported that they didn't drink at all, while over one-fourth said they had had five or more drinks. One in five college students (this includes those who never drink) reported that, during the previous twelve months, they had drunk so much alcohol that they had forgotten where they were or what they did; more than one in five said that, when drinking, they had done something they later regretted.[9]

One mother said that her daughter had been taken to the hospital a couple of times her freshman year for alcohol poisoning. Parties were a common danger, and, as one mother told me, the parties began right away: "When we were unpacking her stuff at move-in, there were students walking around the hallway handing out flyers for parties. And they tried to hand me one. They're like 'Oh, parent.'" Parents' efforts to counter the drinking weren't especially effective, according to these two mothers:

> She quickly learned that those parties basically were setups. . . . We would tell her, "Make sure you always get your own drink, get a bottle of beer that you can open." We really, really did a lot of educating. We thought we were doing the right thing. We talk a lot about it now, and [she'll say things like], "Quite frankly, Mom, that's not feasible. There are drinks everywhere and you can't really be responsible for your own drink. People make them and hand them out, and it's not like I can say, 'Oh, I'm gonna go make my own,' especially when you're making new friends."

> I was always checking in on her and reminding her if she goes to a party, you go with your friends and you stay with your friends, and if they leave, you leave with them, you don't stay behind. And don't drink, I mean, it's okay to have one, but you're illegal, you're not of drinking age, it is illegal and don't do it. My daughter was the partier, which is really surprising because she never partied in high school . . . she's so tiny and small – she can't drink a lot – and it really has a huge effect on her.

Alcohol use by hormone-fueled, boundary-testing late adolescents presents challenges in multiple ways.

Sex and Relationships

Colleges and universities also seem to assume that students will be sexually active. Long gone are curfew hours for girls, prohibitions against having members of the opposite sex in one's room, and, if such visits were allowed, for the door to be ajar and feet kept on the floor. Many of those same residence halls are in use today and, as Jennifer Hirsch and Shamus Khan point out in their book *Sexual Citizens*, the physical landscape of dorm rooms matters: "a desk, a chair, a bureau, and a bed. To sit apart would be awkward. But sitting together means sharing a bed."[10]

Most parents of today's college students grew up after birth control became legal for all persons in the United States, regardless of marital status, in 1972. And today's students, if exposed to school-based sex ed before they go to college, probably know a fair amount about the biology of sex and not much about intimacy and safety. Nowadays, rather than trying to prohibit sexual activity among students, campuses address safe sex and consent.

Much has been written in the past decade about the hookup culture of college campuses. Although intercourse is relatively common among college students (43 percent report having had vaginal, 41 percent report having had oral, and 5 percent report having had anal intercourse in the previous thirty days[11]), it isn't necessarily what students mean when they say they "hook up." Hooking up can include kissing, "making out," and what used to be called "heavy petting" without intercourse. Students themselves use the term rather loosely, sometimes meaning sex in general (including "making out"), whereas others emphasize the interpersonal and social aspects, and yet others refer to specific sexual acts.[12] Lisa Wade's book *American Hookup*[13] describes the hookup scene as "more heartening and more harrowing than we thought" and reports that undergraduates say they feel as if they are *supposed* to have casual sex.

Students have described hooking up to me in utilitarian terms: they have sexual desires and are attracted to someone else with similar desires, so why not? Some are busy with classes, jobs, volunteering, and extracurricular activities and schedule appointments with their "hookup buddy." In discussions in my classes, students have described hookups as being economical in terms of time (scheduled) and finances (why bother with dinner?).

The arrangement often is transactional. They might like each other, and the sexual aspect might grow into more, but often the two parties place strict limits on emotional involvement. As one undergraduate said in a class I recently taught, "I broke it off because I was starting to 'catch feelings.'" The concept was unfamiliar to graduate students in the course, just two or three years older, who looked on with puzzlement and mock horror.

In essence, hookups tend to be individual oriented rather than relationship focused. A "real" relationship is seen as getting in the way of individual achievement and satisfaction; "settling down" in a relationship is perceived as a risk to everything that students and their parents have invested in their success. Although students talk about relationships and want to partner, few date (as "dating" is traditionally defined), and romance is generally considered to be something for the future.

These views appear not to be linked to gender: both college girls and boys seem to perceive sexual activity in terms that some might consider practical, others cavalier. There are exceptions to the ethos, however, and based on my conversations with students, the exceptions tend to be students who hold (or come from families that hold) certain religious beliefs and cultural ideals that value chastity.

The bottom line, if there is one, is that sexual relationships are not easy for college students. In her book *Girls & Sex*, Peggy Orenstein deftly captures what she calls "the complicated new landscape."[14] Those in serious relationships, sometimes the focus of both ridicule and envy, are seen as a bit odd. Those endeavoring to have it all so as not to compromise an imagined future career and income – to be close but not too close – can exhaust themselves.

The parents I spoke with seemed to think that their daughters are growing up faster; one mother asserted that their peers, society, and self-survival are forcing them to grow up faster. It's complicated, as these parents conveyed:

> Our daughter says that [her college] is very much a hookup community. Even her friends, girls, are very open about wanting to have sexual relationships with guys and to have it be no more [than that], which is very different from when I was there . . . our daughter says there is pressure. People will be, like, I think that there was that obscene term – I think it was like, "Oh, do you wanna be fuck buddies?" – and talk about it openly, it's totally acceptable. I think it's hard for my daughter, who's a real romantic, I think it's very unsettling for her in some ways. —Mother

I think sex seems to be more . . . "aggressive" is not quite the right word, although it probably is more aggressive, too – more extreme than when we were younger. . . . When I was in high school, having someone give you a hand job or a blow job or having sex in the back of a car was way out there. And talk about that would last for months and months. And now at high school parties, as far as I can tell . . . there's a lot of swapping, there's a lot of homosexual experimentation, there's a lot of kind of—I don't wanna say "bullying," but pushing kids to do more, boys kissing girls to make out or have sex. . . . I never heard about things like that in high school, and now it seems to happen fairly regularly in high school and college seems to be about more of the same. —Father

There's a lot of transient relationships there. Like we know each other, we have a good time, but then, you move on. And that's the way it's gonna be in the workplace when they get out there. It's a very mobile group of people out there today. —Father

Most students are responsible when it comes to sex. While withdrawal continues to be a common means to prevent pregnancy (about one-third used it the last time they'd had vaginal intercourse), multiple forms of contraception are used by college students. Fewer than 1 percent reported that they had been treated in the previous twelve months for a common sexually transmitted infection.[15]

Condoms can be used to deceive and violate as well as protect. "Stealthing," in which a couple agrees to intercourse with a condom and the guy removes it without his partner's knowledge, is a troubling appearance on campuses. (A post labeled "A Comprehensive Guide" in an online forum for perpetrators provides a detailed description.[16]) The nonconsensual removal of a condom during sex is not limited to college students though, and legal thinking is beginning to address the issue.[17]

And finally there's the issue of men who think they are owed access to women's bodies, a deeply ingrained part of many cultures. One counterpart is that women sometimes feel as if they don't have equal power and, as such, think they haven't much of a choice. An extreme example of men's sense of entitlement and resentment was brought into focus by Elliot Rodger, a good-looking, affluent, white college student. In 2014, he posted a video in which he described "being forced, ever since I hit puberty, to endure an existence of loneliness, rejection, and unfulfilled desires all because girls have never been attracted to me. Girls gave their affection and sex and love to other men but never to me. I'm 22 years old and I'm still a virgin. I've never even kissed a girl."[18] The next day he killed six people and injured fourteen others near the campus of the University of California, Santa Barbara. He was a troubled young man, to be sure, but he is not alone; he became a hero for "incels": men who are involuntarily celibate. In 2018, the Southern Poverty Law Center, which tracks U.S. hate groups (such as the Ku Klux Klan) and their activities, added a new category to its monitoring list: male supremacy.

The belief that women "owe" men sexually and that revenge should be exacted on women in general, as well as those who don't "put out," fuels some men. For example, a male student, accused of sexual harassment that escalated to an assault at Brown University, posted on his fraternity's Facebook page: "there is a special place in hell for girls who seek revenge against those who don't text them back and ignore them by claiming that they were sexually assaulted."[19] Social media gave him the opportunity to be very public with his disdain.

Technology

Information and communication technologies have exploded and continue to change rapidly. Laptops and tablets, words that had either no or a completely different meaning a generation ago, are among current college necessities. Mobile phones and apps that allow for video chatting provide an easy and convenient way for parents and their college students to stay in touch. Colleges and universities have websites and apps that connect to a wide range of resources on and off campus. And the Internet provides easy access to lots of free pornography. None of this existed when the parents of today's students were of college age.

Pornography

Some are concerned that campus sexual assault might be a "natural" product of hookup culture. Others point to Internet pornography, which seems to have become a primary means of sex education for substantial numbers of adolescents.

The Internet has provided a generation with quick and easy access to pornography, and what is available online is similar to what used to be considered "hard core." The most recent research on online material finds that "mainstream" pornography has not gotten worse in that it does not depict more or more severe violence than it did a decade ago.[20] Depictions of nonconsensual sex and coerced sex were relatively rare in four hundred popular pornographic Internet videos. However, women were substantially more likely than men to be shown as having been manipulated into having sex.[21]

The question remains as to whether watching pornography is associated with sexual aggression. Some research suggests little to no association, whereas others find a modest association between violent pornography – only violent pornography, not pornography in general – and verbal sexual aggression and, to a lesser extent, physical sexual aggression.[22] Perhaps the most pervasive outcome of watching online pornography is, as nationally syndicated sex advice columnist Dan Savage suggests, "It's not so much that the more extreme porn instills desires, as it instills anxiety. These kids are convinced or afraid that things they've seen are expected of them – and they may not be interested in, or looking forward to it."[23]

Smartphones and Social Media

Individual mobile phones have taken the place of hallway and in-room phones on college campuses. Introduced in 2007, the Apple iPhone was the first "smartphone," essentially a handheld computer that could connect to the Internet and came equipped with a camera. Mobile phones had obvious benefits and were quickly adopted by the general population. Nearly every young adult has a mobile phone that they use to surf the web, share photographs and videos of their activities (often as "selfies"), send text messages to friends, and finally make phone calls.

Social media platforms and apps (short for "applications") developed for smartphones exploded information sharing. Facebook gave way to Twitter, Snapchat, Instagram, and TikTok among young people. Social media facilitates connections among people who otherwise would never know one another. It also facilitates those who abuse and assault.

Although social media and smartphones can connect survivors to one another and to needed resources, they can also be used to bully and destroy. Negotiating these shoals is new and not easy. Tech designers likely never imagined that homicides and rapes would be filmed and sent to buddies, recorded and uploaded to hosting sites such as You-Tube, or livestreamed on the Internet. (One example: a sixteen-year-old taped and sent to his friends a video he made of his "encounter" with an intoxicated twelve-year-old along with a text: "when your first time having sex was rape."[24]) Hosting sites such as Facebook, Twitter, and YouTube are struggling to address consumer and government demands that they monitor postings and remove those deemed to contain objectionable content. Victims whose sexual assaults are filmed and distributed (or threatened to be distributed) can be expected to have a complicated recovery.

The agreed-upon filming of consensual sex acts can seem like harmless fun when a relationship is in its prime. And sexting – generally defined as the sharing of sexually explicit images of oneself – appears to have some popularity. If the relationship sours, women (far more than men, from all we know) can be victimized by a partner's decision to make such images public. The nonconsensual sharing of the images has been labeled "revenge porn," and statutes have been enacted to criminally prosecute those who share and distribute the content. Although it is increasingly recognized as a form of abusive behavior, none of the students who spoke with me experienced online harassment or abuse.

Texting is a primary mode of communication for adolescents and young adults, sometimes to the consternation of their parents. (I'm certain that I'm not the only parent who has texted, in exasperation, "Enough of this, just CALL me, okay?!!") In addition to being used for routine communications, text messages can be used to threaten and harass others, for example, "You better not tell anyone." Among the college girls who spoke with me about having been sexually assaulted, I was surprised at how many had subsequent texts from the guy saying things like "You don't remember? You better take Plan B" (a form of postcoital contraception) or "I'm sorry, I should have stopped," or "Hey, that was fun, want to get together on Friday?" These young men seem to be unaware that text messages can be incriminating evidence in a criminal case as well as a campus hearing. I didn't necessarily expect what I was told: that some assaulted girls respond – or consider responding – receptively to such texts. Perhaps the college boy sees sexually aggressive behavior as normal and the assaulted girl wants to revise the incident in hopes of making it less traumatic.

New Technology and Sexual Assault

Technology also has changed how women can summon assistance when they sense danger. "Rape whistles" were common for many years. A woman was to blow the whistle when attacked, which would scare off the attacker or bring others to her aid. More recently, technology has entered the market, and profit has motivated the creation of new and novel options. A search of "rape whistle" on Amazon yields hundreds of items, ranging from aluminum whistles to alarms that emit loud, piercing noises when a button is pressed.

Some apps and devices can be programmed to notify specified others – police, friends, family – of one's location when in distress. There are many other products on the market or in development, including nail polish that a woman can apply that, if she dunks her fingers into a drink, will turn color if the drink contains a date rape drug. It gives a whole new meaning to getting ready for a party. Although some of these ideas are stunningly creative, the marketing largely reinforces the idea of stranger danger[25] when we've known for decades that the person most likely to sexually assault a woman is a man she knows. I'd be surprised if a college girl would apply date rape drug–detecting nail polish as she prepares for a Saturday night with a guy she knows. And of course it would take far more imagination to design products to impede men from committing sexual violence.

Costs and Status Differentials

I am among those who worked multiple jobs to put themselves through college. In many cases, that isn't an option anymore. Tuition costs have risen substantially and are extraordinary at some schools. From the 1989 to 1990 academic year to the 2019 to 2020 academic year, tuition and fees tripled at public four-year universities and doubled at public two-year schools and private four-year universities.[26] And then there are the books, room and board, laptops, and what can seem to be a sometimes endless stream of other costs.

At the same time, colleges and universities are trying to make themselves more accessible. Programs have popped up at colleges and universities across the country in an effort to recruit and retain students who might not otherwise have a chance to attend. Such endeavors are important given that higher education continues to drive upward mobility in the United States, with mid-tier public universities moving the most students from the bottom fifth to the top fifth of incomes (that is, from the low income of their family of origin to their own high income).[27] More than half of first-generation students leave college without a degree, however, because they can't afford to continue.[28] Costs include things as basic as housing and food; for example, more than one-third of 43,000 students at sixty-six schools reported that they don't have enough to eat.[29] In response, some universities have established food pantries, altered their dining plans, and partnered with nonprofits to obtain unused meals for hungry students. Worry about how and where they will get food and difficulty concentrating when blood sugar is low take their toll; food insecurity is related to poor mental health and lower academic performance.[30] Whereas expanded needs-based scholarship and grant programs have made it possible for many low-income students to go to college, there's an unintended consequence. In having to forgo other college experiences that cost money – fraternity and sorority membership, travel, unpaid summer internships, special parties and the associated formal wear, and so on – they can be socially isolated.

In the good news category, racial and ethnic diversity in college student enrollment has increased. A higher percentage of young people of all races and ethnicities are going to college, and the gap between the enrollment of white and Black, Hispanic, and Asian young people has decreased over time.[31] Campus racial and ethnic diversity predicts friendship diversity, and most of the benefit goes to white students who have the opportunity for greater interaction with minority students.[32] Being a minority student at a predominantly white school now can be socially isolating like it was it was decades ago; students describe benefits as well as problems related to "experiences of interacting in the majority culture, perceived social pressures to conform, [and] issues relating to personal identity."[33]

Status differentials play out on campus much as they do in the rest of society. In addition to income and wealth, race and ethnicity, whether one's family is from the United States and how long they have been here, whether one is street smart, and other personal and familial characteristics contribute to status differentials on campus that sometimes play out in the most intimate of relationships.

All-Male Groups

Title IX, instituted in 1972, states that "no person in the United States shall, on the basis of sex, be excluded from participation in, be denied the benefits of, or be subjected to discrimination under any education program or activity receiving Federal financial assistance." The federal "Equal Access" Act helped create a wave of female high school athletes. As has been widely documented, myriad coaches and team doctors have engaged in inappropriate behavior toward their players, male and female alike, for which they and their colleges have been held accountable.

The more common concern on college campuses, however, is the behavior of male athletes, on whom some schools stake their reputations. Some athletes comport themselves and treat others with dignity, but some create problems for themselves and others, and certain athletes seem to be "untouchable." In fact, as one mother told me, some athletes seem to zero in on certain girls: "They are the worst in terms of taking advantage of vulnerable girls, and the girls feel like it's a privilege to be associated with them. The guys know that they are in demand, so, even if a girl says no, they'll push her, 'Why should you say no when I can get anybody?'" Financial settlements related to such activities of certain athletes cost the universities the athletes attend and, in the case of public universities, the taxpayers who fund them.

College girls who are athletes themselves are vulnerable to harassment and assault from both other athletes and coaches. Two parents related how their daughters who were athletes had to deal with such behavior: "Apparently on her team, they had this horrible culture of assault. It was almost customary to deflower the freshman girls—the boys [on the boys' team of the same sport] knew what they were doing and the girls didn't" and "The assistant coach was totally sexually harassing another teammate. The girl was really uncomfortable and she was showing my daughter the texts. My daughter was getting angrier and angrier and she finally confronted the assistant coach. The other coaches seemed oblivious to it." The bad behavior of certain college athletes and coaches and that universities enable such behavior are not new problems, nor are they solved problems.

Another long-standing, unsolved problem is the behavior tolerated and promoted in some fraternities. Parents can know that fraternities can be problematic but also really want their sons to join one. The promise of academic achievement (maintaining a certain grade point average often is required), leadership (fraternities proudly list the political and business leaders who were members), and a built-in social group that begins in the first year of college and lasts long afterward (perhaps the ultimate in "old boys' networks") can be compelling.

At the same time, fraternities remain largely segregated with racist incidents coming to light with some regularity; excessive alcohol consumption is common. One father had a particularly harsh assessment of fraternities:

> I always worried that stuff like this would happen. And I was always most concerned about fraternity parties because . . . the only reason they exist is for men to abuse alcohol, drugs, and women. . . . There may be some special interest ones but, by and large, that's why they exist. I've said that to my daughters and I have many times warned them not to go to fraternity parties because that stuff happens there.

Fraternities are allowed to host parties with alcohol but, by the decision of the council that governs the country's twenty-six major sororities, sororities are not.[34] Young people want to party, and in order to do so in the Greek system, girls must go to fraternities, where they are not familiar with the physical layout of the building and, as such, are out of their element.

Hazing continues despite being officially frowned upon. Hazing and sexual assault are similar in terms of the power dynamics that play out – humiliation, demands for risky and sometimes outright dangerous behavior in order to be accepted – and the normalization of predatory behavior. In addition, first-year students in particular are not sophisticated about the sexual aggressiveness and even predation that is part of the ethos of some fraternities. Unwanted sexual touching on college campuses – specifically touching that occurred through physical force or because the college girl was unable to consent (that is, she had too much to drink, was drugged, or was otherwise not able to make a decision) – occurs most often at fraternities.[35]

Study Abroad

Study abroad continues to be an opportunity for college students, but the larger societal context has changed in the past generation. New media (the Internet, social media, and more) facilitate previously unavailable person-to-person connections, and greater travel has resulted from lower airplane fares and Airbnb; families with children travel to places that simply would have been cost prohibitive twenty-five years ago. One result is that students are more aware of other cultures and ways of being, and they know that the United States is perceived unfavorably in some locales and at some times.

Several of the daughters who spoke with me had traveled a fair amount, solo as well as with their families. Some had the means to do so, whereas others did fundraising for program-based trips. The goal was the same: to learn about the rest of the world, different cultures, and different ways of thinking. But a family vacation and lessons gleaned from books, videos, social media, and online chats are very different from living and learning in a country for months. For one thing, talking and thinking in another language, even for students who consider themselves fluent in the language of their host country, can be exhausting during the first few weeks. Although acknowledging the joy and excitement of residing in another country, parents also spoke of the challenges, which included illness and stress. An uncomfortable sense of vulnerability and isolation is common, especially as the study abroad begins.

Study abroad has obvious parallels to the first semester of freshman year. Students choose to apply, are pleased to have been selected to participate, and are excited to be in this new place. They are in their element (school), yet the setting and culture of the new locale are unfamiliar. They might know one or two other students but don't have a friendship network. And they often desperately want to appear "cool," knowledgeable, and at home; they might be all of those things in some ways and not at all in other ways. The novelty of the setting, lack of a friendship network, and less familiarity with the culture, customs, and laws – as well as concern about not wanting to come across as an "ugly American" – can combine to create special vulnerabilities.

Love and Peace Reimagined

Today's college students seem to have heightened sensitivities – sensitivities as in understandings, compassions, and sympathies rather than prickliness – about issues and concerns outside themselves. They are eager to discuss and understand how social and economic structures shape one's experience and perspective.

Gender and gender fluidity have emerged as hot topics on college campuses in the past decade. "Preferred gender pronouns," "cisgender," "nonbinary," "sex assigned at birth," and "person who presents as male" – along with "toxic masculinity" and "rape culture" – are part of everyday conversations on many campuses. Some students come to campus as one gender and leave as another. Things are not as straightforward as they once seemed.

Although students have frank conversations about sex and gender, other conversations are less welcome. It's not as if the past is blemish free, but news media coverage seems to present current campus speech skirmishes as being a horse of a different color. Student protests have shut down guest speakers and they have been roundly criticized for doing so. Universities incur substantial costs to their budgets and reputations too. Currently both the political left and right are censoring speech that they find objectionable.

At the same time, students seem to be particularly attuned to and accepting of differences and of one another; perhaps they truly are kinder and more accommodating than the bullying-tolerant students of prior generations. "Sensitivities" can be perceived as a problem but increasingly are seen as a window into the life of someone else. Microaggressions – comments or actions that *Merriam-Webster* defines as "subtly and often unconsciously or unintentionally expressing a prejudiced attitude toward a member of a marginalized group (such as a racial minority)" – are an acknowledged reality. It's not *if* they exist, it's whether something *is* a microaggression and how to deal with their routine frequency. Things that older adults might dismiss as unimportant, truly "micro," can be intensely important to college students.

The idea of a rape culture is not new, but it has gained traction and articulation on college campuses. As defined by author Emilie Buchwald, it is "a complex of beliefs that encourages male sexual aggression and supports violence against women. It is a society where violence is seen as sexy and sexuality as violent. In a rape culture, women perceive a continuum of threatened violence that ranges from sexual remarks to sexual touching to rape itself. A rape culture condones physical and emotional terrorism against women and presents it as the norm."[36]

At the university where I teach, the term "rape culture" became a sustained topic of conversation after copies of a fraternity's email invitation to just-arrived first-year female students were brought to light. The message read: "May we have your attention please / We're looking for the fun ones / And say f**k off to a tease. . . . Wednesday nights will get you going / With bankers flowing all night / Tonight is your first showing / So please wear something tight." (An aside: if you, like I, haven't any idea what a "banker" is, here's the definition from the online slang dictionary urbandictionary.com: "A banker is the girl you know you can get with no matter what. She is the one you go for when all else fails, or you simply can't be bothered to make any effort for others. You may have one, or several bankers.") Within a day or two, the message was plastered across campus on flyers that were stamped with "THIS IS WHAT RAPE CULTURE LOOKS LIKE" and "WE ARE WATCHING."[37] The mother of one of the fraternity boys scoffed to me a few weeks later, "It might be in poor taste, but it certainly is not rape culture." The undergraduates who posted the flyers evidently thought otherwise. As feminist author Rebecca Solnit put it, "I find in young women a clarity about their rights."[38]

Columnist George Will might not have coined the term "snow-flake," but he certainly helped make it a widely used descriptor implying that today's college students are fragile: the least bit of heat and they melt. I see it differently. First, the dismissive characterization of "snowflake" ignores experiences that are understandably troubling and can result in harm. I am repeatedly impressed by the resilience of the students in my courses. Second, Will might be picking up on – and judging harshly – that students sometimes seem to express a desire for colleges and universities to fulfill a protective parental role. They aren't looking for a parent who enforces rules inflexibly and reduces their agency but for one who offers a supportive environment to create a "brave space" in which they can engage in controversial content with civility, challenge themselves by choice, and expand their agency.[39] How best to do this isn't always clear. We're in the midst of all this, and university administrators, as well as students, are trying to figure it out.

Sexual Assault

"Sexual misconduct" is the umbrella term that many colleges and universities use for sexual assault, sexual harassment, and sexual relationships in the workplace. "Misconduct" puts such behavior squarely in the context of the college's code of student conduct and, according to some, seems to put the behavior on par with plagiarism, drinking, and other "lesser" actions.

Many parents pay attention to news stories about colleges and universities. Fewer seem to be aware of or pay attention to crime statistics that are publicly available and easily accessed. (Release of the numbers is mandated by federal law.) Such information might reasonably affect perceptions of a school, so colleges and universities are motivated to keep crime, violence, and sexual assault under the radar, out of the news.

Many parents told me that they didn't think to consider such information, whereas others were attuned to the topic. One father complained that colleges and universities "certainly don't talk about it at the welcome weekend for kids – at least when parents are on-site, they don't talk about it at all. . . . [They don't say] 'You're dropping your daughter off. Just want to make sure you know something – really bad stuff could happen here.'" But sometimes parents bring it up. I was impressed with the mother who, at a recent new student orientation with over a thousand parents, asked what the university was doing to address campus sexual assault. Everyone left orientation a bit more educated.

Like the military, the entertainment industry, the tech field, and other institutions, colleges and universities are trying to figure out how best to address and respond to sexual violence. Some have done poorly – horribly, even – and their failings have been ridiculed, written about, and the subject of lawsuits.[40] On the other hand, some invest considerable resources at multiple levels across their campuses, and some university administrators make a point of the values that undergird the education they offer. Controversies can be expected to continue.

Looking back, parents who spoke with me were divided as to whether campus sexual assault is a relatively recent phenomenon. (It isn't – more on that in the next chapter.) There is, however, greater acknowledgment of its occurrence. One father told me, "Back when I went to school, we had other problems, it was the Vietnam War. But I think the guys who tell you that it [campus sexual assault] is a recent thing are either naïve or mistaken."

Parents with fond memories of their college days might be surprised when they listen as their children talk about their lives on campus. There are wonderful things, to be sure, yet today's students navigate shoals that their parents couldn't foresee. Technological innovations have changed how they take notes in class and communicate with their parents and one another. Tuition and other costs have skyrocketed. Competition and competitiveness seem to be higher than ever in recognition that the labor market has become truly global. Sexual assault is discussed openly, and traditional understandings of gender are questioned, as are appropriate limits to free speech. Good grades are important for those wanting to pursue another degree but continue to be an outsized marker of personal worth for many who plan to end their studies after four years. Students experience considerable anxiety and depression and turn to alcohol, casual hookups, and mental health services.

Amid the pressures, college students, as did their parents, have fun, enjoy themselves, make lifelong friends, and grow. The parenting function of colleges and universities that focused on making and enforcing rules faded a long time ago. Students today seem to want a different sort of parenting – one that provides a kind and supportive setting in which they can figure out their way. Unfortunately, the college journey for many includes sexual assault. But is it new? And how many are assaulted? That's what the next chapter will address.

CHAPTER 2

The Big Picture

Although the same violations are perpetrated, society generally takes a place-based view of sexual assault, categorizing it according to the location and context in which it occurs: in war, jails and prisons, religious settings, schools, the workplace, and elsewhere. It is in this splintered perspective that we consider campus sexual assault.

In historical context, one can see vestiges of the past in how rape and sexual assault are viewed today.

A Brief Look Back

"Rape entered the lawbooks through the back door, as property crime of man against man, with the women viewed as the property involved."[1] As such, punishment was severe. In her 1975 book *Against Our Will*, the first book ever about rape, Susan Brownmiller recounts how the Code of Hammurabi, one of the oldest sets of written law, considered the rape of a virgin to be damage to her father's property.[2] Mosaic Law directed the Israelites to stone to death an unmarried woman who was raped within city walls, along with her attacker, the rationale being that she must have consented or the townspeople would have heard her scream. If she was not betrothed, the pair was ordered to marry and the rapist to pay her father fifty pieces of silver in compensation. If she was betrothed, the arrangement was canceled and her bride price was marked down. In Assyria, the father of a raped virgin was allowed to rape the wife of the rapist.

In England prior to the eleventh century, the penalty for rape was death and dismemberment, but only if the man raped a "high-born propertied virgin." In 1066 the penalty was reduced to castration and the loss of both eyes. Trial by jury was introduced in the twelfth century – a trial that occurred only if the victim filed a civil suit and "ran through the town immediately after the attack making a 'hue and cry,' and showing her injuries and torn clothing to 'Men of Good Repute,' thus the roots of . . . rules of corroboration."[3] The thirteenth century saw major advances in the law: the Crown was involved in all cases (not just the rape of virgins), statutory rape was recognized, and the Crown could prosecute; thus rape became viewed as a problem of society as well as a private matter. The penalty for rape, however, was reduced to two years of imprisonment.

The perspective of women as property was most evident in the United States during slavery. Slaveholders could "take" an enslaved woman whenever they wanted. Perhaps, as the legend of President Thomas Jefferson and Sally Hemings goes, love and kindness were sometimes involved, but it is nigh impossible to imagine freely given consent in the context of one human owning another. The effects on the women must have been devastating, and their offspring served as a constant reminder of the assault. Slaveholders who didn't want visible evidence of their behavior could and would sell the child; the cruel practice of rape contributed to the destruction of the family. More-over, the rape of enslaved women by slaveholders served to demoralize enslaved men, who risked severe punishment and even death if they tried to intervene. Most states excluded African American women, both free and enslaved, from rape laws. As Yale historian Crystal Feim-ster notes, African American women couldn't bring a charge of rape against a white man until 1871, six years after emancipation.[4]

Acquaintances and coercion – not just strangers and force – were part of the focus of reformers in the 1800s. Activists worked to hold accountable the "licentious man" who used a false promise of mar-riage to obtain sex. Stanford historian Estelle B. Freedman notes that although it was considered a lesser crime than rape and the penalty was less severe, the activists' efforts had succeeded in most states by 1900.[5] A similar national campaign garnered tens of thousands of signatures, long before online petitions and before women were able to vote, and persuaded most U.S. state legislatures to increase the age of consent to somewhere between fourteen and eighteen. The prior age of consent had been ten years of age.

In 1927 the FBI defined rape as "the carnal knowledge of a female, forcibly and against her will." The definition was to stand for eighty-six years. Some people, including elected officials and law enforcement officers, seem not to know that the definition of rape they grew up with is no longer the definition. But I'm getting ahead of myself.

In the 1970s and early 1980s rape began to be viewed as a threat to women's safety and autonomy more broadly. Criminal laws regarding rape underwent multiple changes as a result of what was known as the "rape law reform" movement. The effort was, in no small part, an attempt to reduce women's experience of the criminal justice system following rape as a "second victimization." Among the changes were:

- *Mens rea* was removed as a criterion for conviction. *Mens rea* – Latin for "guilty mind" – was required for a man to be convicted of rape. He had to know, to be aware, to realize that what he was doing was rape. If he didn't, he couldn't be found guilty.
- Special jury instructions, unique to rape cases, were eliminated. As jury members went into deliberations in a rape trial, the judge used to advise them that "a charge such as that made against the defendant in this case is one which is easily made and, once made, difficult to defend against, even if the person accused is innocent. Therefore, the law requires that you examine the testimony of the female person named in the information with caution." Rape was the only crime for which juries were routinely instructed to approach the victim with skepticism.
- The victim's prior sexual experience became largely off limits. Before then, defense attorneys could ask the victim, under oath, whether she had been a virgin prior to the assault and cross-examine her about any and all sexual experiences. It was a routine tactic by which to demean and discredit the victim that harkened back to an earlier time when it was thought that only a woman

who is "pure" could be "defiled." I said "largely off limits" because under some circumstances (for example, if the victim and suspect had a prior sexual relationship) the nature of their sexual relationship continues to be admissible evidence.

As one might imagine, thinking shifted even more as we learned that a man known to a woman, often someone she trusts, is the person most likely to rape her. Two other changes were made:

- The requirement of victim resistance was modified but not eliminated. Rape is the only crime for which victim resistance was required. One needn't have resisted if faced with a robber; "He took my wallet" was sufficient. But victims of rape were expected to have resisted "to the utmost" – the message being, evidently, that women would prefer death to "dishonor." Physical injury and torn clothing were evidence of resistance. During the rape law reform period of the 1970s and 1980s, the victim resistance requirement was recalibrated as needing to be proportional to the threat presented by the assailant, although the idea that you had to fight your attacker continues to hold sway. Resistance to a known person isn't likely to be the same as resistance to a stranger.

  (As an aside, I recall being interviewed by the news media about a paper our research team published in the early 1990s about resistance to sexual assault and how women's efforts to resist could reduce their chances of being raped. A police officer presented an alternative view, advising women not to resist because he thought they would be hurt worse; instead they should "lay back and enjoy it.")

- Spousal rape became a crime. English Common Law, on which the U.S. legal system is based, stated in 1847 that "the husband cannot be guilty of a rape committed by himself upon his lawful wife, for by their mutual matrimonial consent and contract the wife hath given up herself in this kind unto her husband, which she cannot retract." Although marital rape became a crime in all fifty U.S. states in 1993, some states continue to draw distinctions based on whether the two parties are married.

A new FBI definition of rape went into effect in 2013: "The penetration, no matter how slight, of the vagina or anus with any body part or object, or oral penetration by a sex organ of another person, without the consent of the victim." The definition was changed because many agencies interpreted the old definition as excluding a long list of sex offenses that are criminal in most jurisdictions, such as offenses involving oral or anal penetration, penetration with objects, and rapes of males. Also oft-disregarded were alcohol- and other drug-facilitated sexual assaults and sexual assaults of unconscious victims. In other words, the definition shifted so that consent became central. The law made it clear that people who are asleep, unconscious, or in a drug- or alcohol-induced haze are not in a position to provide clearheaded permission for sex.

In summary, the rape of women went from being viewed as a crime against a man's property to a crime against individual women to being viewed as a pervasive threat against the autonomy of women as a group. Women became more widely acknowledged as sexual beings who are in charge of their own choices. As the "no means no" of the 1980s morphed into the "yes means yes" of the early 2000s, laws changed and, along with them, at least some beliefs about rape.

Laws are a reasonable reflection of social norms; they are the written expression of unwritten expectations for behavior. Like norms, sometimes they reflect things as they are; other times they are aspirational and reflect how we hope things will be. For example, Sweden criminalized the spanking of children in 1979. Does that mean that Swedish parents never spank their children? Probably not, but it is a strong statement about what Swedes don't want in their society in terms of child rearing. It's important to note that spanking was common in Sweden: in the 1960s, nine of ten Swedish preschool children were spanked – "smacked" is the term Swedes use – at home. By 2018, nearly forty years after the behavior was deemed criminal, only one in twenty were spanked.[6] Since Sweden banned corporal punishment in 1979, fifty-two other countries have enacted similar legislation. Laws can change behavior.

Campus Sexual Assault in the Twentieth Century

Campus sexual assault is not new.

The first peer-reviewed research on campus sexual assault was published in 1957 in a highly regarded journal of the American Sociological Association. The authors, Clifford Kirkpatrick and Eugene Kanin, found that many college women had been "sexually offended." In fact, "20.9 per cent were offended by forceful attempts at intercourse and 6.2 per cent by 'aggressively forceful attempts at sex intercourse in the course of which menacing threats or coercive infliction of physical pain were employed.'"[7] The acts were perpetrated nearly equally by acquaintances and by a "steady date." The investigators described their study as grounded in a conceptual framework of "a person-to-person relationship that is characterized by exploitation and shared stigma," one that does not lend itself to public disclosure.

Twenty years later, one of those same authors and a colleague replicated the initial study and concluded that there was "little modification in incidence and frequency. Approximately 50% of a sample of university women report being victims of sexual aggression during the academic year."[8] Two things had changed, however: how peopled paired off (the 1960s had occurred) and the characteristics of the "offended" females. The investigators concluded that "all females appear to have become suitable sexual targets regardless of the stage of premarital intimacy, including the most casual and impersonal." That was in 1977.

Three decades passed from the publication of the initial study of campus sexual assault until other scholars picked up the topic. This new generation of scholars who studied sexual assault was mostly women – women's enrollment in PhD programs had increased substantially in the intervening years – and most of them were psychologists. Sociologists didn't seem to have much interest in the topic, even though sexual assault was increasingly being framed as a social issue rather than a personal problem.

In the mid-1980s Mary P. Koss, with funding from the Antisocial and Criminal Behavior Branch of the National Institute of Mental Health, surveyed 3,187 women and 2,972 men enrolled in thirty-two U.S. colleges and universities.[9] Koss and her research team found that 27.5 percent of college women reported that, since they were fourteen years old, they had experienced an act that met the legal definition of attempted or completed rape. In the previous six months, thirty-eight of one thousand women reported experiencing an attempted or completed rape. The victimization numbers were ten to fifteen times higher than criminal justice estimates, probably because most such assaults are never reported to authorities. Looking at sexual assault more broadly (not limited to rape or attempted rape), the researchers found that just over half of the college women indicated that they had been sexually victimized.

These numbers contrasted starkly with public knowledge about sexual assault on campus. Following the rape and murder of Jeanne Clery in her dormitory room in 1986, her parents advocated for greater transparency regarding crime on college campuses. The Clery Act, which became law in 1990, requires each college and university that receives federal funding to issue an annual security report that details, among other things, the number of rapes and attempted rapes on their campus as well as information about their efforts to prevent and respond to sexual assault.[10]

Around this same time, the first epidemiological surveys of sexual assault in the general population were under way, conducted with federal dollars made available through the National Center for the Prevention and Control of Rape, established as part of the National Institutes of Health during the Ford administration and quietly eliminated during the Reagan administration. Three studies were launched in the mid-1980s covering diverse populations: 930 women residents of San Francisco; 3,132 English- and Spanish-speaking Hispanic and non-Hispanic men and women in Los Angeles; and 1,157 Black and white women in North Carolina.[11] These studies, based on in-person interviews and published in the late 1980s, all found that the person most likely to sexually assault a woman is a man she knows and often with whom she has some sort of relationship. I recall the team of researchers in Los Angeles, of which I was part, questioning our work – Was a variable coded wrong? Was the analysis wrong? Could that really be the case? – questions that were later put to us by skeptics. The findings came out in the midst of a highly publicized preschool case in southern California, which, despite its many flaws,[12] drew attention to what research was beginning to document at that time: the most common perpetrators of the sexual abuse of boys and girls, as well as adult women, are adult men they know and trust.

"Stranger danger" was coming up against a huge challenge. From childhood, girls had been brought up to fear men who offered candy or a chance to see a puppy, or who sought directions from little kids. Later we were taught that men who lurked in the bushes, in poorly lit parking lots, or in the backseat of our cars were the men who were intent on doing us harm. Susan Estrich's book *Real Rape: How the Legal System Victimizes Women Who Say No* describes what now is called "stranger rape" and depicts it as what the criminal justice system – and society – views as "legitimate" rape.[13] The idea that we are at highest risk from a man we had been taught would protect us from those other men was, for many, unfathomable. For some it still is.

It's important to note that researchers studying sexual assault didn't ask, "Have you been raped?" or "Have you raped anyone?" We had learned from previous work that it was advisable to use the legal definition of rape that was in use at the time rather than leave it to the study participant to define the term. A substantial portion of college students said "No" when asked if they were the victim or perpetrator of rape but said "Yes" when asked the behaviorally specific question that reflected the legal definition of rape at the time (for example, "Have you had sexual intercourse when you didn't want to because a man threatened or used some degree of physical force [twisting your arm, holding you down, etc.] to make you?").[14] Avoidance of the term "rape" continues to this day: although all 174 women in a study published in 2018 indicated they had "experienced completed vaginal, oral, or anal penetration by force, threat of force, or while incapacitated due to substance use and unable to give consent" (the legal definition of rape when the research was conducted), a full three-fourths of them said "No" when asked if they had been raped.[15] College women acknowledge the behavior but turn away from calling it rape.

Young men's self-reports of perpetration buttress the accuracy of young women's reports of victimization. Of the 2,972 men who participated in Koss's survey, most (about three-fourths) reported that they had not been sexually aggressive.[16] However, about one in twelve (7.7 percent) said that, since age fourteen, they had perpetrated an act that met the legal definition of attempted or completed rape that was in effect at the time. In the previous six months, nine of one thousand men reported that they had perpetrated an act that was consistent with the legal definition of attempted or completed rape. When the researchers asked about sexual assault more generally (that is, not limiting their inquiry to rape or attempted rape), one-fourth (25.1 percent) of the college men acknowledged that they had been sexually aggressive. As the researchers noted, "The number of times that men admitted to perpetrating each aggressive act was virtually identical to the number of times women reported experiencing each act. Thus, the results of the present study failed to support notions that a few extremely sexually active men could account for the victimization of a sizable number of women."[17]

Around this same time, UCLA psychology professor Neil Malamuth began to explore "rape proclivity" among college-age men. He and his colleagues reported troubling, unexpected findings when they explored the possibility that rape might be an extension of normal sexual patterns. The young men

> believed that a high percentage of men would rape if assured of not being punished and that a substantial percentage of women would enjoy being victimized. While both genders shared these beliefs, very few females believed that they personally would derive pleasure from victimization. Surprisingly, more than half of the males indicated some likelihood that they themselves would rape if assured of not being punished.[18]

To help make sense of that response, the researchers asked anonymous male study participants in a series of studies if they would commit armed robbery if they could get away with it; 26 to 29 percent expressed some willingness to do so. Asked whether they would rape a woman if they would not be punished, 16 to 20 percent expressed some willingness to do it, as did 38 to 44 percent who were asked if they would force a woman to have sex if they would not be punished for it.[19] (Note the parallel to findings from studies cited earlier in this section – the term "rape" is avoided.) Let me repeat the key study result: more college-age men said that they would be willing to force a woman to have sex than would commit armed robbery if they were assured that no one would know and that they could get away with it. Sexually assaulting a woman appears to be more acceptable or more satisfying to them than stealing goods or money.

A subsequent large national survey of college women led by Bonnie Fisher found that, on campuses with 10,000 female students, more than 350 would be raped each year.[20] The survey of 4,446 women attending a two- or four-year institution of higher education in the fall of 1996 concluded that "many women do not characterize their sexual victimizations as a crime for a number of reasons (such as embarrassment, not clearly understanding the legal definition of rape, or not wanting to define someone they know who victimized them as a rapist) or because they blame themselves for their sexual assault."[21] As Julie Samuels and Jan Chaiken, acting director of the National Institute of Justice and director of the Bureau of Justice Statistics, respectively, noted at the time, these findings have "serious policy implications for college administrators."[22]

Although there wasn't a groundswell of change among campus administrators, students themselves took action. Student-led organizations that address campus sexual assault have been in place for many years. For example, the University of Pennsylvania, where I teach, has Abuse and Sexual Assault Prevention (ASAP) and Men Against Rape and Sexual Assault (MARS) as well as other student-led organizations. The names might not be the same, but similar organizations exist on many campuses. Activities such as Take Back the Night marches and rallies have been around since the mid-1970s. And Eve Ensler's *The Vagina Monologues*, a series of sketches that address multiple topics, including rape, has been an annual performance staple on college campuses across the nation for decades.

Campus Sexual Assault in the Twenty-First Century

Student activism in the early twenty-first century propelled rape and sexual assault on college campuses into the spotlight once again. Throwing off the cloak of anonymity traditionally provided by the news media and using the emerging power of social media, young women spoke out about their experiences. They rejected the long-standing stigma of being a victim of sexual assault that was based in part on rape myths – that is, judgments about the culpability of women when it comes to rape.[23] Was it easy or painless for them to go public? No. But many had been exposed to the idea of sex positivity – that all sex acts are healthy as long as they are pleasurable and consensual – and knew that what they had experienced was not mutually pleasurable or consensual. Defying and denying invisibility and the idea that women don't, can't, and shouldn't trust one another, determined campus sexual assault victims across the country refused to be dismissed.

Activism was fueled in part by disappointment, anger, and disgust at how their institutions of higher education had handled – or more accurately bungled or even stonewalled – their reports. Their acts were a harbinger of the writings of Brittney Cooper (*Eloquent Rage*) and Rebecca Traister (*Good and Mad*), which recounted how women's anger often is decried as incivility and even pathology yet is a force for social change.[24] High-profile cases – such as that of Jameis Winston, whose exploits on and off the football field and during and after college are well documented, and Stanford swimmer Brock Turner, whose "twenty minutes of action" (his father's words) involving an intoxicated and unconscious woman next to a dumpster resulted in a sentence of six months in county jail (he served three months)[25] – highlighted how protecting men's futures appears to be a higher priority than women's safety. Eloquent first-person accounts resulted in previously unseen empathy for campus sexual assault victims. For example, the 2016 victim impact statement by Turner's unnamed victim, filled with powerful statements such as "You don't know me but you've been inside me," was viewed online millions of times. In her 2019 book *Know My Name*, she disclosed her identity: Chanel Miller.[26]

Showing remarkable strategic skill, women college students filed a Title IX complaint with the Department of Education in 2011, asserting that women's access to education was circumscribed because of campus sexual assault. (Before this, Title IX as it relates to gender was perhaps best known for increasing women's participation in school sports. As I write in 2020, the Department of Education's website indicates that hundreds of complaints about sexual violence are active.[27] And hundreds have already been settled.) In April 2011 the Office of Civil Rights in the Department of Education issued a "Dear Colleague" letter that began with the soaring language characteristic of the Obama administration: "Education has long been recognized as the great equalizer in America." Colleges and universities were directed, for the first time, to investigate all reports of sexual assault that were brought to them. Cases were no longer to be swept under the rug.

In 2013 End Rape on Campus was founded by a group of students including Annie Clark and Andrea Pino (both of the University of North Carolina at Chapel Hill) and Sofie Karasek (University of California, Berkeley). In that same year, Know Your IX was founded by Yale students Alexandra Brodsky and Dana Bolger, and Columbia student Emma Sulkowicz began her senior thesis art project, "Mattress Project: Carry That Weight," in which she carried around campus her senior year a mattress similar to the one on which she reported having been raped. College students who had been sexually assaulted testified before the U.S. Congress; wrote pieces published in the *New York Times*, the *Wall Street Journal*, *The Nation*, and elsewhere; and were interviewed on television and radio. They framed campus sexual assault as a public, not private, issue.

In September 2014 and in response to recommendations from the White House Task Force to Prevent Sexual Assault, the It's On Us campaign was launched. The organization created a thirty-two-second video titled "It's On Us," featuring multiple celebrities, to underscore that everyone has a role in stopping sexual violence. The 2014 video[28] became the template for campus-specific videos across the nation and, later, an organization by the same name worked with more than five hundred campuses to change attitudes and actions about sexual assault. They report that over a quarter of a million students have taken a pledge "to recognize that non-consensual sex is sexual assault, to identify situations in which sexual assault may occur, to intervene in situations where consent has not or cannot be given, [and] to create an environment in which sexual assault is unacceptable and survivors are supported."[29] Bystander education programs, which endeavor to increase the willingness and effectiveness of bystanders to intervene in incidents that might result in a sexual assault, became more popular, and careful evaluations document that they can be effective.[30]

In 2015 *The Hunting Ground*, a film by the same team that had produced *The Invisible War* about sexual assault in the military a few years earlier, was released. *The Hunting Ground* began with scenes of high school girls opening letters and emails notifying them of college acceptances. The offers of admission, typically met with joy, surprise, and pride, gave way to students' accounts of sexual assault and parents' accounts of their daughters' struggles, some of which ended in suicide. Rape survivor Lady Gaga cowrote and performed a featured song – "Til It Happens to You" – in which she gave voice to the pain and isolation of victimization, which brought further notice to the issue. The film unfortunately lent credence to David Lisak and Paul Miller's assertion that most campus sexual assaults were due to a handful of serial perpetrators, a claim that was inconsistent with prior research and about which subsequent careful research studies have not reached consensus.[31]

In 2014 the Obama White House urged colleges and universities to survey their students to assess, among other things, the scope of campus sexual assault. The action was motivated in part by recognition that higher-education crime numbers reported under the Clery Act did not reflect the scope of campus sexual assault. The idea of such a survey evoked negative reactions from researchers who had spent their careers studying sexual assault and from university administrators across the country. The researchers asserted that the proposed survey did not use the best available methods, and college administrators resisted the idea of a government-mandated survey.[32] Working on behalf of the Association of American Universities (AAU), an organization representing sixty-two of the nation's leading research schools, university administrators and a handful of researchers rapidly developed a survey that was administered at twenty-seven of their member schools in the spring of 2015. The resulting online survey, the Campus Climate Survey on Sexual Assault and Sexual Misconduct, measured victimization and knowledge about and perception of services.

Coinciding with the first weeks of classes across the country, a report of the overall findings of the first wave of surveys was released in September 2015, and shortly thereafter individual reports were generated for and provided to the participating campuses. The reports generated substantial media coverage that contained quotes along the lines of "I had no idea" from college presidents. Their astonishment was, well, astonishing. College presidents obtain briefings on a remarkable range of topics – from nanotechnology to demographic shifts that might affect application rates to investment strategies to maximize return on their endowments – and ask probing questions so as to best inform the future of their institution, yet many were taken aback by the information provided by their own students.

What did the report say?[33] Nearly one in four (23.1 percent) of the undergraduate girls reported having experienced "nonconsensual sexual contact by physical force, threats of physical force, or incapacitation" since beginning college. One in nine (10.8 percent) were penetrated in the assault. (Men's reports of such victimization are about 80 percent lower; for example, 5.4 percent reported that they were the victim of nonconsensual sexual contact by physical force, threats of physical force, or incapacitation.) Rates were higher among undergraduates than graduate students and higher among students who identified as transgender, queer, nonconforming, questioning, or gender "not listed" rather than heterosexual. (Nonbinary, a gender classification that has become more common since the 2015 administration of the survey, was not among the options from which students could self-identify.) And more than one in ten (11.7 percent) undergraduate girls reported that they had been sexually assaulted more than once during the current school year.[34]

A finding surprising to many college administrators was how many assaults didn't involve alcohol. Some college administrators had so closely linked sexual assault and alcohol that it was as if they were saying, "It's drinking. Drinking is the problem. If we can fix the drinking, this will get fixed too." And a good portion of it might be. Lower alcohol consumption at Historically Black Colleges and Universities (HBCUs) is posited to account for the observation that sexual assault rates are about one-third lower for female undergraduates at HBCUs than for women at other institutions of higher education.[35]

Concern about alcohol use is warranted, to be sure – being drunk reduces one's ability to read and react quickly and effectively to cues of danger, and alcohol can be used as a tool to incapacitate a potential victim. The report stated that "among undergraduate females, about as many individuals reported penetration by incapacitation (5.4%) as by physical force (5.7%). For sexual touching, a larger percentage of the undergraduate females reported being physically forced when compared to being incapacitated (12.8% vs. 6.6%)."[36] Moreover, "Nonconsensual sexual contact involving drugs and alcohol constitute a significant percentage of the incidents."[37] But a substantial minority of the incidents in which there was "nonconsensual penetration involving physical force" involved *no* consumption of alcohol by the woman victim – 30 percent at the University of Pennsylvania, 33 percent at Yale, 36 percent at Harvard, and 40 percent at Brown.

Consistent with common perceptions, the first year of school is a particularly risky time for girls: about one in six female freshmen reported unwanted sexual contact by physical force or incapacitation. The number drops to one in eight during the senior year.

Remarkably – and, to many, disappointingly – similar numbers were documented in reports of the second wave of surveys, conducted in 2019.[38]

The AAU survey can be critiqued for being limited to several dozen campuses, its relatively low response rate (albeit higher than for most surveys these days), and the fact that responses can't be verified. But it's the best we've got. And the findings are not all that different from what was obtained in other national surveys about campus sexual assault. Perhaps most damning is that by focusing on individual victims, the survey locates the problem of sexual assault at the level of the individual victim and unwittingly reinforces the idea of victims being responsible for their victimization. It does not focus on perpetrators nor, as its title promised, on the campus climate.

Many students personally know a victim or a perpetrator of campus sexual assault. At one university, two-thirds of undergraduates reported that they personally know a woman who is a victim of at least one sexually abusive act; over half reported that they personally know a man who is a perpetrator of those same acts.[39] Most students reported knowing multiple such people. From my classroom experience, I know that some students have a sophisticated understanding of and knowledge about sexual assault, while others might best be described as clueless. They are clueless about the topic despite the efforts of their colleges and universities to bring attention to and to prevent sexual assault.

New student orientation is commonly the setting in which colleges and universities provide information about campus sexual assault. Skits, role plays, and videos about consent are featured prominently these days. One cheeky video that's worth watching is "Consent, It's as Simple as Tea."[40] It draws a parallel between sex and making a cup of tea for someone: you can offer the tea and they might excitedly accept, not be sure they want it, say no thank you, or say yes and then change their mind. In less than three minutes, the video presents several variations – someone has changed their mind, someone has passed out, someone said yes one day but it doesn't mean that they want tea again – on "the important thing": if they don't want the tea, don't make them drink the tea, don't get annoyed at them for not wanting tea, just don't make them drink the tea. When used in new student orientation at the University of Pennsylvania, the simple and seemingly absurd parallels in the video were met with lots of laughter and, perhaps, recognition.

A clever public service announcement–type video that has been viewed millions of times is "What If Bears Killed One in Five People?"[41] In it the host of a football watch party nonchalantly minimizes the fear of his four guests who discover a bear in the kitchen: "I don't think it's going anywhere but I don't know what to do about it, so I just ignore it." His guests are less sanguine about his reassurances that "it's not going to eat all of us; it only eats, like, one in five." "One in five?!!" "I said *only* one in five, man." "You gotta get rid of this thing." "Or at least warn us!! . . . we gotta look out for each other!!" "Hey, what happens between you and the bear is none of my business." The video deftly satirizes university administrators' long-standing indifference to a documented danger.

All institutions of higher education that receive federal funding, which is nearly every college and university in the country, are required to offer sexual assault prevention programs. In April 2017 the AAU described the efforts of fifty-five universities to address campus sexual assault. The executive summary indicates that, during the previous three academic years, 100 percent of the schools changed "or are in the process of changing their education and training for students and faculty."[42] And 100 percent "developed, redefined, or enhanced programs to assist victims of sexual assault and misconduct."[43] This is remarkable. The federal initiative appears to be accomplishing its purpose: administrators began to acknowledge campus sexual assault and do something about it.

In late 2018 the Trump administration proposed changes to Title IX rules administered through the Department of Education's Office for Civil Rights that pertain to campus sexual assault. The proposal was designed to "clarify and modify Title IX regulatory requirements pertaining to the availability of remedies for violations, the effect of

Constitutional protections, the designation of a coordinator to address sex discrimination issues, the dissemination of a nondiscrimination policy, the adoption of grievance procedures, and the process to claim a religious exemption."[44] In essence, to correct for a perceived bias toward victims. Following a period of comment – over 124,000 comments were received[45] – new rules were issued and implemented in 2020.

Also in 2020 Jennifer Hirsch and Shamus Khan published *Sexual Citizens: A Landmark Study of Sex, Power, and Assault on Campus*. Based on years of research, it "reveals the social ecosystem that makes sexual assault so predictable, explaining how physical spaces, alcohol, peer groups, and cultural norms influence young people's experiences and interpretations of both sex and sexual assault."[46] I anticipate it will be an influential book for students, parents, and college administrators.

In closing, it is important to consider campus sexual assault in a larger social context. Community organizer Tarana Burke reports that, when a thirteen-year-old girl told her about being sexually assaulted, she wishes she had simply responded, "Me, too." More than a decade later, in the midst of disclosures about the abusive and assaultive behavior of filmmaker Harvey Weinstein and a second trial of comedian Bill Cosby, each of whom reportedly sexually assaulted dozens of women, actress Alyssa Milano encouraged women to speak up via Twitter and used the hashtag #MeToo. It quickly went viral as women recounted their experiences; within a year, #MeToo had been used more than nineteen million times by Twitter users around the globe. In September 2018 many people were spellbound by the testimony of Christine Blasey-Ford at a hearing intended to determine whether Brett Kavanaugh was fit to serve on the U.S. Supreme Court. It was not a quiet time.

Campus sexual assault is far less hidden than it once was. Moreover, student activism presaged broader social phenomena. These are not end points, of course, but they're a good start.

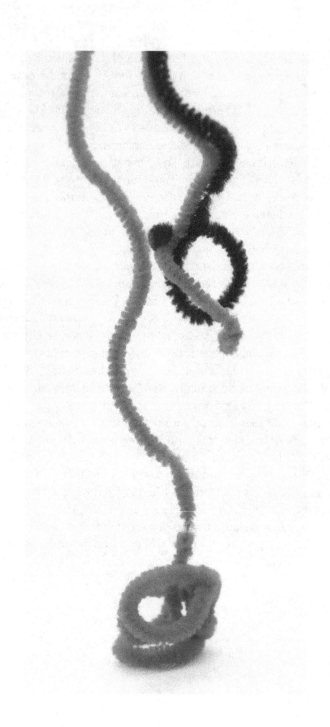

CHAPTER 3

How Families Work

Because there's another victim here – it's not just her, it's us – there was a violation of all of us when that occurred. —Father

It's a gift as well, to have the kind of relationship with your child that they can tell you something like that in their life. I've told her since she was tiny that I want to be part of it all, whatever you'll let me know. I mean, that's what family does – we're just there. —Mother

I never feel like I'm in my sweet spot. It's always "Am I saying the right thing? Should I intercede? When should I not?" It's an ongoing feeling of perpetual inadequacy, I guess. But you do the best you can, right? —Father

I've learned that no matter what you tell your kids, they're going to do what they want. I learned that you just have to be ready for whatever life throws at you. I never thought we would have to deal with that. . . . I think we all found a strength that we didn't know we had. —Mother

Chances are that you're reading this book because you are in the minority, the minority of parents whose daughters tell them shortly after they have been sexually assaulted. You aren't alone, but there aren't many of you. Your daughter turned to you because she wants you to know, might need your help, and sees you as central to her life. You are important enough to her that she came to you.

So that you have an idea of how few are told, let me give you some numbers. In a pathbreaking study of campus sexual assault more than sixty years ago, only two of the 414 "sexually offended" female college students had told a parent.[1] And of the 644 nonoffended students, only twenty-six thought that they would tell a parent if it happened to them. That means that 96 to 99.5 percent of the parents wouldn't have had the chance to be a source of support to a daughter who had been assaulted. More recent research focuses on disclosures to family members in general rather than specifically to parents.[2] But it is widely understood that girls in college rarely turn to their parent(s) after being sexually assaulted. (Please see the introduction as to why I call them "girls.")

When your daughter shared it with you, you were most likely taken aback, maybe shocked and stunned. Your system might have been pushed into overload. Maybe you said something you later regretted; maybe you regret not saying something you could have said. Few if any of us are ever prepared to receive such news.

We love our children with a fierceness they don't understand and probably won't until they have children of their own. Even with a nearly grown son, I find myself sometimes going into Momma Bear mode, much to his chagrin and perhaps occasional unspoken relief. We want to protect our children from harms they can't imagine, harms that we can imagine all too well.

But despite how you tried to prepare her for and inoculate her against all things awful, a horrible thing happened. Sexual assault can be deeply traumatizing for victims. Less well appreciated is how crucial a victim's family can be.

Families respond to crises – and learning of a daughter's sexual assault often is a crisis – in different ways. Let's step back from the immediate circumstances and think about families in general and yours in particular.

Like people, all families are unique. They differ along superficial dimensions, such as food preferences and the sorts of vacations they favor. They differ along dimensions far more likely to be consequential, such as whether both partners are employed outside the home or whether there is a single parent or, at the other extreme, a large, extended family that can be relied upon to help with day-to-day things and pitch in during a crisis. What works well for one family in meeting a challenge might not work well for another. And your own upbringing affects how you view the world – a reality that my Manhattan-born husband and I, from an Iowa farm, remind each other of with some frequency.

To provide an initial appreciation of such variation and to lay a foundation for subsequent chapters, I start by taking a look at some ways in which a family's characteristics and history can shape its dynamics, particularly when a child is a victim of sexual assault.

In the Context of Your Family

Families have histories that shape their identity and their views of one another. Years of interacting about music lessons, sports, homework, and social activities become shared, foundational memories. There also are challenging things: parents with a fractured marriage, a daughter with an eating disorder, a father with cancer, a mother with depression, family members with alcohol and drug problems, bankruptcy – you name it. We've all had "something" in our families. None of us emerges from life unscathed. We're touched by things based on who we are, and it affects each of us differently. Two parents described it this way:

> Our family is unique in many ways. But the main one is all three of our children had some issues in childhood, the biggest one being our son was diagnosed with autism at five. He's high-end Asperger's, now at [university] and doing extremely well. . . . It was a hard road in the early years. What that did for our family was all three of our kids are extremely open to talking – talking about differences and talking about challenges – because we just had to. —Mother

> She had to take on responsibility very early in life. And maybe I also contributed to how she is because she had to come to this country, where we don't have a lot of support. She had to do a lot, like help me take care of her brother. —Mother

So by the time a child goes off to college, the parent-child relationship most likely has faced a challenge or two. Much like toddlers testing limits and patience, conflict with a parent is common during adolescence, and the stakes can be high. The relationship between the parent and the college student daughter is not a blank slate. At times, parents and children handle the inevitable growing up and apart with grace; at other times, not so much. In this context of varying warmth, stability, struggle, and resolution, a daughter decides whether and what to disclose, as this parent and daughter explain:

She started a relationship with what turns out to be her current boyfriend, who is much older than she. And I guess she, in her wisdom, felt that we would be very against the whole scenario. So she decided that she would go on the sly and, for maybe about six or eight months – or maybe a year or more – basically lie to us. I was not shy to tell her that I felt very, very betrayed. I did not agree with her pursuing this relationship. She was right on that. But I don't think she gave me or us enough benefit of the doubt. And so, by the time that we had learned that this was actually happening, we were pretty angry and we did become the ugly people that she thought we were going to become. —Mother

I have always had issues with telling my parents things. Like in high school, I had an eating disorder. I hated myself. I used to cut myself. It was bad, and my parents didn't know about it. They found out when I started passing out and all that stuff – the dramatic stuff – and were like, "Why didn't you tell us? We're so upset." My mom was really hurt with that. When I got to college, there were a couple times where I had just not told her things, I guess I was still growing out of that. —Stacey

Children can be surprisingly perceptive, noticing things that adults think they are keeping hidden. The mistaken belief that things are secret can distort relationships and at times the child does the caregiving:

I knew a lot more than they thought I did. They thought I didn't know that my mom had tried to kill herself multiple times, when I totally did. They thought I didn't know that my dad had cheated on my mom, and

I totally did. They thought that I didn't know that my mom had also cheated on my dad, which I did. —Trish

My husband and I never fought in front of them. I only would share a little with her, but every day I'd come home and find that she had written a note to me. She would say, "Mom, it will be okay" . . . she knew I was not happy . . . she was eight. —Mother

I've always felt like I need to be the one who is mature. I feel like my mom and my sister can be emotional and that I can't, and it's really hard for me. Like when my stepfather committed suicide and when my dad left and that kind of thing, I was the one who took care of my mom and my sister emotionally. I don't feel comfortable being the person who is upset – I think that's part of what colors the interactions with my mom. —Julia

Sometimes a family's history includes assault and abuse victimization – the mother's, another daughter's, the father's. In some cases, such history can be an unanticipated bonus in that it can produce a generosity of spirit toward the daughter and what she's going through. The prior experience also can add a layer of complexity, especially if long-buried memories are brought to life. One mother told me "it would totally affect the way I respond now" if she herself had been assaulted. Regardless, how the experience was handled in the past can serve as a template, a guide for what to do and what not to do. As one daughter told me:

When I was in seventh grade, my uncle molested me. I wasn't sure what to make of it – it was breast fondling – but it stuck with me. I kept it to myself for years. When I was a junior in high school, I told my parents. We had this big argument, I was acting out, and that was just the first thing that came out of my mouth. Upon hearing it, they took action, and it was something that we had to deal with as a family. But after that, we never spoke about it again.

If news of your daughter's assault comes in the middle of a difficult time for your family, you might want to think that it won't affect how you respond, but it will. In one family who spoke with me, the mother had cancer, the father had heart problems, and the daughter had serious health problems too. They had their hands full. We rarely get to choose when bad things happen to us. We do what we can with the resources we have at the time.

Many Ways to Be a Family

Traditional family structure in the United States has consisted of a mother and father and their biological children. Times have changed. Fewer than half of U.S. children under eighteen years of age are living in a home with two married heterosexual parents in their first marriage.[3] The rest of the parents might partner with someone of the same sex, with a series of partners, or not at all. Bloodlines still matter, especially in legal terms, but the definition of "family" these days is largely social, relying heavily on parent-child roles and emotional attachment rather than genetic lineage.

Family interaction patterns likewise encompass a wide range of emotional closeness and expressiveness. Some are like a fire hose – everything seems to flow at full volume – whereas others feel almost pinched, only a little bit of information, a little bit of emotion ekes out, often in concentrated form. Paradoxically, but understandably, when a family that's been really close or simply been able to talk about nearly anything experiences a break in the face of an unexpected event such as campus sexual assault, it can feel even bigger than in a family that hasn't had as much emotional closeness. Decisions can be carefully considered or on the fly. Communication ranges from direct and clear to circuitous to diffuse based on the family, the individual family member, and the topic.

Here's how it played out in a few families:

I didn't tell anyone because it was something that I don't think she wanted anyone to know. I don't remember if she asked. I think it's up to her to tell her sister. And her dad. I wouldn't tell anyone. —Mother

The kids understand that whatever my wife learns, I learn. The people in our family, including sisters-in-law, brothers-in-laws, other in-laws, parents, they all understand whatever is communicated to her ends up coming to me and whatever is communicated to me ends up going to her. We then spend a lot of time talking between the two of us about how best to parent in different situations. —Father

My relationship with my parents is very interesting because it's very open. I'm very transparent with my parents. But at the same time . . . I'm not asking for permission each time I'm open, right? I'm not asking for validation. . . . Recognizing that I'm expressing myself and not asking for permission – and then getting them to see it that way, too – is new in my own growth. But it's hard . . . I don't want to be the cause of this much pain to my mother. —Abbie

Sometimes conversations have more than one level and can help a family address a topic that otherwise might be too difficult to handle directly. A father told me about a heated family conversation about the assault that, on the surface, was about school dress codes. He said:

It was actually one of the worst arguments I have ever had with my wife and daughter. . . . My son and I had a very particular position that was opposed, if you will. And then our middle son ended up being the diplomat who ultimately shuttled between the two rooms because we weren't talking to each other anymore. It was a remarkably heated conversation, and I know that a lot of it was because of what she had gone through at school.

We look to our own upbringing to help determine how we do and don't want to parent, but it's often not enough, especially when it comes to campus sexual assault. We often didn't have much modeling regarding how to handle such things. Yet we can see traces and shadows across the generations:

She's like her father in that way. Her father came from an abusive family background and he channeled all of his energy and talents into his work. I see that in her right now. —Mother

The problem for me is that what my parents needed and wanted always took precedence over what I wanted. As a consequence I have kind of swung the pendulum completely the other way. I will tell my daughter my opinion, but I'm never gonna say to her, "This is what I want you to

do." She has her own issues about reaching out to me. She'll say, "I'm struggling," but not in a way that says, "I want you to take this over for me." She will articulate and express all of her anxiety or whatever it is that she's feeling . . . [but] she wants to come up with her own solution.
—Mother

Importantly, parents told me that they, themselves, would not have turned to their parents had they been sexually assaulted in college.

Feeling caught between cultures was common among those whose parents or grandparents had immigrated to the United States. The girls described growing up in a restricted, protected environment that "wasn't at all like a Western view of sexuality." As one girl said:

My mom [born in South Asia] has these visions. Guy likes girl. Girl doesn't like guy. Girl's about to get engaged to marry somebody else, so she says no to this guy, right? That would be a very normal thing to happen in the U.S. Guy might be creepy and stalkerish or whatever, but generally, it's okay, right? Guy would finally leave, right? No. In [country name], guy goes and buys acid and throws it on the girl's face, and then is like, Well, if I can't have you, nobody else can.

Our cultural backgrounds, our family of origin, and our history of partners all affect how we view and create family. And how we deal with the disclosure of a sexual assault.

Relationships in the Family

Families are a network of relationships and roles. We like to think of roles being assigned on the basis of competence – someone was hired for a job because they're a good fit and have the requisite skills for it. In families, however, roles are ascribed. Parents are parents because they are the oldest and gave birth to or otherwise acquired a child. Children are children because they are the product, intentional or not, of their parents' desire and intention. Sometimes a parent is not so good at parenting and a child learns how to fulfill that role. It takes a lot to keep a family going and someone needs to do it.

Each person has a connection to every other person in the family, and alliances form and shift over time and across topics. Alliances can cut across genders and generations. As a mother and father reported:

> Our older daughter is a spitting image of him . . . they're very, very tight. Whereas this daughter is more like me, and I drive him crazy, so she drives him crazy, too.

> My daughters and my wife consider me a blithering idiot and insensitive troll, a man. They'd be horrified to hear me say that, but they would laugh about it, too. And they would say, "Yeah, we put you in your place," that's how they would put it.

Now for the roles.

Parenting

When we reflect on the entirety of life with our child, we typically start with the beginning – birth or maybe even conception. Even with a network of friends and extended family members, parents lament how they occasionally must parent "without a net." Parenting can be a source of apprehension for nearly all of us at one point or another:

> I always laugh and tell her – and I say this to both of my kids – you didn't come with directions, you really didn't. And we may make mistakes along the way, but it's all part of learning to determine where you're headed. —Father

> It does puzzle and worry me that she is kind of unemotional about things. There's a lot of psychology behind that. Is it the divorce? I was so emotional. Did that affect her? I mean, oh, my gosh, I often think how did I screw up her life? —Mother

As the child grows, day-to-day parenting can be grinding upon occasion, yet the mundane routine provides a concrete basis for the relationship. Both the daughters and parents who spoke with me talked about the importance of a sense of safety with one another. And some lamented its absence. Some parents seemed to serve as safety nets, whereas others focused their efforts on preventing their child from needing a safety net. As one mother said, "I'm not there to catch. I'm there to prevent having to catch." It can be exhausting:

> She gives me a run for my money. We've been at loggerheads more than I have been with my other daughter. She's a challenge for me. I don't think she fully respects a lot of what I do for her or bring to the table for her. And she's always judging me. I feel like the roles are reversed at times, way too often, actually. She's a tough nut. —Father

> Parenting is always hard. Parenting in the current environment, I think, is a little harder, a little riskier. You don't wanna make a bunch of steel-skinned children. You want them to be open and receptive and willing to experiment and try new things. Those are important things. —Mother

Parenting styles differ not just across families but within families. As they mature, children learn which parent is good for what and turn to that specific parent. (In chapters 6 and 7, I will address fathers and mothers.) Even those who pride themselves on parenting together well, regardless of whether they remain a couple, sometimes vehemently disagree. Such couples are likely to disagree about how best to address a daughter who tells them that she's been sexually assaulted.

One mother was clear about how she and her husband parent in very different ways, and another told me how they fill different roles for their offspring:

> I'm always there for her. But I let her know pretty straight when I'm really upset and when I'm really disappointed in her, whereas her father is like her constant cheerleader. No matter how bad it is, "It's okay, honey." And I'm like, "No, it's not okay." We have different parenting styles.

> Our daughters call their dad just to chat, and it's a beautiful thing. I'm not always part of it, and I love that they have their own relationship with their father. I'm sure that there are things that he knows that I have not been party to, and that's fine. We handle things differently. Not good cop, bad cop, but there's just certain things that they talk to their dad about, and certain things they talk to me about.

Coupledom

The relationship between the parents often gets less attention during the demanding hands-on years of parenting. At least it does in the United States, such that when the last child leaves home and the couple has survived, adult partners sometimes talk about the transition as an opportunity to get to know each other again. The parents who spoke with me had various paths to becoming a couple; some had met in high school and others were nearly twice as old as that when they met and married. No matter the age at which they became a couple, both mothers and fathers talked about how the labor of parenting often found them falling into traditional roles:

> In some respects, we each have a role and as long as they're covered, it's good. But as I'm thinking about it, that's the traditional kind of 1950s parenting where the father has these defined roles and the mother has those. I like to think of myself as a more enlightened dad but, in some respects, I'm not all that. I tend to go to safe zones, areas that I'm comfortable in, so to speak. —Father

> She gets herself into big things and then hands over the tough stuff. . . . Usually I take it on. He doesn't take it on. He doesn't want any part of it. He can't. He's not organized enough. He's busy enough with his stuff. He just can't. It'll never get done. And she knows that with me, it'll get done. —Mother

Mothers and fathers also spoke about how they managed one another in relation to their children, a task that became especially salient and charged when a daughter disclosed that she had been sexually assaulted. The length and depth of knowing one another could serve them well, whether in words or the set of a jaw, averted eyes, or the emotional heat that the other partner could simply sense.

Two such examples:

> I have to keep my wife in check sometimes because she will begin to fire questions at our daughter and stuff. And I just give her a look, and normally she gets the drift. Without me saying anything, she will just back off when I think she's being too stern. She is much more forceful with what she wants than I am. So I guess maybe I'm the good guy. She's the bad guy. And I guess that, for me, is a fortunate place to be. —Father

When I was annoyed at her or mad at her, I did not tell him. The reason I didn't is because he was mad at her and I was trying to not fuel that, trying to keep him from showing that to her. Because if he showed that to her, I felt that it was going to crush her – in her mind, Daddy was always okay. . . . He's mostly calm, but if he gets really pissed off at something, he'll go on this rant for about twenty minutes or a half hour. And she would have been devastated. And I kept reminding him of that. I would just sit there and I'd say to him, "You listen to me. If you say that to her, I'll never forgive you. You will destroy her if you do that." . . . He'd say, "I'm not going to say it to her." But I know it's brewing in him. I could just feel it . . . I mean, being married for twenty years . . . —Mother

Parents were aware that the daughter's disclosure didn't affect both of them the same way. Two parents' comments were particularly poignant:

The news was devastating for my wife; it hit her at her core. There were times when I was concerned that this was going to destabilize her to the point where she would need professional help. But that was the initial reaction. She's a very strong person. . . . She figured out the ways to support herself, support me, and support our daughter. . . . But she had quite a lot of emotion, anger and frustration and concern for our daughter and sadness. It really opened up a lot of sex stereotypes for her. It was kinda like if you spend a lot of your life as a police officer and then you actually have a family member get shot and killed. You always know that these kinds of things happen and the world is sometimes a shitty place. But then it comes right into your goddamn bedroom. —Father

She thinks he blames her, but he doesn't. He's just devastated that he didn't do his job as a parent. And I've tried to help him understand that it's not his job to protect her from everything. —Mother

Several parents who spoke with me were single. And those who weren't counted on the strength of their marriage to help them through the difficulties associated with their daughter's disclosure:

My husband and I didn't get married until we were in our late thirties – first marriage for both of us, and these are our only two kids. . . . I think if you're older, you deal with it a little bit better. I'm probably calmer than I was twenty years ago. —Mother

My wife and I just have a special relationship, and I think that helps with the kids, too. We don't fight over anything. What's important to her is important to me and vice versa. So I'm blessed – the Guy upstairs is looking out for me. —Father

I was thankful that I had him [her husband] around with his totally different perspective. I respected him for it. I was thankful and really glad that she has a father like him. —Mother

But it wasn't always rosy, as one mother recalled something that affected her relationship with her husband and, at least initially, her perception of its connection to their daughter's sexual assault:

When my daughter – the victim here – was a junior in high school, she caught her father looking at pornography of college girls at frat parties. I blamed her wanting to go to frat parties on her wanting to please Daddy. I know I shouldn't have, but I did. He and I have gotten past that, but it was really a big deal for me to get over in the first place. And then to take trips with him and my daughters looking at colleges – oh, it was really rough. —Mother

Couples can grow closer when dealing with their daughter's disclosure that she's been sexually assaulted. But not always.

Siblings
One child can cut a path, be the test ground if you will, for other offspring. In the abstract, children of the same parents are in the same family, but it isn't the same. In addition to differences in personal temperament, birth order, sibling constellation, and the family's financial situation, the parents' comfort with and confidence in their parenting changes over time. And there are simple preferences as well; one mother told me how her other daughter "avoided the lower-class stereotype and never considered herself Hispanic, whereas [the one who was assaulted] embraces it and learns Spanish. Her sister could care less; she's going to learn Italian. So they're just very different that way."

And sometimes siblings have painful things in common:

When her sister was three or four there was a big scandal at her day care . . . a worker got arrested for sexually abusing these little girls. Well,

guess who finally fucking told me [many years later] that she was one of
the girls? Yeah. So here you are thinking your life is one thing, right?
That really broke me. . . . [Our] two very strong, beautiful, independent,
smart-as-a-whip girls [were both assaulted]. —Mother

Sometimes the first person in the family the daughter tells is her
sister, even a sister with whom she has a classic sibling relationship
in which they love each other one day and are at each other's throats
the next day. One girl relayed that she told her fourteen-year-old sister
and asked her not to tell anyone. It was a decision she came to regret
because it weighed heavily on the high school freshman.

How the sisters relate to each other in general affects how they
handled information about the assault. The history they have together
is long, as one mother relayed:

> From the moment she was born, her sister treated her as though she was
> some foreign animal that just wound up in our house. She was born in
> early December, so we dressed them up in little Christmas outfits, and
> I'd put her sister in a chair and her on a pillow next to her. I was trying
> to get her sister to put her arm around her, so I could take a picture. And
> she's looking at her like "What is this thing?"

A disclosure isn't neutral; it affects the subsequent connection of the
sisters, and one sister can serve as an information conduit for another.
As two mothers told me:

> I think she's talked to both her sisters at length. The sisters always seem
> to know things before I do, so I'm sure that they communicate a lot with
> each other. They're so supportive of each other, they really have the
> best possible relationship. Even if someone messes up, the other two go
> straight to their defense. So it's great for them.

> She really didn't want to tell her sisters. And I'm like, "Well, you at
> least have to tell the one that's going to college so she can be aware of
> the dangers."

Brothers seem to be turned to less often but were reported to be
very supportive when they were. One girl spoke very fondly of her
twin brother and another relayed how her brother visited and helped

her rearrange her dorm room, where she had been assaulted. Mostly, though, brothers were simply part of the larger family constellation and, especially if younger, not made aware of the incident, at least not right away.

As two fathers said:

> We have had a couple conversations with our kids. Our older boy, our middle child, is smart, but he's a little clueless. And our younger is about the same. So I don't know what they've pieced together. But again, there were a couple conversations where it was very clear that my wife and daughter were becoming quite emotional around the topic. If you were listening carefully, you would figure out that our daughter has gone through things that she hates having gone through. I don't know what they [our sons] know.

> We made an agreement of sorts that we weren't going to share it with other people in the family. We weren't gonna share it with our other children at the time. Although, I think over the intervening year or so, that's been relaxed a bit. I think the boys probably have a good sense that something bad happened to our daughter because we've had family conversations about date rape and college abuse.

Each of these relationships enter into how the sexual assault is initially addressed and subsequently managed by a family. And we must remember the girl herself.

Who Your Daughter Is

Of paramount importance in a family dealing with the aftermath of a campus sexual assault, of course, is the girl who has been assaulted. What is her temperament, her basic personality? Has she been a person who is focused inward? Tentative in the world? Confident? A risk taker? Serious? Easygoing? Is she book smart, street smart, relationship smart? Does she seek your guidance and support routinely (one mother relayed how she hears from one daughter multiple times each day but not from the daughter who was assaulted), or does she come to you only when she needs help? Is she generally cheerful, doubting, cynical? Does she prefer being with older people and choose an older boyfriend,

or does she like being with those of her same age? Her years before the
incident and the nature of her connection with you during those years
will guide you during the days, weeks, months, and even years ahead.

These mothers put it this way:

> My daughter's a starfish – she regenerates fairly well. . . . She had a
> poster in her room for a long time about a bunch of starfish that got
> washed up on the beach and a little boy going along the beach and he
> starts tossing them back into the ocean. And a gentleman comes by and
> says, "What are you doing? This is a waste of time. You can't save them
> all." He said, "No, but I can save some." That's my daughter, that's her
> attitude.

> Her general character is that she's one of those who leaps before she
> looks. And so I've kind of got to be there to help her along. I love the
> fact that she's successful – she's got that real go-getter kind of personal-
> ity, she's kind of magnetic and it's fun to be around people like that. . . .
> I'm lucky to have her. I really am. She's a light in my life.

Regardless of structure or communication style, families are marked
by concern for one another. The parent-child relationship changes
over time – often going from a task-oriented, getting-it-done connection to a less frenzied hanging-out-together bond. Parenting, an oft-
cherished role, is never done:

> You worry about your kids being, God forbid, killed stepping off a school
> bus and somebody passes it on the right. Those thoughts go through your
> head every week. And it's no different now. The bigger the kids, the big-
> ger the problems. —Father

Even if you're ready and eager to let go of some of the responsibility – as many parents are when they drop their child off at college –
your daughter has turned to you in this troubled time because she wants
you to know what happened and because she might need you. This is a
time to parent as best as you can:

> It will hurt you quite a lot and it will be natural – I think, almost inevi-
> table – that you will have many different mixed feelings [*pauses, clears
> throat*]. And it will be hard for you, but it is nothing compared to what

the daughter has gone through. It's a violation of almost every aspect of her being, physically, mentally, emotionally. I mean, it . . . it happened to her. So listen to her and try to take your guidance from her. It's certainly what I have tried to do and it seemed to have helped, for what it's worth. —Father

We try to protect our children, but things that worked well for a stretch suddenly don't work at all. Sometimes we misjudge and choose wrong or could have chosen better. As one parent told me, "As soon as I get this figured out, the kid is onto something else and I've got to catch up again. I always feel a little behind." Feeling as if one needs to catch up and figure things out quickly is heightened at certain times. Parents expect certain changes, events, and shifts to occur as a child grows up. A daughter being sexually assaulted is different, however, and can require a departure from parenting as usual.

CHAPTER 4

So What Happened?

She just told me exactly what happened. I hope that she told me every-thing. I'm not sure that she did tell me everything. —Mother

I don't think my dad would ask too many questions, because I think he'd be scared to know what I've been doing. But my mom was asking a lot of questions, and I didn't want to talk about it. If I'm not telling you the answers to your things and I'm not telling you at the beginning, don't ask, because I'll tell you when I'm ready or I won't tell you at all. —Jocelyn

I am reminded of a book I read many years ago, *Stories Parents Seldom Hear: College Students Write About Their Lives and Families*, by Harriet Harvey.[1] Harvey, who taught writing at Yale, gathered the assignments of eleven undergraduates into a compelling book about growing up. As the book jacket notes report: "All of the tales were written – con-sciously or not – for parents. It was as if these young people wanted their parents to see them as independent individuals before they could step into adulthood with confidence."

A daughter's sexual assault appears to be a story that parents seldom hear for at least two reasons. First, many parents are not told, and second, those who are told often don't learn about the details. Parents whose coping relies heavily on intellectual understanding might want to know the specifics of the assault and yet *not* want to know. It's a tough position to be in. As one mother told me: "I didn't really understand the details, the step-by-step, like 'We were doing this and then we went there and then this happened.' I want to know the whole step-by-step and the truth is, I never really, really understood exactly what happened."

The specifics of sex continue to be a topic of limited conversation across generations. Although a sexual assault often is not about the sex itself, the fact that the incident involved sex in any form is sometimes too much for parents and daughters to manage in conversation. Because of this, some daughters don't disclose the details of their assault; they infer that the parent doesn't want to know the specifics. And in some cases they are correct. As one father relayed:

> I didn't get into the graphic information of exactly what he had done relative to her. I asked her about penetration and rape. That was one of the things that kind of like in my mind, did he go that far. And when she said no, I kind of backed off – I didn't get into or ask further questions. I just wanted to understand the scope of it. And so, I'll be candid with you, when I found out that he – it did not extend to a rape – I remember that feeling of relief. I was still quite angry, but like thank God it didn't go to that length.

Daughters also want to protect their parent's image of them. Some do not talk about the fact that they date, go to parties, drink alcohol, or are sexually active; thus telling a parent about their sexual assault risks unraveling mutually held constructions of who the daughter is and how she behaves. Several students who talked with me said that they had always been a "good girl" and feared that their parent would view them differently or, more accurately, as less. This perception was heightened when daughters were expected to adhere to cultural norms that are at odds with behavior typical of U.S. adolescents and young adults (for example, going to parties of any sort); youthful experimentation is seen as a violation of one's heritage and family. The strategy of these girls, if they told a parent, seemed to be one in which they left out key pieces of information. As one daughter told me, "I didn't give her details. She still doesn't really know what happened."

In addition, the daughter might not share specifics about the incident with her parent out of a sense of privacy. Some described it simply as a decision to maintain a boundary with a parent. One daughter said, "I wouldn't talk about my sex life with them normally, you know, and this is an extension of that, I guess. It's weird. I don't think they even know I'm having sex, so I wouldn't bring it up like that." Another likened not telling her mom to keeping a secret: "I've kept secrets from her before but, I guess, it's the biggest one. Because this is like something that seriously impacted my life that she doesn't know, which is weird. But I'm not telling her."

Also entering into the decision of whether and how much to disclose is the sense that telling a parent will do no good and perhaps even do harm. That said, if you are reading this book, it's likely because your daughter has come to you and you want more information.

What Happened

In this chapter, I address a single topic: simply what happened. Rather than describe or try to explain the incidents, I will convey each account as it was told to me. The students and their experiences don't apply to all college students or all college settings. At the same time, their experiences and the issues they raise generally will resonate across a wide range of educational institutions and students.

As you read them, I encourage you to keep in mind that your frame of reference is bound to be much different than the frame of reference of someone who is eighteen, nineteen, or twenty years old. There is a generational difference; things have changed. The old fraternity prank of mooning the sorority or the boy who exposes himself is viewed differently now than it was thirty years ago. College campuses are not the place where certain behaviors that were commonplace in the past – "Hey, I was a waitress in college and got grabbed every day" or "I used to slap everybody's butt all the time" – are seen as acceptable. Moreover, I get the sense that many in the general public think that there is a bright line somewhere but there isn't. A more accurate depiction might be gray, different shades of gray, especially when alcohol is involved.

You might consider some of the incidents recounted here to be simply uncomfortable situations, others to be "not that bad" (I recommend

Roxane Gay's book *Not That Bad*[2]), others to be largely a betrayal of friendship, and others to be wrong or outright horrible. The judgments you make as you read the accounts reflect the same evaluative process that your daughter went through before she spoke with you.

You might have held your breath as she spoke and let out a long exhale at the end, relieved that she wasn't raped. And you might even have said that. One parent expressed how "real rape" served as the basis for judgment in their family: "My other daughter has friends who had actually been raped, scenarios where there's been much more aggressive sexual assault behaviors. And so, she was talking about this being not as big a deal as that – she was kind of grading it on a scale, such as it is."

Your daughter's frame of reference, however, might not have been rape; it might have been "nothing." So what happened might be very traumatic for her. A father compared his daughter's sexual assault to that of a longtime friend: "[A woman friend of forty years] was the victim of rape at knifepoint. She never married – it was really difficult for her to open up to men because of that, it stayed with her all her life. I don't think my daughter's was a knifepoint or gunpoint rape or something like that, but it's still traumatic and it still has really long-lasting impact." He's got it right. Legal definitions are not central here; your daughter's psychological reality is.

These young women's accounts document a range of behaviors that comprise sexual assault. I organized their reports by a salient characteristic of the incident. Some accounts are brief, others long. In fair warning, they can be difficult to read.

Groping

In a massage, I got touched in a way that I don't get touched by anyone but my boyfriend. There was a massive language barrier. [*The student was abroad on a university-sponsored trip.*] And the only English word that he said was "fine." As he was touching my breasts, he kept on saying "Fine, it's fine, fine." But not in a way of asking, "Is this okay?" It was like, "This is fine, and this is what's happening and you're not gonna speak up about it." It was this insanely well-manufactured power dynamic – ingenious, now that I think about it – because it made me think that this was fine, that this was normal, when it wasn't. If anyone had come up to me in the street and just grabbed my boob – oh, my God, I would have been shocked, I would've jumped back. But it was the nature of the situation in a good establishment – [my friend, who also was getting a massage] was right there next to me. The fact that he was saying that this was fine, it was – it genuinely seemed – the only thing that was telling me that it wasn't fine was my gut. —Sophia

Grabbing

We were having a really wonderful time. We had gone to a house party, which was a little off campus and all students. I wasn't drinking, but I think the crowd there was very intoxicated and it was a really crowded place. We were dancing, having a really nice time. A lot of our friends were there. And then, it was really weird because, all of a sudden, I felt somebody touching my butt, just really aggressively groping. But when I looked around, there's nobody there, it's just a sea of bodies. I'm like, Oh, am I imagining things? But then this happened twice. And then thrice. And then four times! And so at this point, I'm just so paranoid – who keeps groping me so aggressively?! I felt very uncomfortable. I had my back to a wall, and was like, Oh, my God, we need to get out of here, I don't know what's happening.

I told my friend I am experiencing this sensation, I don't know if I'm imagining this, like it's an accident. And she was like, Oh, my God, that happened to me, too, but I can't seem to figure out who it was. So I thought it was just this sea of bodies; I didn't know somebody was being so intentional about it. It was painful, the grabbing and pinching. It almost seemed like somebody was targeting just girls or us. The last time it happened, I saw this body just move, right? And I was, like, Oh, my God, it must be that guy because every time I see this guy it happens, but I didn't process it – he was just moving through this sea of bodies and touching girls, and you can see him, not even dancing, not doing anything, but just touching girls, groping girls as he walks by. And then he walks by again and does it again. His hands are very traveling, right? Your personal – your private area – he just kind of gropes that entire area. It's so uncomfortable. It's so invasive. It's almost like he doesn't even see that these are people. It's like he's just using it for his own experience. —Trish

Oral

The person who did it was someone who I had been seeing – someone who actually is a serial offender, as it turns out. But basically, I was sleeping in my room and he came in, in the night. My roommate liked to leave the door unlocked in case she wanted to . . . [*drifts off*]. I don't remember certain parts of it because of the trauma of it all. To having done – against my will – a hand job, there were oral components, too, that I'm not gonna go into, if that's okay. I come from a traditional family where I was told as a kid, you do not close the door when you're with a boy, the door needs to be open, there needs to be someone else in the room, you should never be alone. So it basically was one of the first sexual interactions I had with someone. It just was really difficult. I still haven't been able to do a lot physically with partners. I haven't felt comfortable. —Emily

Changed My Mind

So then we went into a stall and he sat down on the toilet and he asked me to give him a blow job. And so, I started doing it. I was like, Okay, whatever. And then when I was doing it, I realized, I don't want to do this. So I just pulled away. I was, like, I don't really want to do this anymore. He's like, No, just come on, just do it. And so I kept doing it a little bit. And then I [said something] like, No, I really don't want to do this. He didn't ever force me to do anything physically. Eventually I just like got up and ran out of the bathroom and I went straight to my room. —Veronica

Charitable Sex

I was tired, I wanted to go to sleep. But it wasn't like I was being hurt, right? I love him and I want him to be happy, so I was perfectly . . . okay with him being happy and like having sex with me. But I wasn't happy doing [another sexual act]. So that's when I, my knowledge, I guess, of, like, the labels or of sexual assault in general made me say [that] this isn't right. Even though I want him to be happy, my happiness is also as important. So we need to have – we need to both be happy in order to have sex. —Maddie

Sleeping

I knew him. We were very close and involved with each other, socially and extracurricularly and stuff. I was sleeping over one night, and I woke up and he was having sex with me. It was very strange. I hadn't experienced anything like that before. I didn't say anything. I just let him finish, because I didn't know what to do. And then, I'm a very nice person, so I was planning on waking up earlier than him anyway and making him breakfast, so I continued to do that. We ate breakfast and I just went home. I wasn't really sure what to do. I didn't even know whether it was good or if it was bad or I should be upset about it. I was very confused. —Alicia

We were at a formal together, and there was an after-party, and neither of us were drunk or anything. We both had one drink at the party, and we were pretty sober by the time we got back to his place. We were kissing a little bit. I guess in retrospect there were like red flags because he started doing things and I was like, No, let's not do that, and he'd [say], Why, or he'd like try to push me to do it. And I'm not – I clearly was telling him no, I'm not comfortable, and he would be like, Oh, are you sure? Just kind of like trying to pressure me and keep going, even though I'm telling him to stop. And then later, like the actual incident was . . . I was asleep, and then I woke up and realized he was like doing stuff, obviously without my consent. And it was just like very confusing, and just like disorienting, and I'm like – he kind of pushed me aside and fell asleep. I felt very like used, and like objectified. And it was just a very scary thing. —Lily

Drinking

He was liked by everyone. That night was the first time I'd ever met him. We made out at a bar, but that was it. Nothing else. Didn't go back together. No suggestion of anything. So I thought that that was just it. [She went to another location where there was a dinner and dance.] After the dinner, after the ball thing [a formal dance], I [had been drinking a lot and] was very clearly not in a good state. Within five minutes he found me and basically brought me to his room. He laid me down on his bed. I couldn't even get up. He took my glasses off. My dress didn't even come off. He just pulled down my underwear. There was absolutely no foreplay. All I remember was asking him to put on a condom because that was just the only thing I could think of in that moment – I don't wanna get pregnant, I don't know if he has STDs. So it was basically in my head that this is what's gonna happen – that there's no alternative. He took my virginity. —Abbie

Not Conscious

I thought he was cute and I'd had a crush on him for a while. We were at a party and I was very intoxicated. I blacked out. I don't remember anything until I wake up the next morning to him having sex with me. I wake up and I'm confused about where I am, what's happened. And so I'm still incredibly drunk by the time I leave the house. So once he finishes I just get up, put my clothes on, and leave and go home and sleep. —Veronica

We had done more drugs once we got to his room, and I kind of passed out. And then I assumed – when I woke up the next morning, I had seen – and he wasn't there, and then I just was really sore and I couldn't really walk. But I felt like I had to get out of there. And so, what had happened was he had sex with me multiple times while I was unconscious, one being where I remember being like, I don't really want this, like no. And I tried to get him off of me, but he wouldn't stop. —Catherine

Got Her Drunk

It was a mutual friend of my and my boyfriend's at the time. Someone told me my boyfriend had gone home with another girl and I was upset. He [the mutual friend] was like, Wow, that really sucks to hear, do you want to hang out with me and we can just like drink, you don't have to worry about it. I was like, Okay, yeah, I know this guy, we're friends, he's friends with all of my guy friends. And then we were drinking, and then I just didn't want to keep drinking because I felt myself losing control. And he was like, No, no, no, you need another, you need another. And at that point, I was just like, Okay, I guess, sure. And so we were just dancing, it's probably like 2:30 in the morning and he started making out with me against the wall, and I'm like, Oh, okay, he's cute, whatever, if this is as far as it goes, it's fine. And then he just kept telling me, Keep drinking, keep drinking, keep drinking. And I was like, Okay, I guess, I trust this guy, it's fine, he wouldn't make me do anything I didn't want to. And so at this point, I'm sort of blacking out and in, which is a really unfortunate thing to be doing. I don't ever remember leaving the party. I remember blacking in, in my room and really making out, but then he asked me if I wanted to have sex and I said no. He asked me two or three or four times, and I just kept being like, No, no, no, I don't want to, I don't want to. And then I sort of blacked out again. And so I couldn't tell you how long it was going on for. And then the next thing I remember I kind of became conscious again and was crying and we were already having sex and I was in tears, covering my face, asking him to stop. He was like, No, just let me finish, just let me finish. And I was like, No, no, stop, stop, but he didn't, I guess. I guess he didn't, because I kind of blacked out after that. And then I woke up in the morning, he was gone. He sent me a text, You should probably get Plan B [*a post-coital form of birth control*], and I was like, Okay. And that was pretty much what happened. —Julia

I didn't really know what to expect in college, I guess. Drinking had never been a big part of my relationships. We [my boyfriend and I early in freshman year] ended up going to a date night at a frat, and he's, like, how much do you think you can drink? And I was, like, I think I should probably cut myself off at like thirteen drinks. I was very drunk; I didn't cut myself off at thirteen. He had me playing in a drinking game for him, taking his spot because he thought that he might be intoxicated. He told me later that he didn't wanna get intoxicated because he wanted to have sex with me that night. But I guess he didn't seem to think it was a problem if I was. I completely had control over how much I drank; I chose to drink that much. But anyways, I was really drunk. We went back to his place, and I took some shots of tequila in his room, and he didn't drink anything. And when we were having sex, I told him that I wanted to stop, that I was too drunk. I think what I said was, Please stop, I'm too drunk, I don't want it anymore, please stop. I was crying. And, yeah, he sort of looked me in the eye and didn't change anything . . . I just kind of gave up, I was just kind of trying to pass out. His roommate was knocking and came into the room, and the first person I told about it was the roommate. I was crying and telling him that I didn't want what had happened. —Kimberly

Age and Power Difference

He knew a bunch of my friends. We were friendly and I thought he was cute. We always flirted a little bit, but it just kind of was never really gonna happen. My friends were like, Bad idea, bad idea—just because he was old [*she was a sophomore, he a senior*]. I was of the mindset like we can just flirt and stuff, but it's never gonna go anywhere. But I think he might have had other thoughts. We were out. I saw him. He just kept buying me drinks, kept saying things. He knew me pretty well and he's really smart, and I think he knew kinda what he needed to do, needed to say. And, yeah, so that happened. I mean, I guess I went back with him, but at a certain point I was saying no and that wasn't being listened to. And then finally, I was able to leave at 4:00 or 5:00 in the morning. I left and walked home and went back to my room. —Liz

I don't know how long I'd been there maybe a couple of weeks. [*Student was working with a local organization while on study abroad.*] My boss seemed so cool to me. He was probably in his late forties and he had dedicated his life to doing work to help kids and he took a special interest in me, which I found incredibly flattering. I was really enamored with him and his life's work, and he seemed to think that I was really intelligent and special and that I was gonna do great things. He started [paying] more attention to me than the other interns, and that still felt okay. I was moving to different apartments because the housing didn't work out, and he offered after work to help me move, and I politely declined. I was kinda getting a sense that he was more interested in me than the average employer . . . something he did every week was take the interns out for drinks and food. . . . My boss really seemed to think that I was some very brilliant student who was about to do something amazing. I really wanted him to think that I was cool and I could, I don't know. Something like that. But anyway, he encouraged us to drink and, as you would imagine, I blacked out. I mean, I guess I'll never know, but I still think that I probably was drugged because I blacked out for a long time. When I came to, the other interns were gone. It was just my boss and me, and he was naked and he was on top of me and I was naked. And I was really confused and dizzy and disoriented, but I told him to stop. . . . We were on this couch, and he said, Why do you say that to me? It makes me so upset, it makes me so sad. I kind of pushed him away again and tried to sit up, and I was like, No, this is making me uncomfortable. And he was like, No – you're just being like an American. And it's all kind of a little bit blurry in my mind. And then he started saying these weird things to me about how he wanted to marry me. He had singled me out and he knew from the start that I was the one for him, and I was kind of like, No, this is not okay with me. I wanna go home. And he, he refused to let me go home. And eventually, I started crying, and I was just like I just really, really wanna go home. Please stop. And then he let me go home, but not after touching me and – yeah. —Sara

Betrayals

I was dating a guy at the time, and I would say for the longest time he was just verbally and kind of emotionally abusive. And then it escalated to a day where there was a lot of alcohol involved and we were arguing, and he and his friend took advantage [of me] when I wasn't conscious. I found out later because they told their entire fraternity. A friend of mine kept kind of saying to me, or hinting to me, that I should talk to him [the boyfriend] about something that happened earlier and that everyone is talking about. I confronted him and he told me what happened. It was so humiliating. I feel like it would have been different if it was something that I could have remembered or stood up for myself about, but since I wasn't conscious it just – it was very, really humiliating. Well, so his whole fraternity knew and so that trickled down to some girls in my sorority. So I had to kind of tell my closest friends because the way that my ex-boyfriend and his friend framed it when they told their entire fraternity was that I was aware. And so what was going around was that we all did this together, and I had to explain to my friends that that's not what happened. So my closest friends in my sorority know – probably three or four girls. —Hannah

My suitemates were like, Oh, there's a party, let's all go. One of them was wild. And I was like, I've never – but they were like, You should come. I told them I had never been to a party before. Even in high school, I was always at home. So we were like, Okay. Let's all of us go. So we all went. And one of the girls was like, Alright, I'll be the mom of the group. And I said, But that's my job. And they're like, No, you're going to have fun. And I was like, Okay, I'll have fun. That was the first time I drank alcohol, and I hated it. But they were like, You can keep going. And so obviously we were intoxicated after a while. And then the girl that was going to be the mom was gone, and I felt really uncomfortable because she was supposed to be the one to get us home and everything, but after a while I stopped thinking about it. And then these guys came over. And you know when you feel very uneasy? I could sense them watching me – my mom calls it the sixth sense that every female has – and I felt very uncomfortable. It was my first time drinking and I couldn't really act on the feeling. So when they came over, they were like, Hey, do you want to go back to our place? I was like, Are you kidding me? I'm not going back to their place! My suitemate was like, Oh, we're gonna go and smoke weed or something. And I was like, I can't do that – my program does drug tests and everything, I don't want to do that! So I just went with them, and I sat. They did stuff. They were like, Hey, give it a hit. I was like, No, I can't. They were like, Wow, you're so strict. They were mocking me and everything. I was like, I really don't care what you're saying, I just want to go home. So I went to my dorm and sat on the couch.

A few minutes later, the one that was supposed to act like a mom came in and she brought the guy with her and they were like, We can continue having a party in here. I was like, Why'd you sign him in? We don't know him! I just sat on the couch and eventually fell asleep. And then I woke feeling someone grabbing my arm, and I thought, No one's here, who is that? It was the guy they signed in. And then he was like, Have you ever done anything before? And I was like, No. And then he was like, Okay, but then he was touching me, and I didn't say anything, I didn't know if I could. My roommate was asleep in the room, so I could have said something, but I didn't. He unbuttoned my jeans and did whatever – he couldn't really do anything because it was like – I guess I was a virgin, and I wasn't sexually aroused or anything, so he couldn't really do anything. I wanted to say something, but I just – I don't know. I've never been – I've always thought of myself as very – I know I'm sensitive and I know sometimes I'm gullible and naïve, and people take advantage of that, but I've always been very – I know it's two contradicting personality traits to have, but I've also been very upfront and very – if I say no, it's no. But I just – I don't know. Maybe – I don't know what it was, but I just couldn't. Maybe I'd – because I'd never been in a position like that. So it was like – I knew I didn't want it because – I don't know. I was talking to someone already, and I really already knew how I felt about that one person. So I don't want this at all. I know it's very stereotypical, but if I was going to do something, I wanted it to be with someone I loved, especially if it was going to be my first time doing anything. I had never even been kissed before that night, so it was like – so it was like – I just didn't want to do it. I'm a hopeless romantic, sad to say. He was bigger than me, so what can I do? I know I could've done more, but I just couldn't find my voice. He started touching me, my arm first, and then he moved my head because I was sitting up straight, but I was – I was sitting, but I was slouched over because I was asleep and everything. And then he tried kissing me, and I pushed him away. It felt weird. It wasn't what I imagined kissing to be like. So I was like, No. And then he was like, Oh, okay. Then he was – then he came back – like oh, okay to the kiss, but then he went, and he tried unzipping my pants. And that's when I was like, I don't know what to do. And then he – I think he put like – I don't know. He was reaching for something, and I think that was a condom or whatever. He did that, and then he tried. I remember what he said to me, and it just makes me so disgusted. And then he really couldn't do anything, so I – that's when I kicked in. I pushed him away. I was like, I'm going to sleep. And I pulled up my pants, and I went into my room, and I fell asleep. —Jocelyn

Wanting Traditional Roles, Romance in the Age of Hookups

There was a fraternity party that I had gone to, and I met one of the new guys, a freshman, that wanted to join or whatever. We had talked way into the night at that first party. I was attracted to him. I liked him. I wanted him to like me back. So when I heard that there was this mixer going on, I definitely wanted to go so I could see him again. Maybe something could happen, who knows? The problem is that because I was so anxious about it, I got very drunk. I was still kind of an anxious mess, even though I was drunk and he wasn't making the moves I wanted him to make. So I enlisted the help of a friend – I told him about how I was feeling and whatever. I didn't expect him to, but he just went up to the guy and said, "She likes you, just kiss her," or something like that to spur him into action. So he did kiss me. We started making out. It was fine. My memory's a little fuzzy here, but the mixer was going on, on the ground floor, and at one point I think he went to the basement to clean up something. I'm not sure. But I followed him down there. I think it was late, everyone else was gone.

We started making out again in the basement. And things started heating up. Things started getting intense. And I thought, Okay, we should probably move this somewhere. And I think I paused and asked him, Do you want to come back to my apartment? And I offered that to him. And he said some excuse like, No, if I do I won't be able to make it back in the morning. And I didn't want to go to his dorm because he lived really far away. I think he said something along the lines, Follow me, I know where we can go. And he led me through this door in the basement, to either this room or this hallway. It was dark and I was drunk, so I can't really remember. I think he was really drunk, too, but I'm not sure. I don't know if it was a mattress or something, but we started having sex on that. I never explicitly said no or not to do this, or whatever, but – so that's what made it tricky for me to come to terms with this. Because I did want him and I did want this to happen. It was just not under those circumstances at all – it was an unfamiliar place, I was scared, I didn't want to be there – it was not pleasant. At first I was like, Oh great, this is going the way I wanted it to. But then as reality sank in of, I don't know where I am, I don't know him that well, he is not – clearly not caring about me, because he just pulled me into this random room in the basement to have sex with me. So then the one thing that I clearly remember of this whole timeline or action of events, or whatever, is that I was – I guess I was on my knees and elbows or something, because I woke up with scrapes the next day – I remember thinking I just want this to be over. That's what was going through my head – When will this be over? When can I go home? —Jessica

Negotiating

I had never done anything, but I smoked for the first time with him and I was like, Wow, this is living on the edge. And so he invited me back multiple times to his room. And I said no. And he kept pushing night after night. And he asked me why I said no. And I said I was a virgin and I intended to stay that way. And then I feel, this is just my speculation, but after that, he just got more and more persistent because it became more of a challenge kind of thing. . . . [The next night] we had been drinking. We started kissing and that was consensual. And then I tried to leave. The bathroom was right next to the door and he pushed me into the bathroom. I was so disoriented, I didn't even know what to do. I guess I should have fought back harder, but I was really disoriented. And he took my dress off and he – I didn't even know what to do with him, to push him back or what. So I said no. And then I just put my hands over myself to try to cover myself. And then he pulled my hands apart and held them together, and then he penetrated me and then I started saying that it hurt and that he should stop and that I didn't want to lose my virginity. And then I told him I would give him a blow job if he would stop. So whether or not the blow job was coerced is a question mark. So that happened. And then the next morning I woke up there and I ran out. And I had blood and I was just so freaked out. But I wasn't really sure what had happened. I just thought, Oh, well, that was a shitty way to lose your virginity. I didn't realize that what had happened was not consensual. It didn't click back then. —Leah

"No" Is Ignored

There was a bathroom – a public bathroom once you entered, and then
the lobby area of the building before you went upstairs to the dormitory
rooms. He said, I need to use the bathroom, and I said, Okay, go ahead.
And so he went in and then came back outside and said, Actually, let's
both go into the bathroom. And I said, What are we both doing – why
would we both go in the bathroom? And he just said, I just want to talk
to you about something there. And I was like, Why can't we just talk
about it here? And he said, No, it's private. And I was like, All right. So
we went inside. And this was at a time, I guess I would say, that I had a
lot of difficulty saying no to people in general. I don't know whether –
as I said I'm from [country name] and I later realized that – it's like a
very cultural thing where women are kind of taught to be submissive in
nature. And I don't know whether that contributed to me being unable
to be assertive in general. But anyway, we went in and at first we were
just talking and it was fine. But then he kind of pushed me against the
wall and started kissing me, and I asked him, What are you doing? I
already said that I don't want to have sex or anything – I was a virgin.
He said, No, we're just kissing, it's nothing big, really. And I said, Okay.
And I said again, like I had said, I don't want to have sex. And he said,
Yes, yes, I understand, okay. And we kept kissing, yada-yada. Then
he pushed me to the floor, onto the ground, and I started asking him,
Now what are you doing? This is when I was like, What exactly are you
doing? And he just said, Be quiet, don't make noise, people are gonna
hear outside, I guess, in the lobby area or whatever. And I was like, Why
should I be quiet, what do you mean? And I remember he got a phone
call from someone, I don't know who it was, but he had already – by this
point, he had already taken off his clothes. I still had my clothes on, I
don't think he had taken off my pants. And when he went to answer his
phone, he had left his phone on the opposite end of the room, and he
went to answer it, and I remember just sitting there, almost immobile
because I tried to get up and leave. I don't know why I didn't leave, I
was just there. And he came back after being on the phone, and I said
I don't want to have sex. And he said, Yes, I understand, you've said it
over and over, I get it.

But then he proceeded to take off my underwear and then he forced
himself into me. I remember just asking him, I said I don't want sex,
what are you doing? And he said, Well, this isn't that big of a deal, and
he just kept repeating that. And I don't remember what I was thinking

really, or how I was feeling at the time. All I remember is after he had done this, he stopped all of a sudden and put on his clothes quickly and ran out and said, I'm leaving, you can't come out of the bathroom before or at the same time as me, you have to wait here. And I was still on the ground without my pants on, and he just left. And I think I just – I lay on the floor for a couple of minutes, trying to just understand what had happened or – I don't know – trying to put together the pieces. But eventually I did put on my clothes and I walked out. I just kept repeating to myself, You're okay, you're okay, and this didn't happen to you, you're okay. I was crying, but I just kept repeating that over and over. —Jenny

My dad's family is from a country where it's kind of ingrained in the culture to have a glass of wine at dinner. And so I've had a taste of alcohol before going to college, but this was one of the first times that I kind of let myself go a little bit. I wasn't to the point where I lost my wits about me or anything like that, though. I just felt dizzy, and I just knew that I wasn't in an awesome state, so I wanted to be near my friends if possible. And I had gone to the bathroom all by myself because I knew what the house was like because I've been here before and there weren't too many people [at the party]. I was actually followed into the bathroom by someone who had been trying to dance with me earlier in the night, but I didn't want to dance with him. He kind of pinned me down to the ground and I fell while trying to get back up. And I couldn't scream just because I was in shock of what was going on. I just – I wasn't sure what was happening, and I was drunk and, although I had my wits about me, I didn't have enough self-control or the strength to kind of protect myself as I would have if I was sober.

He kept asking me, Let's have sex, let's have sex, and I kept saying No, no, get away from me. [She had not had sex.] And I tried my best to try and push him away, but he was very violent in terms of trying to rip my clothes off. And when I took my stuff to the lab, I mean, parts of my clothing were ripped. And he – yeah, it came to a point where he had just his boxers on and I had my underwear on and I was – at that point, I started yelling, and he was very close to me and was almost about to put it in before my friends actually knocked on the door. It's miraculous how they came in such perfect time, but that's when they saw that he had basically almost no clothes on – he only had a shirt on, and he grabbed his pants and he ran off. And I was in the bathroom and I was kind of in a frozen state for a while. —Theresa

Earlier in the day I went to my friend's dad's funeral. It was very emotional for me. When my friend and I got back, we went to the local bar; it was really fun, drinking and dancing and stuff. There was one guy who kept dancing with me, but I didn't want to dance with him, so I'd just kind of lose him. When we were leaving, my friend started talking to some guy and he invited her over. I didn't want her to go alone, so I was like, Okay, I'll go with you. Turns out the guy is the roommate of the guy I was trying to lose. So I was like, Oh, great. I was really tired. It was a long day for me and I had been drinking, so I just kind of wanted to go there and just sit and chill out, but my friend and the other guy started making out. And so the other guy started making out with me and then that kind of led to the incident where I was so tired, I was like, Can I just go to sleep. I just want to fall asleep. And so I just went to his bed and then he violated me. It wasn't intercourse, but I had told him to stop several times and even pushed him away and he didn't. I was just so tired and, I don't know, just over it. I just kind of – I don't know, stopped trying to push him off. And then I woke up in the morning and found out that my friend had left way earlier; she had come up to check on me and she saw that I was asleep, so she thought I was fine. I got up and just kind of got out of there as quick as I could. —Stacey

The accounts of sexual assault conveyed to me by these twenty college students represent a range of behaviors and outcomes by both them and their perpetrator. Some incidents you might consider to constitute rape, others to be less extreme forms of sexual assault, others yet to be sexual coercion or harassment, or maybe to fall outside the definition of abusive behavior altogether. As you will see in chapter 5, the daughters considered a similar continuum as they struggled to name and label their experiences.

If you found yourself focusing on the daughters and their choices – whether and how much they drank, whether they accompanied a guy to his room, how they handled situations in which they did and didn't want to be sexually active, and so on – you're not alone. As recounted in subsequent chapters, the girls questioned themselves about these very things and, in anticipation of how others would evaluate them, decided whether to talk with others about the incident.

Likewise, if you found yourself judging the perpetrators in these scenarios, you probably aren't alone. In several cases they were persistent, in others they sound predatory. With limited exception, the girls described good use of their communication skills – both nonverbal through physical avoidance and verbal through straightforward statements of "Stop . . . no . . . I don't want this." Listening intently to the girls, I was struck by the frequency with which they continued to be polite, to not want to offend the guy, to respond from an "I'm a nice person" image of themselves. Yet the college boys continued in the face of clear "no" and "stop" statements from the girls.

I was not surprised that each incident involved someone the girl knew. Rapes and sexual assaults by strangers are a reality for women. Far more common, however, are rapes and sexual assaults by men known to and even loved by the women who are victimized. This society-wide pattern is evident on college campuses. When the perpetrator is someone they know, more than their body has been violated. Their trust in others and their confidence in their choices regarding whom to trust can be deeply shaken. Moreover, their sense that they are supposed to be safe in the world – or at least safe at college, a place that they chose and, in turn, chose them – is challenged.

I *was* surprised by how public bathrooms figured into several of the incidents. We tend to think of sexual assault as occurring in private spaces. And public bathrooms, simultaneously public yet private, are typically not all that clean, showing signs of their primary purpose – a repository for the expulsion of human waste. The risk of someone walking in during the incident may have heightened the experience for both individuals – for the perpetrator in terms of getting away with something in a brightly lit public space, for the girl in terms of confusion about the reality of the situation and perhaps a particular sense of debasement associated with the setting.

Several of the girls experienced "frozen fright" when they determined that they were in danger. It might be helpful to call to mind the work of Hans Selye, the founder of stress theory. Selye proposed a model of human stress response that consists of three stages: alarm, resistance, and exhaustion.[3] He posited that, during the alarm phase, humans will flee or fight back when under threat. But sometimes we just freeze, perhaps most often when there is an intense conflict in our assessment of what is and what should be. Girls described this circumstance well – they believed they should be safe (safe with someone they know, safe in a public bathroom) at the same time that they were aware that what was happening was not safe for them. They froze, which often was a source of consternation as they looked back on their experience.

The experiences of these girls do not involve weapons or physical brutality. Nor do they necessarily involve forced penetration. If parents focus on physical force and penetration, they will likely be perplexed when their daughter is having trouble "recovering." Again, quite often sex is not entirely what it's about for the girl. As the girls told me and as will be addressed in subsequent chapters, the event can be traumatic and the damage psychological.

Alcohol- and hormone-fueled boundary testing is common in late adolescence and young adulthood. Sexual assault on college campuses occurs in a complicated matrix of social norms and a range of relationships. Some of the girls considered the incident to be part of "the college experience," whereas others perceived it to be outside the norm. Regardless of how you or I or anyone else might judge these experiences, the girls considered them to be traumatic. Their assessments were based on characteristics of the incident itself, their relationship with the perpetrator, and the personal history each had developed during nearly two decades of life.

Your daughter told you, in generalities or in detail, about the incident because it's important to her and she wants you to understand, perhaps to help in concrete ways, and, foremost, to *know* her. What comes next is crucial. In the next chapter, I discuss giving and getting the news.

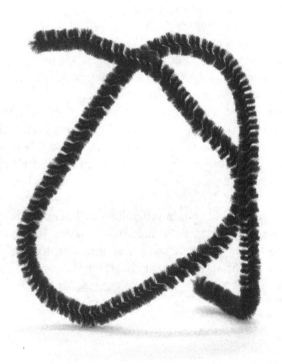

CHAPTER 5

Giving and Getting the News

What a terrible thing for a kid to go through and then not have an avenue to talk to their parents about it. Wow. That's a lot for a young person to deal with. —Father

I am really close with my dad. If it were really traumatizing, I probably would [tell him]. . . . I would definitely go to my mom first and probably would open up to my dad about it. I can't decide right now, but I would consider it at least. —Sophia

I did not want to tell my parents whatsoever because of the whole you-shouldn't-have-sex-until-you're-married deal. I was pressured to tell, and I really wish I hadn't. —Catherine

It allows me to parent her forward, because I'm sure the parents that don't know don't get why their child's being resistant to this and this and this and just figure they've had a change or they're going through a stage or whatever. —Mother

It's a burden for parents to know about their daughter's sexual assault, but being told is a gift. It might not feel like one at the time, but you matter enough to her that she wanted you to know.

Most of the girls who talked with me had not told, and did not plan to tell, their parents about their assault. The reasons rested largely on their perception of the parents – that it would upset them and that there wasn't anything they could do anyway. This sentiment can serve as a general guide for parents.

But first, I want to acknowledge that your foremost reaction likely is that you feel terrible about what happened to your daughter. The emotions might be so intense that it might feel as if it happened to you. But it didn't. It's important to remember that. Your daughter needs you now. When you need comforting or a place to be angry, turn to someone else. It is not your daughter's responsibility to tend to or even to respond to your emotions right now. Maybe one day you can tell her more fully about your reactions, but this is not the day. It might be hard, but it's important to know that a common reason girls don't tell their parents is that they want to protect them; they think such news would be too hard for them to bear. It will be hard, no doubt. And you'll say that if you need to say it. Such a statement is best followed with kind and firm reassurance: "This is hard for me, but I can handle it. I have [fill in the blank here – friends, family, church, whatever and whomever you turn to] and will be fine. Maybe one day it will make sense for me to talk about my feelings with you, too, but not now. This is a time to focus on you."

But maybe she told you and you went right to your pain or your fear. It happens. Certain news can shock us so much that our usual ways of being, our usual efforts to be helpful, can become overwhelmed and our own primitive emotions leap out. If that occurred, your daughter probably didn't take it so well. She needed you and instead you gave priority to your own reactions, to yourself. It happens. None of us are perfect parents, perfect friends, or perfect humans. We sometimes mess up in the big picture. The issue then becomes how to reconnect and move forward.

Maybe it hit something deep inside you, something that cried out when touched. Sexual assault itself is not new – many adult women and some men have been its victims. Many of those victims are parents, and some of those parents have a college-aged child who has been sexually assaulted too. A parent having been sexually assaulted – often, like the daughter, at a young age – can be a complicating issue. More on that later.

Some college students tell their parents everything. Others tell them nothing, no matter what. Most are in a middle ground and make decisions about what to tell and when, consistent with their sense that they are becoming adults and figuring out how to handle things on their own. If you're the sort of parent who has always thought of your daughter as a friend, her disclosure might be a reminder that you are her parent first and foremost.

Telling Is a Choice

The #MeToo movement and both civil and criminal sexual assault charges against high-profile men have raised awareness of a woman's decision to talk about having been sexually assaulted and the timing of her disclosure. Multiple considerations go into the "when" decision. Let's focus first on the "if" decision.

Telling someone else about having been sexually assaulted is a choice. When I sought college girls who were willing to talk about their decisions, I sought those who had made what I called "for now decisions." This name recognized two things: first, that there was a choice to be made, and second, that other choices might be made in the future.

In that context, let's consider why some of the girls who spoke with me chose not to tell. Those who had not told, and didn't plan to tell, their parents focused on protection – protecting themselves or protecting their parents. In both cases, they believed it would be harmful if the parent knew. Those who seemed to be protecting themselves by not telling spoke about how they thought they would be – and didn't want to be – pitied, treated differently, blamed, or have their judgment questioned. They also were concerned that their parents might act rashly and pull them out of school (like the perpetrator, the parents would take away her choice) or, when the perpetrator was known, harm him. These young women were also concerned that a parent would feel helpless or sad. As one daughter's comments illustrate:

It happened. And there's no use in telling her and hurting her. She can't do anything. I don't want her to be burdened, like I am, with "I could've done this, I could've done that." She wasn't even there, she didn't even

know I was going to the party, she didn't know what was happening, so
I know I won't tell her. —Liz

The fact that the act, which often included a betrayal of her trust
and sense of safety, had a sexual component was relevant for some,
especially when the parents had a "good girl" image of their daughter.
Talking about sex in general, let alone about one's own experience, can
be difficult for parents and their offspring. And quite frankly, quite a few
parents are afraid of conversations about the body and human sexuality.
How does a daughter go to a parent like that and start perhaps their
very first discussion about these issues with rape? If she was robbed at
gunpoint or someone stole her car, there likely would be no hesitation
in telling. But if she's sexually assaulted, her calculus might change.

Some felt torn about their decision and continued to struggle with
the question of whether to tell their parents. A few students asked me
outright, "Do you think I'm doing the right thing by not telling them?"
They felt as if they *should* tell their parents, even if they didn't want to
and didn't plan to. But I understood how it could be hard, especially if
they came from a household where there hasn't been a lot of communication, to suddenly introduce this huge topic that requires so much
dialogue and feels incongruent with how life works in the family.

Others managed their ambivalence by providing a partial truth:
they didn't tell about the sexual assault but conveyed that there was
some sort of serious problem. One told her parents that she had been
bothered by a classmate and was having difficulties with him. Another
called her dad and said she was upset and needed to come home
because she got a C on a midterm. ("I hadn't, I don't get Cs.") One
said she was suicidal but did not say that she attributed it to the assault.
And another told me that her "parents are really hurt, they know there
is something I'm not telling them . . . my mom tries to emphasize that
every time she talks to me. She's like, 'I know you're going through a
lot of stuff.' . . . I just couldn't tell my dad, I couldn't tell my mom. . . .
I just feel like it's not for them to know right now."

I found the comments of one daughter particularly poignant:

My mom was talking to me like I was a stranger. She has a voice that
she uses with people that she's just meeting, I can't describe it really, but

she was using that voice with me instead of talking to me like she always does. . . . She's gotten back to normal, but if I were to ever bring it up again, she would revert back into that weird-like stranger voice . . . it's still a relevant thing in my life, obviously, but I haven't talked about it with her because of that. —Hannah

The voices we use with close friends and family do differ from those we use with people we don't know. Perhaps the daughter, in conveying that there was a problem but leaving it at that, did call forth her mother's "stranger" voice – the mother saw the daughter as suddenly being unknown.

Others took an it-could-be-worse perspective when they decided not to talk with their parents. If their life hadn't been disrupted much – their academic performance wasn't badly damaged, they felt happy enough – they kept the news to themselves.

A few girls perceived not telling their parents as simply a choice to set a boundary. They told me directly that "this is mine" and that they might tell their parents someday but not now. I had the impression that some almost savored the separation that was inherent in the decision not to tell their parents. One girl declared her separateness through her decision:

It's my thing. It's me. I'm the one who was raped. I'm the one who has to live with it. I'm the one who lived the consequences of it and the results of his actions. So it's my decision whether or not to share it. —Kimberly

Many of the girls who had told their parents also voiced some ambivalence about their decision. They expressed shame, a fear of being judged harshly, and concern about parental fury at the boy, particularly if the parents knew him. In telling – whether impulsively or carefully thought out – the daughters had to overcome all of that.

When Matters

How a family deals with a crisis varies widely, and both when and how a daughter discloses her assault shapes the crisis. *How* she tells is typically linked to *when* she tells. If she calls right after she's been assaulted, it's her crisis, her parents' crisis, and their crisis together. She might express confusion, even disorientation, and, if not yet having a label for her experience, use phrases such as "something bad happened." She needs help, and she and her parents must figure out what that could be. If, on the other hand, she waits to tell her parents, she has had time to think about the incident, experience a range of emotions, and actively decide to tell them; when she tells, the parent might be stunned by the news and the emotional impact of the information might reverberate through the family, but the immediate crisis has passed.

None of the daughters who spoke with me called their parents immediately after the assault. About half told a parent within a week, often within a day or two. The others waited several weeks, months, and sometimes more than a year.

Daughters who told a parent about being sexually assaulted did so in all sorts of ways and in all sorts of contexts. The settings varied a lot: over the phone, in person, in writing, and while in the family vehicle. I recall several important conversations in the car with my teenage son: sitting side by side, facing forward, not looking at each other for much longer than a glimpse, and both of us having a good idea when the journey would end. Car rides provide a unique setting in which to have a private conversation for a limited amount of time.

One mother found out on a hike, a routine activity that she and her daughter shared:

> "Mom," she said all of a sudden, "I don't remember. I have vague snippets of some memory." And then I'm looking at her and I'm realizing she's wearing a heat-gear long-sleeved shirt, and I'm putting pieces together. So I say to her, "Can I see your arms?" And she looks at me and goes, "Do you have to?" "Absolutely not. But I would like to." She's black and blue – she's black and blue here, she's black and blue here, her thighs are black and blue. . . . Now it's slowly starting to seep in . . .
>
> I say, "Okay, so you don't remember. Tell me what you do remember." She says, "I remember we left the dorm. We were walking. Everything is so hazy." I said, "As in you were drunk and you blacked out?" She's like, "Mom, I had two little tiny drinks, and I don't even mean shots. I just don't know. I don't know if somebody put something in my drink. I just know that one minute I'm talking to everybody, and the next minute there's a merry-go-round, like on a playground . . . I remember people lugging me back up. And then I remember waking up the next morning.

I'm in my sleeping bag on the floor and I'm naked and I'm black and blue." I listen and I say, "Okay, so what did you do next? Did you call the police?" "I took a shower," she said, "and I couldn't find any bleach to shower with, so I scrubbed and I scrubbed and I scrubbed." [*Question: Does your daughter usually shower with bleach?*] No.

I turn now from whether she tells to when she tells.

Near-Immediate Disclosure
A daughter calling shortly after she's been sexually assaulted is a crisis. The stakes can seem higher and the news be more keenly felt by the parent. In contrast to the parent who is told months or years after the fact, the parent receiving a near-immediate disclosure doesn't know how things will turn out or even what might come next.

No matter our age or gender, when we reach out to someone when we're in crisis, we're distressed, frightened, and agitated. We're seeking solid ground, familiarity, and reassurance that what is known still exists and will continue to be. We reach out, sometimes without much forethought, to touch base with our foundation.

Parents, particularly when students are in their first year at college, are a big part of that foundation. Parents provide psychological and social continuity, as well as tangible support: information, economic assistance to a greater or lesser degree, and help with problem solving. Thus a primary task when responding to a crisis is to establish a sense of stability and security.

This can be easier said than done. If the parent–child relationship has begun to take on an adult–adult quality as well, it can be jarring for parents to have a daughter call crying and vulnerable. She suddenly is not the young woman talking about friends, classes, and plans for the future but is much more like the child she was many years ago – full of fear and pain and needing comfort.

Parents must deal on the spot with the news, no matter how stunned they are. Our reactions to unexpected bad news often begin with an "Oh no, how could this have happened?" followed by a period of disorientation as the information sinks in while we scramble to sort out competing feelings and thoughts as we try to respond to the person who delivered the news. The reactions don't necessarily occur sequentially, nor is it a one-time thing; the process is rather like a continuous loop that reorders the pieces as it cycles. Simply put, we don't think as clearly or as quickly as we otherwise might. Taking stock and assessing the need for immediate action often is a key component of the conversation, and emotions can run high.

These next three quotes illustrate the intensity of the interactions that occurred, as well as the internal processes that the speaker was aware of at the time. The first is from a father concerned about whether his daughter had been raped, the second is from a mother with regrets, and the third is from a daughter; all three illustrate how quickly the tables can turn:

I said to her, "Okay" – and I didn't wanna be insensitive – I said, "Are you telling me this didn't lead to you being raped?" And she said, "Oh, no, no." And then she shifted to the other side of the spectrum, and she said, "But, Dad, I was sexually assaulted.". . . I kinda stayed away from my feelings about how relieved I was that she hadn't been raped, so much so that I think I underappreciated the significance of what he did to her. —Father

I don't even know if it's possible for a parent to not judge their child's responsibility, unless you are assaulted by a stranger in an innocent situation. If this is somebody that she's dating, did she lead him on? Did she give him the impression that by drinking and coming home with him that night that something was going to happen? And do you have the right to press charges against someone for that? I think I said to her, "You realize that you could destroy his life by pressing charges, and you don't even want to tell me what happened? How are you going to tell an attorney what happened?" My hands are buzzing just talking about it. I feel so . . . I wish I had just said, "I'm so sorry. How can I help you? I'll get on the next plane." —Mother

I called them late afternoon [I had been assaulted the night before], and I talked to my mom. I didn't have words at first, all I could do was cry. And then I told her what happened – that was the first time that I used the words, that I said I was sexually assaulted. My mom screamed and said, "What?!!" and hung up the phone. I was very upset and freaked out. It took a lot of guts for me to even make that call. I mean, I deliberated for hours in my room whether I wanted to call. But I felt so alone. . . .

I got a call about ten minutes later, it was her again. She started yelling and saying, "What do you mean? What happened?" I explained and then she asked me, "What's wrong with you? Why did you put yourself in this situation?" and started going off on how I dressed that night and how much alcohol I drank and why it was my fault and that she was very disappointed in me. I kind of expected it. She and I have always had issues when I was growing up . . . so I knew that I was risking to hear those things again. After that she passed the phone to my dad. He just asked me, "Do you want us to come tonight?" I said, "No, I don't think that will be necessary, I think I want to be alone for a while." And then my mom said, "We're coming tonight." And so they did.

After the phone call and until they said they were coming, it was the first time that I had suicidal thoughts, the first time that I actually had thoughts about really wanting to kill myself. I was scarred by the experience that I went through, but a lot of it was also the disappointment that I felt I gave my parents. I'm the only child. I know they've provided me with all they've had. And so for them to feel this upset and disappointed in me just destroyed me. Once they arrived to campus, my mom told me that right after we talked on the phone, my dad cried. I've only seen my dad cry about two times, and that really, really devastated me. I already felt like I disappointed them, but at that point I felt awful – it was not a good time. —Lily

One mother relayed a puzzling and trying phone call with her daughter. As the mother spoke, I found myself wondering if the daughter was displacing her righteous anger from the perpetrator to her mother and, in doing so, finding a way to pull herself together. As I listened, the mother seemed to have come to a similar conclusion:

I felt mad at her. I felt brokenhearted, really brokenhearted. She hung up on me, I called her back, and we talked, and I just wasn't able to give her what she needed me to give her. I still don't know what she really wanted – I don't really know if she knows exactly what kind of response she wanted from me either – but I didn't give her whatever it was. She told me that she was deeply, deeply hurt that I didn't understand, that I did it wrong. I was not able to offer anything other than "I'm so sorry I handled this wrong," without really understanding what was wrong about how I handled it . . . she's yelling at me and I'm being quiet and thinking, "You know what? I don't need to defend myself. It's not constructive. This is not about me. It's not about my mothering. It's not about my feelings. I have to take myself out of this conversation and let it be her and let her talk." She just needed to vent, and it was venting about me. Like the whole incident was transferred from him and what he did to her to me and what I did to her or what I failed to do.

Delayed Disclosure

When disclosure occurs later, she has managed the immediate crisis with greater or lesser success. And she's spent some time thinking about whether and how to tell her parent. One daughter, for example, waited more than a year to tell her mother, in part because she knew her mother had been raped and was concerned about what effect the news might have on her.

Some of the parents who talked with me saw the delayed disclosure as a betrayal of sorts. They were hurt that they hadn't been told sooner, disappointed that their daughter hadn't come to them earlier, troubled that she had kept it "hidden" from them for so long. And some of the daughters who hadn't told their parents seemed to feel as if the moment had passed, that if they told them now, their parents would focus on why they hadn't told them sooner rather than on what happened or on the fact that they *had* decided to tell them.

I understand that reaction. At the same time, I tend to see it differently and hope that a parent who is told long after the fact considers alternatives. For one, when someone enacts some kind of power over us – as is the case in a sexual assault – part of healing is to find ways in our lives where we can take power back. Delaying telling her parents might be one way a sexually assaulted college girl retains (or perhaps regains) some power. She wants her parent to know what is shaping some of her decisions and actions, to know what she carries with her. It is precisely because she wants a closer relationship with her parents that she tells them.

But it can be difficult for a parent to know this in the initial crush of being told. One mother was upset that her daughter withheld the information while maintaining her usual pattern of communication: "For Christ's sake, you call me five times a day for this and for that, and then *this* thing you don't share with me? That was so hard for me." Another voiced her surprise and disappointment that she wasn't told sooner, especially when the daughter waited until she had been home for two weeks during semester break before saying anything:

> She sits down on the couch and says, "I'm going to read something to you and you may not interrupt me." And I'm like, "What the hell?" I thought she was joking; it was so out of character . . . but within the first sentence she says, "When I was on study abroad, I was raped," and she just keeps reading. And I'm sitting there like, "What??!! I'm your mother!" I'm pretty good in a crisis situation, I would have been willing to get on the plane and gone out there and beat the ass of whoever. I mean, I would have! . . . I will come in there on a white horse and I will have that kid for breakfast.

Aside from the parent sometimes feeling a sense of betrayal for not being told sooner, conversations tended to be less volatile than if the disclosure was right after the incident. Commonly, a lot of emotion was expressed by both daughters and parents, but it typically was less raw than in the conversations that the near-immediate disclosers reported. Parents were sometimes puzzled by their daughter's composure; they seemed to expect her to be more distressed, perhaps reflecting how they were feeling when learning of the assault. In waiting to talk with her parents, the daughter sets a boundary; she directly or indirectly is telling them, "I want you to know what happened and that I dealt with it." Parents in that situation seemed to begin, if they hadn't before, to see her as someone who could get along without them, as someone who *was* getting along without them. She might have fared better by turning to them sooner or she might still need their help, but she had managed without them. Whether aware of it or not, they were responding to the fact that she had made a choice, actually two choices: first not to tell them and then to tell them.

Parents sometimes put together more subtle cues after the fact. As one mother said, "If you watch her feed from Facebook, you know exactly when it happened because of what she started posting on that kind of stuff [sexual assault]." One father said that the problems that had developed for his college daughter made sense once he learned, nearly a year later, that she had been sexually assaulted. And one mother understood the salutary effect of her daughter's disclosure: "I hope she doesn't feel as ashamed as she did when she was trying to hide it. I think that burden of guilt has been lifted by her revelation. It's not a dirty part of her that she needs to hide."

Why she didn't tell them sooner is a reasonable question, and the answer might help parents better understand their daughter and her sense of their relationship. Sometimes the delay is related to simply not knowing what words to use.

What to Call It

Language is a crucial way to make sense of one's world. We use language to describe ourselves to ourselves and, should we choose, to others. Thus words have great importance: they help us explain what happens in our lives and what sense we make of it. It's part of how we cope.

It's also part of growing up. Very young children are largely reactive. Awash in transitory emotions, they can go from gleeful laughter to foot-stomping rage to heartfelt sobs at dizzying speed. A key developmental task is to acquire language, which requires children to have an awareness of themselves and the world around them. To identify what is happening to or with themselves, and to convey it to others, requires awareness and sufficient distance to be an observer, a spectator of sorts of one's self and one's life. A similar awareness and distance are essential for sexual assault victims.

Each of the college girls who met with me described their efforts to find words that would make sense of their experience. The recruitment flyers I used asked for students who had been sexually assaulted rather than for students who had had a bad sexual experience, had been raped, or some other term. So the girls who spoke with me had tried on the term "sexual assault" and decided that it fit to some degree.

Attaching a label to one's experience is a process shaped by knowledge and time. For some, including this girl, the lack of experience was central: "I was really inexperienced. I just didn't know. I woke up and was like, 'Oh, I guess this is just kind of what it's supposed to be like.'" Her childlike trust in the college boy who became her rapist is heartbreaking. Sometimes it simply takes time to find words that fit. As another girl said, "I definitely wouldn't have called it 'sexual assault' at the beginning. I knew it was not consensual, but I didn't know how to put words to what had happened to me." Not having words that convey how one views an experience makes it almost impossible to process it or communicate it to someone else.

The process of choosing words to describe these experiences and emotions often involves comparisons to known phenomena. Does what happened fall under the definition of "rape"? How does what happened to me compare to what happened to my roommate and what she called it? Would other people call it abusive? As one girl told me, "I feel like rape is very specific. It's like vaginal penetration and it implies a lot of violence. I mean, I guess maybe that did happen. But . . . I prefer 'assault' because it's just more general and – I just use 'assault.'"

Naming the experience is intensely personal, yet not necessarily private. Others are often actively recruited to engage in the process. Some of the girls turned to organizations and individuals who might be considered experts – the local rape crisis hotline, campus mental health services – for help in naming what had happened. Most, however, turned to friends. And as these two girls conveyed, sometimes the friends could see and say things that the girl wasn't ready to see or say herself:

> The next day I got breakfast with one of my closest friends, and I told her what happened. And she's like, "That's kind of like rape." And we were laughing because it felt uncomfortable. She wasn't making light of it. —Jessica

> I called one of my friends from back home and I was, like, "I don't know what's going on, this happened." Obviously, they're not trained or anything, but they named the incident for me . . . they were just, "Yeah, I think I would call that 'assault.'" And something in me felt like it broke – I was, "No, I don't want it to be that." —Maddie

Some girls described feeling confused and conflicted, wondering if they were making a big deal out of what happened. As one girl said, "I was like, 'Oh my God, is my incident enough of a sexual assault? Does it even count?'" Rape seemed to be the standard against which they evaluated their experiences. One girl told me that "neither times were rape. The reason I mention that is because that's been part of my process of coming to terms with it, because at first I was, like, because it wasn't rape, it was nothing, it doesn't really matter." And others won-dered whether their own actions somehow invalidated the incident such that a widely known label wouldn't apply. Such doubting seemed to be particularly common among those who had been drinking prior to the incident or who had in some way "participated," as these girls expressed:

One of the things that was hard for me was that during the process, he told me to do things and I did them. That was hard for me to come to terms with – I did it, so is it really rape? But it's rape. —Emily

Part of me was confused because it wasn't intercourse; it was oral sex. I'm still a virgin, haven't had sexual intercourse, and I didn't know if it was considered sexual assault or not. I think the other part of it was I just didn't want to think about it. I felt really stupid the next day. I'm like, "Oh, I shouldn't have put myself in that situation," so I just didn't want to bring it up. I didn't really talk about it at all. —Alicia

Being in a relationship with the perpetrator made finding a name for the experience even more challenging. His actions didn't match her belief that she cared about and was involved with a "good guy." One mother understood why her daughter would override cues: "She didn't want to overreact. And I understand that, because you don't want to make a jerk of yourself. But at the same time, all your red flags are up, going 'Okay, this is not right.'" When it came to an after-the-fact label, some took the advice of others; one girl told me that she took her therapist's advice when she "basically told me that was sexual assault and you probably should not be seeing this person again." Others struggled – sometimes alone, sometimes with the partner – to reconcile their romantic feelings for their partner with what he had done. Their struggles reminded me of how marital rape had long been framed – if a woman said yes once, it was yes forever, and sexual assault was some-thing done by "bad guys," that is, strangers, not someone to whom you had pledged devotion for the rest of your days. Although today's college students talk about the importance of freely given consent and are aware that the person most likely to assault a woman is a man she knows, the idea that someone they care deeply about could also harm them continues to be nearly incomprehensible. As these girls said:

I had stayed over at his house previously and in the mornings when we woke up together, it would be a "the birds are chirping, the sun's coming up" kind of feeling, and he would say something really cheesy. . . . [After the incident] that feeling was gone. Something in me just felt different. I felt weird – it wasn't a bad weird, it was just weird. I didn't know what was happening, and I was, like, Okay, I need to leave. —Jenny

I saw him a few times after [*she woke up to find that he was having sex with her*], because I was also very in love with him. It was very confusing – I wasn't even sure if what he did was wrong. Now I know, but at the time it was very confusing, separating my feelings for him from this bad person that he was all of a sudden. —Veronica

I had the sense immediately that it was an assault because it was something I couldn't remember, so it automatically felt demeaning – I mean, there was no consent given. Right away I felt very upset about it. But then he made it seem like, "Well, we're dating, so you shouldn't be upset about it." And so that's why I kept saying, "Okay, I should just normalize it." —Stacey

Some eschewed labels altogether. Their way of handling it made me think of the title of the report of the first national study of campus sexual assault – *I Never Called It Rape* – and subsequent research on "unacknowledged" rape.[1] Perhaps to protect themselves and to defend against the judgment of others, some sexually assaulted college students simply avoid applying a name to their experience or apply a more socially acceptable label. One girl told me: "I mentioned to people that we'd hooked up because in my mind for a really long time that's what it was, a bad hookup." Another said: "I don't really say I'm a survivor because it's not who I am. It's what happened to me. I also don't say it because then people know that someone forcefully stuck his penis in me. And I don't want people to know that." Avoiding the label might help her avoid judgments of others. The initial rejection of a label can change over time, but the ambivalence and the implication of labels can be powerful, as is evident in this comment:

I started thinking about it and I read more stuff. And then I was like, "Whoa, this might have actually been sexual assault." And then I was personally conflicted. Do I really actually want to go to a counselor and

. . . then be defined as someone that has experienced sexual assault, not that being defined as that is a bad thing. Does it really matter that I define it as this or that? It's not like I was raped. —Julia

Parents were confused and conflicted too. Perhaps they weren't given the explicit information that would allow them to apply a definitive label, or maybe they didn't understand the meaning of the labels. But occasionally, being a step removed, the parents understood in a way that the daughter didn't. One mother captured it well:

She called me at 1:30 in the morning and she just said, "Mom, I have to tell you something." And she said, "You'd better sit down." And then she started to describe this sexual experience that she had. But she didn't understand that she was raped. She just said, "Well, I was – I'm not sure what happened. I just was drinking a lot and we were singing" – he plays guitar, my daughter plays piano, and they were doing this together – and she said just one thing led to another and we had sexual intercourse. And I said, "Well, how do you feel about that?" And she said she wasn't sure, but she wasn't talking to him anymore. She said that she's just not sure what happened, and he's apologizing to her and he's coming to her and talking to her, but she's not enjoying that. And she was confused, but she was laughing the whole time, too, sort of shrugging it off and laughing but confused. But my heart was broken because I understood what had happened. . . . I knew that this was something very, very crushing. And I was very sad, but at the same time, I didn't want to make her feel that way because I could tell that she didn't understand what had happened yet. But she knew she was very, very upset. So I tried to shrug it off too. And I said, "Well, that's okay, we'll figure this out."

Labeling is powerful. Regardless of what is being named, the chosen label affects a person's view of herself as well as others' view of her. A label becomes shorthand for what happened and can facilitate communication. "Sexual assault," the term commonly used on college campuses, is an umbrella that covers a variety of experiences. It is a useful label when the speaker wants to convey a general concept but not specific details.

Who Is Told

Girls who are sexually assaulted in college typically turn first to their friends. One girl told me: "The first time I talked about this to a friend, I couldn't even get it out. It's been only a year and I'm still trying to process it, but my friends have definitely been there for me." And often it stops there, with friends. But as one girl reported, friends sometimes encourage reaching out to a larger circle:

> My friend was the first person I told. It helped me to be comfortable with telling other people. . . . [She said,] "You really need to talk to someone, not someone like a therapist, but people that support you and love you. They need to know that this happened so that they know why when you lash out at them – not that it [the assault] is an excuse – but so they have a context of what happened. You're hurting them by not telling them." So I took that advice and ran with it. And it helped. —Leah

If they do tell someone in their family, the question of who to tell first can be answered in one word: Mom. The news reverberates within the family. As one girl said, "It was definitely weird for everyone, and there's nothing you can do about that, I guess." Parents' reactions shape what follows.

Initial Parent Reactions

Giving the news was hard for the daughter. Getting the news was hard for the parents. Support might have been offered in most initial conversations, but expressions of support typically paled in the context of the parents' shock and questioning of the girl. The initial conversation typically was a bit of a mess.

When I asked one university service provider how parents could best be supportive in that first conversation, she said, "Being responsive, being compassionate, believing whatever you're told, not making any judgments, asking how can I be part of your healing going forward, expressing empathy that their son or daughter was hurt." I remember raising my brow and narrowing my eyes in skepticism – her advice was a tall order – and she replied, "I think this is what happens to victims of sexual violence in general: people bring all of their ignorance, their fears, their own projections to the victim-survivor, so there's little room for the victim-survivor to get what they're looking for or what they need in terms of support or healing." Yet sometimes it worked out well, as Liz relayed:

> I went to therapy, and we talked for a couple sessions about me disclosing to my mom. I told my therapist that I feel like I can't really completely heal without having my parents' support. It was really important to me. But I was also confused, because I was really scared that my mom was going to blame me, and if that happened . . . I don't know if I can deal with that, especially because, being an only child, I've been extremely close to my mom – she stayed at home and raised me. . . . My mom was very taken aback, and she was "I'm so sorry this happened, I'm here for you, I support you, screw him." And I was, like, "What? – This is awesome, she's so supportive." I felt so fulfilled, because, finally, my mom knows that this happened, and she gets it, and she's here for me.

Parents generally seemed to be forthright when telling me about how they received and reacted to the news. In addition, some seemed to treat our conversation almost as a confessional, telling me how they regretted that they hadn't had their wits about them when getting news that they were completely unprepared for. One mother, answering a phone call from her daughter who was many time zones away on study abroad, told me how they "talked a little bit . . . and then I told her, basically, that I had to leave to go to work, but that we would talk again." Some had flagellated themselves for years for posing questions that, in hindsight, they wish they hadn't asked. It was not uncommon for parents to be haunted by not having been the kind of parent they wanted to be in that moment. Some told me how they responded with gentleness in kind and loving ways. That, however, was not the norm. At least not according to the girls, mothers, and fathers who spoke with me.

Shock was the most common immediate reaction of parents when their daughter told them that she had been sexually assaulted. Some mothers were so stunned that they behaved in ways that were not typical for them. One mother, who was quite reserved when she met with me, reported a strong reaction in a public setting:

I remember screaming and screaming. I was on the bus, and I was screaming. Fortunately, I was just about to get off. . . . I remember praying, "God, let that not be true. I don't want that to be true. Let me hear that it was all a dream, a bad dream." Unfortunately, when I talked to her I was crying uncontrollably. It was very, very difficult. And for a long time, it was very painful, very, very painful.

Anger was another common first reaction of both mothers and fathers. Anger was directed at the daughter, the perpetrator, and, on occasion, the university. Sometimes the anger wasn't voiced, as one mother explained: "My instant internal reaction was 'I'm going to kick your ass. You're not even twenty-one. What were you doing drinking?' But I didn't say that." The sentiments of several fathers were in line with this father's: "My initial reaction was I just wanted to go and beat the hell out of him."

Fear and relief were also common. One mother, from a country and family devastated by AIDS, was scared about her daughter contracting the disease, as well as becoming pregnant. More than one father expressed relief that "it wasn't a full-blown rape." One father asked directly, "Did he rape you?" and when his daughter said no, he backed off and didn't ask more.

Asking questions can be a tricky venture at this time. Parents might want answers to the questions they pose, but in the context of a daughter disclosing that she's been sexually assaulted, their questions are not likely to be well received. Some parents seemed to be outright accusatory and others might have been trying to gather information but, to a vulnerable girl, it can feel like a cross-examination.

In that initial conversation, she probably isn't ready to move into problem solving for the future either, as was clear from the comments of one mother: "I was meaning to ask her questions to sort of brainstorm how she could protect herself next time or if it happened again, and she took it as 'These things I was doing wrong' – as 'Why didn't you?' instead of 'Did you?' And so, that first conversation was very tense." A parallel could be drawn between the assault and the subsequent conversation with her parents: the line she draws merits respect and her silence means something.

Your daughter may well be looking for a kind of loving acceptance that she has had – and still might have – difficulty extending to herself. She likely is already feeling responsible and blaming herself. These three mothers sought information in ways that their daughters didn't appreciate:

And I was asking her, "So why did you not run?" She kept on saying, "I said no, I said no." "Then why didn't you run?" . . . She said he had used protection. And I was just wondering, at that time when he was putting on protection, why could she not – she told me she was paralyzed. She was the one paralyzed, she couldn't do anything, maybe some fear, I don't know.

She was visibly upset as she was telling me. And so, I didn't want to upset her more by prying or prodding or saying the wrong things, which I did say the wrong things anyway. But I didn't know what to say. She took my questions as if it was her fault that she didn't do all these things. . . . I thought I was being careful about what I was saying. I asked, "Did you drink out of someone else's cup?" And, of course, the answer was yes. I said, "Well, when you go to parties, you should always have your own cup. If you put it down, it's garbage." I thought I had said that before, but you know. "Did you signal your friends when he was taking you away?" And I probably asked what she was doing when he took her. I probably asked if she was dancing or where were her friends when this happened. I don't recall the conversation 100 percent, obviously. I might have asked what she was wearing, which I know would be taboo. You should not ask that question. But I might have asked that also.

I said, "So what were you doing? What did you . . . ?" – this was the worst thing that I said to her, but I had to say it, and my husband said it too – "What did you think was going to happen in the apartment of a twenty-eight-year-old man who had been drinking? Did he think you were teasing him? Do you understand what that does to a man? – I mean a jerky man, not a nice man, but a jerky man. You don't know him well enough." All these things that I was saying to her she took as it being her fault, she's bad. "Oh, so it's my fault, so now it's my fault, you're so sexist, no means no," blah, blah, blah, blah. I was just like, "Oh, my God, I don't even know how to rewind and more delicately say what I was thinking."

It's important to attempt to recoup if you want to have a subsequent conversation. One girl captured it well: "'Hey, parents, remember yesterday how you yelled and screamed at me for being drunk at this party and being raped, well, I'm gonna bring it up again so that I can face more scrutiny about my poor life choices.' Hey, nobody's setting themselves up for that."

Some daughters put limits on the conversation – *don't interrupt me, read this* – so that they could get their story out. One mother described how "I sat there and I'm listening . . . and this was the kicker – I was not allowed to ask her any questions, and I was not allowed to talk about it. Obviously, you want something from me, or you wouldn't have shared this. But you want full control of it." Yes, she likely does want control over talking about a time when she didn't have control, a situation in which she was controlled.

Concern about their daughter's well-being might be the foundation for some of these reactions, but not always. And it's easy to understand why a girl, reaching out in vulnerability, might not take kindly to a parent's anger, relief, or general distress – especially when she herself is called upon to help parents manage their reactions. One daughter spoke of how her mother broke down and was overwhelmed for days:

> She looked at me and just started crying. I had to drive home. She didn't stop crying for two days. She did the whole typical Mom thing – "I can't believe this happened to you; if you need to transfer, you can." I'm like, "Hey, I'm fine." She would waffle back and forth between feeling really sorry for me, being amazed that I wasn't dying, and then resenting me for being able to handle something that she couldn't handle, which is sort of my entire childhood in a nutshell. —Leah

The memory of being told was somewhat foggy for a few parents, particularly those who had been told years prior. However, it was probably more than memory decay. As one mother said, "It's interesting that with this topic, it is hard for me to really have clear memories of everything. I think because it is so emotionally loaded." Memories are very personal too. After they each had spoken individually with me, one couple sent an email to say that they were surprised at how their memories differed. Subsequent to our conversations, they had discussed getting the news from their daughter and wanted to clarify a few details.

I was aware that their recollections of the disclosure didn't correspond on key points and appreciated how much they wanted to provide clear and accurate information. At the same time, I knew that, as all of us do, they had written and rewritten their individual memories in their heads. Their history would be whatever they agreed it would be.

I don't mean to paint the giving-and-getting conversation as inevitably horrible. It is, however, a very difficult conversation for both the daughter and the parents. There were some daughters and some parents who felt that they all had communicated well, or at least as well as could be expected, but they were in the minority. And even "good" conversations had rough spots. You might be reading this book in part because the news is recent and your own such conversation became a flash point or was otherwise trying. If so, know that you are not alone.

The first conversation can be tough. The daughter has her antennae up and is understandably sensitive, even when she is reaching out long after the initial period of feeling wounded and frightened. But parents, not braced for such news, often bungle their part. Some of the bungling is likely related to what's called the "just world hypothesis": a core belief that our choices and behaviors always lead to appropriate and fair outcomes. The title of a path-breaking book on the topic captures it well: *The Belief in a Just World: A Fundamental Delusion.*[2] Even when we *know* that things happen entirely outside of our control, we try to fool ourselves into thinking that the world is always fair. When your daughter told you she was sexually assaulted, your belief in a just and fair world was shaken, and you probably tried to shore it up by looking to her behavior. She, another believer in a just world, is undoubtedly examining and reexamining her actions too. To some degree, you both are blaming the victim. Maybe you and your daughter will conclude at some point that she could have done some things differently; we call that learning, and it needn't mean she is responsible. The perpetrator and what he did matters. As do the situations and settings.

You likely will have different recollections and perceptions of that first conversation. As one mother said, "She's entitled to her perspective and what it was like for her. It doesn't mean that she's right and I'm wrong – we could both be right. I was shocked and upset more than anything. But for her, it came across as being kind of insensitive."

Another mother told me how it was actually much simpler than she thought at the time. She realized that her daughter was trying to tell her that she needed her "to console me and tell me that everything is going to be okay and that he's a jerk and that I did the right thing in calling her. She just needed me to stroke her. She needed me to be her mom and hold her and do all the things I didn't do."

Attempting to communicate usually involves applying a label of some sort to the experience. The girl might describe the acts that occurred, sometimes without choosing a specific word or words to define her experience. One of the thoughtful campus service providers who spoke with me on background eschewed the idea of labels. As she said:

> Our language has never reflected reality. The reality is when a young woman and young man are kissing or being somewhat intimate and then he gets forceful, she is either afraid or embarrassed or feeling too naïve or uniformed to say no or to even understand what's happening. I've seen this many times with women for whom this is their first time having intercourse – they don't exactly know what's happening – or with women who say, Well, he's so aroused, if I stop now, it would be cruel or he'll be angry or I just don't know what to do. So they just become mute. . . . [they ask] So was that rape?, I didn't say no, I didn't push him off. . . . I say, just tell me what happened. . . . It doesn't matter what label we give it. The label matters if you're going to court, if the police are involved, even if [the office of] student conduct is involved, but I just want to know what happened and how it felt to you and what you're worried about and what you want to happen next. The language is inadequate.

Daughters go through this process and then parents, who often do not know the details of what happened, sometimes argue with the daughter – "It's 'just' such-and-such," "It's not that bad," "It could be worse," "At least it wasn't rape" – often infuriating her. Together they must figure out how to label the incident. Sometimes not knowing what to call it or perhaps shrinking from calling it what it is they create a euphemism, for example, "the Daniel thing." Creating a code word or phrase allows the family to communicate, to acknowledge the incident without using words that any of them might want to avoid. Both parents and daughters simultaneously seek and resist a label.

The effort – and wanting to avoid certain words – involves what I have come to see as a problem: The traditional labels (for example, "rape" and "attempted rape") focus on the nature and extent of the sexual contact. Several fathers, as noted, were less concerned when they learned that the incident didn't involve physical force and vaginal penetration; the federal definition of rape in effect from 1927 until 2013 seemed to be their standard for "serious." However, the dichotomy of rape/not rape is too extreme, and the sexual aspect might not be the most salient component in the long run. The girls acknowledged as much when they talked about what was at play when they evaluated the incident: being dominated resulted in a violation of the trust they had placed in another person, the loss of a sense of safety at a place where they had expected no danger, and the damage to their sense of self-determination.

Keeping the focus on your daughter and what she needs will be central in the time ahead. You are undoubtedly affected by the news, sometimes very deeply, yet putting it bluntly, helping you deal with your reactions is not your daughter's responsibility. You need to find a space where you can cry, be angry, or do whatever you need to do and say without it affecting her. Your words and actions impact your daughter. As one mother told me, "If you're disappointed because they didn't listen to you, you can't let them know that. You realize they're more fragile than you ever thought someone could be."

Many college students I encounter are keenly aware of their parents' expectations and fear the day that they will fall short. I don't know if their parents are putting a lot of pressure on them, but I do know students feel it. Several of the girls who spoke with me felt the weight of wanting to please their parents and perceived having been sexually assaulted as somehow having let them down. Having a parent express disappointment when their daughter tells them that she has been sexually assaulted can devastate her.

If you feel like you didn't do right by your daughter in that initial conversation, know that it can be powerful for a parent to say – and for a nearly adult child to hear – "I botched it, please forgive me. How can I help you?" It is important to reestablish a connection with your daughter and move forward individually and together. Take a breath and think about how you can best support your child after the assault.

CHAPTER 6

Fathers

I felt as though there were a limited number of things that I could do or that my daughter would let me do. But those things, however narrow my role, I wanted to do those things very, very well. —Father

When I think about it, I'm disappointed. I'm disappointed in myself knowing that I couldn't do anything to protect my daughter from this happening to her. But I don't think about it frequently. And the longer it's been since it happened, the less I think about it. —Father

I've kind of safely been on the periphery. In some respects, it's safer and easier. But I'm not sure if it isn't warranted for me at least to open the door for her to discuss it with me if she chooses. I'm her male role model, right? – I guess that's the way you would look at a father – and maybe that would be an appropriate thing for me to do, just open that door. But again, my discomfort with those topics, I guess that's part of it, too. —Father

Fathers often are less visible than mothers in the aftermath of their daughter's sexual assault. But that doesn't mean they are unimportant. Sometimes they play a loving role in few words or in what they do not say. And sometimes their distance accurately conveys strong implications of blame or is simply misunderstood. Families, including fathers, can only work from where they are. There can be fundamental changes in family dynamics in the midst of a crisis, but usually people revert to what is familiar, whether in how they relate or in how they explain and understand the world.

Fathers help their daughters learn how to be a woman. "You're turning four, Molly, how exciting! What do you want for your birthday?" "Roses from Daddy, just like Mommy got."

Freud might have interpreted Molly's reply one way, but there's a less complicated explanation. From a very early age, girls attempt to figure out what it means to be female in our society and often try out phrases, postures, and actions on their dads. The father's diffident response or warm reception shape how she comes to perceive men as well as herself.

"You'll always be Daddy's little girl" can be reassuring to both father and daughter, but the idea often is thrown into a spin when puberty hits. Suddenly the cuddly little girl has long, coltish legs and budding breasts. The process begins in elementary school – girls reach nearly 90 percent of their adult height by the time they are eleven years old – and speeds along. And it can take a while before things get sorted out.

Fathers can be uncomfortable with a daughter's blooming sexuality. I recall a dad at baseball practice say that he'd been ready to punch some guys in their twenties who were ogling his twelve-year-old daughter. Her curves, long, flowing hair, bee-stung lips, and diffident demeanor were interpreted as sultriness, something that the men appreciated but that the girl was wholly unaware of. Her father's jaw was tense and he kept squeezing his hands into fists even though the event had happened weeks earlier. He exhaled deeply as he shook his head and looked down, "I get it, though. She looks like she's eighteen. What am I going to do?"

What many dads end up doing is pulling back a bit (or a lot) from their daughter, physically or emotionally or both. They keep a watchful eye from a distance. If, that is, they are part of their daughter's life.

Many of the daughters who met with me didn't have a father who was active in their life. They aren't necessarily out of the ordinary in that regard: close to half of the children growing up today spend at least some part of their first eighteen years living with one parent, most often the mother.[1] The reasons the daughters who spoke with me didn't have a father in their lives included divorce (most common), death, incarceration, and simply "not getting along." So I knew I would have to make a special effort to reach fathers.

Most of the fathers of the daughters who talked with me (and had told their dads) were willing to be interviewed. After talking to that small group, I did targeted outreach through flyers and newsletters. That yielded a few more dads but not as many as anticipated, particularly when heads of the organizations willing to include information in their newsletter postings said things like "Our dads *really* care about sexual assault and I'm sure a lot of them will contact you." They might care, but they didn't contact me. After several iterations of these efforts, I came to the conclusion that most fathers of girls who had been sexually assaulted at college simply didn't want to talk about it.

The fathers who spoke with me typically were businessmen working in various fields at various levels. Aside from that, they were wildly divergent: some were remarkably insightful and articulate in the language of emotions, some were noticeably uneasy but really wanted to help, and others were so internally upended that they spoke in sentence fragments whenever getting near the topic of the assault itself. But they all were clear that talking to me was a way to better understand their daughter and possibly to help other parents. The quotes in this chapter, unless otherwise indicated, are from fathers.

What Dads Have to Say

The connection between fathers and college-aged daughters is grounded in the many years that came before. When the father is the primary caretaker, even if for a limited time, a particularly strong bond can be created. But even then the connection ebbs and flows. Some fathers had a fairly limited role, at least at the time. One father described himself as "the money man. They reach out to me for the money because they don't want to tell their mom what they're spending. I don't know if that's good or bad." Whatever relationship the father and daughter have established provides the context in which fathers receive news of an assault.

How Dad Learned About the Assault

If the daughter told a parent about the sexual assault, typically it was her mother. But sometimes fathers were told right away. One described finding out when the phone rang in the middle of the night. It was his daughter calling from a hospital, and his wife "just blurted it out." Other times they are told much later. One father said it was months after the incident that he found out. His wife knew but "didn't let on" because the daughter wasn't ready to tell him yet.

One father appreciated having the information withheld from him:

> I had been diagnosed with and was suffering with cancer when all this occurred. My wife and daughter chose not to communicate that our daughter had been assaulted. And then I had surgery and a lot of post-op issues that kind of consumed me for a time. I really wasn't in a place where I could absorb that kind of information. They were probably wise and kind not to share it with me at the time.

This same father also told me, though, that he felt strongly about openness because, although sometimes painful, "it's a safer way to live as a human being."

Most were told not by their daughters but by their wives. These three fathers recalled the moment:

> My wife took me aside and explained what had happened. I believe it was the day after our daughter had talked to her mom. . . . Then Mom [my wife] told me. I kind of block that out, I guess. I think I got instantly so ugly [as he later explained, furious] I really hadn't paid attention to how she had presented it to me.

> I learned about it from my wife . . . there was a lot of crying [father begins to weep quietly]. . . . She told me the details about each event. [His daughter had been assaulted twice.]

> I don't remember much about the conversation [with my wife], I really don't. And I don't know if this is just me protecting my own psyche a little bit. I remember both conversations being at night, and I remember both conversations being very emotional. I remember a lot of sense of disbelief and frustration and concern.

But some learned directly from their daughters. Tears often were involved and sometimes tough questions as well. The range of expressiveness and ease of addressing the associated issues was wide, as these three quotes illustrate:

> I remember comforting her, hugging her. She was crying. And then at some point, I kind of sat next to her. And then my wife came in the room and we went on about our business. I moved over to another chair or to the couch and we didn't talk about it at all, kind of went back to watching TV or doing whatever we were doing.

> She said, "Dad, I have to tell you something." And she was almost sobbing at the time. I forget her exact words, but I think she said something like "I was sexually abused." And I said, "Well, when did that happen" or "How did that happen?" And she said it was at a party. And she said that she didn't know the person and never actually found out who the person was who did this to her. She didn't go into any detail. And the more I asked questions – and I didn't ask too many – she seemed to be fairly, well, obviously very sensitive to it. But almost anything I asked, she either said or got the feeling that I was blaming her. So I just clammed up, tried to comfort her, and we have not spoken about it since.

> I think it was hard for her and for me. Because I said, "Depending on how severe the abuse was, it will probably impact the way that I feel. . . . So you don't have to share it with me exactly what it is, but it'd be pretty important because there's a spectrum here of things that could have happened. And you may not – because you were drinking, you may not have known all the things that in fact did happen, but – and the degree to which you . . . put yourself in that situation and the degree to which he in a sense dragged you into it. And so, help me understand." And that was a tough conversation. But at the same time, she said, "Look, this is not a case where he dragged me into the corner, ripped my clothes off and raped me. This was more of a date rape kind of thing. There was a point where I expressed my displeasure at what was happening, I wasn't aware enough to stop it, and I wasn't even aware exactly what had happened in a sense until after the fact." And so, that was good to know. . . . It wasn't as severe and violent and physical as I had anticipated it could have been – I was prepared for the worst. A clear violation occurred, but it was not a situation where this guy was ever going to get convicted

of rape and that helped bracket my thinking about it. I think that that conversation helped both of us.

Dad's Reaction

Fathers reacted as most of us do to unexpected, unwanted news: with disbelief. The "I can't believe this is happening" kind of disbelief, not the "I don't believe you" kind. It was especially keen for a father who learned about the assault long after it had occurred:

> When I first heard about it [a year or so after the assault], I had a very short period of thinking, "This is a bad B-movie or something, this can't be happening." And as I thought about it, I said, "Yeah, of course it happened because I saw the impact on her: the weight gain, the difficulties with her sport, the grades going down, the diminished self-esteem, the being acutely sensitive to any type of criticism or observation and being much less willing to share."

One father spoke of feeling sympathy for his daughter at the same time as he expressed a sense of inevitability: "I was worried that something like this would happen because that's what happens at frat parties." Another described a fairly calm and cerebral response:

> It wasn't really the time to be lecturing her about personal safety and that type of thing as much as it was consoling her and empathizing with her about it and making sure that she didn't let it overwhelm her moving forward or debilitate her or distract her from more important things – more important, as I would judge them anyway. I was pleased that she would even tell me.

A more typical response was that of dread, anticipating that their daughter had been raped, and immense relief after learning that the assault had not involved intercourse. These fathers describe the tension they felt as they waited to learn something very important to them:

> For the first five minutes of what she was telling me, I was: a) dumbfounded, and b) I assumed the worst. I had thought she had been raped. I waited, I'm not prompting, I'm listening to her because I can tell it's hard for her to tell me this. I'm pretty talkative, so I tamped that

back and I waited, but I was stunned, too. The gravitas of it was just mindboggling.

I think it was very good that I wasn't overly emotional. I wasn't, "Oh my God, oh my God, are you all right?" I wasn't withdrawn, I wasn't closed up, clammed up, I was very – I listened. I listened in sheer terror, but I listened. And I waited. I waited patiently, and then I was – it almost brings a tear to my eyes as I think about it now – I was so relieved when it became apparent that she hadn't been raped. Because everything she had said at first led me to believe that she had been raped.

The most common reaction, by far, was simple fury: the father wanted to harm the guy. Whether it was protectiveness, revenge, rage, or a mix of those and other motivations, most of the fathers unabashedly said that they wanted to hurt the perpetrator. One daughter said she hadn't told her dad for that very reason: she was sure he would find out who the guy was and would harm him, a concern based in reality given that her father had been incarcerated for a violent crime the first third or so of her life. As these fathers said, the anger was immediate and sometimes lasting:

You wanna go kill the person who did it. I know the kid. He was at our house numerous times when there was a prom or whatever. And his parents were there as well. But you know what? It is what it is.

I just remember that tremendous first anger at the guy. I just wanted to beat the shit out of him. And then just relief – the relief over the fact that he – that they didn't go that far. But still, it went far enough for her. . . . There's no excuse for the assault scenario . . . the anger towards that man and what he's done to her – it lives with me, it continues.

I'm reminded of the jokes about dads protecting their daughters as they begin to date. Some of the actions aren't jokes; dads have been known to sharpen a knife or flash a gun or, with less violent implications, to issue a stern warning or, as a popular television series depicted, use their smartphone to take a photo of the boy's driver's license. The implication is that, as another male, Dad knows that the boy is up to no good. And now, with their daughter away at college, they weren't able to protect her and prevent the assault. No wonder they are furious.

Men often are portrayed as unaware of their feelings or as converting feelings of vulnerability into anger. It's hard to tell whether that generalization applies to these fathers or whether anger is a fair and legitimate response to the circumstances. Perhaps some of both apply.

Many of the fathers seemed a bit baffled when I asked how they had coped with the feelings that were brought up by knowing about the assault. They paused, reflecting on what their feelings had been at the time and, most often, didn't seem to recall. Others reported that they dove into work, and others said that they simply resumed their routine.

Who Dad Talked With

Fathers usually limited their conversations about the assault to those with their wives. Talking with others, particularly other men, was not common, and when such a conversation did occur, the topic was typically addressed obliquely. And some dads didn't feel the need to talk about it: "It's never felt like something that I should bring up with anyone."

Wives were the exception, as these two fathers said:

I just talked to my wife. I didn't expand to the circle of any of my friends. I don't have a strong network. I have a couple of very good friends, but I'm not a buddy kind of guy. I don't belong to a golf club or anything like that. So it was no one really that I talked to about it. I didn't talk to my siblings. Just kind of internally processed it and exchanged information with my wife.

I don't want to say embarrassing, but it's an event that you don't really want to share – "Oh, my daughter was sexually assaulted." . . . Even if I did want to feel like I wanted to talk to somebody about it, I'm not sure if I would want to open up about something like that. It's a highly personal type of thing. You don't wanna go around having that conversation because everybody puts their spin on things. So I don't talk to anybody besides my wife.

A few fathers did talk – or try to talk – with others about the incident. Conversations with other men, as these two fathers relayed, were avoided entirely or done in a code of sorts:

There was one conversation with another dad with a daughter in college. We got together to essentially kick back beer and catch up with how things were going. His daughter was struggling and my daughter was struggling, and we commiserated. I certainly didn't tell him about the rapes. But we talked a lot about the environment and how hard it is for college kids these days, particularly girls. I threw out a statistic that I'm sure was wrong about the number of college girls that are raped as just a, "Yeah, it's hard for them." Now that I'm kinda recalling this conversation, I would bet it's a coin toss whether his daughter was raped as well. I think we both said enough that at least we acknowledged that there might be a problem.

People in my generation that I know, I think that there's a great tendency not to trivialize it, but to lessen the significance of it and to try to sweep some of it under the rug. We don't sit around talking about this when dads get together, at least my friends and I don't. I have never had a conversation with another man about sexual abuse or sexual predators or date rape or anything of that sort. And interestingly enough, I've had conversations about that with women, my wife and her friends. I'll be there and it will come up, and there will be a discussion and it'll be fine that I'm there. But you get the dads involved, and it's not like we just sit around talking about politics or baseball, but we don't talk about our daughters, we don't talk about date rape.

Mothers reported that they helped their husbands identify and manage their emotions. Sometimes it wasn't pretty. Fathers reacted with anger and blame when talking with their wives and sometimes their daughters too – reactions that their wives believed didn't reflect their husbands' "real" feelings. Comments by these two women illustrate what they thought about their husbands' reactions and likely feelings at the time:

My husband reacts. And the first thing out of his mouth – can you even guess what the first thing he said was? – "You shouldn't have been drinking." Well, of course, she shouldn't have. She wasn't even twenty-one. Gosh, she shouldn't have. She knows that. You don't have to tell her. But he said it out loud. That's hard because now that's in her head, and that alters things. It alters what she is comfortable telling her dad. He doesn't blame her. He was overwhelmed and he was angry and he was devastated that something like this would happen to his baby. But he can't fix what he said now.

All my husband said to her was "I'm so sorry." He's her father, he wants to strangle this guy, but he also thinks, "What the hell was she think-ing?" He has always warned the girls, "I was a young man once – don't play games with men." . . . Men need to learn how to control them-selves, which is true. But the other side is true too. You can't tease a guy and flirt and stroke – it's like a game, a power thing, it's dangerous, it's dangerous.

Dad Doesn't Talk with Daughter about the Assault

After a first conversation with his daughter, it was common for fathers not to talk with their daughters about it again. And if the father learned about it from his wife, he typically never or only obliquely talked with their daughter about it. It was rare for a father to speak directly with his daughter about the assault more than once. I was surprised to learn that one of the fathers who spoke with me about his daughter's sexual assault hadn't spoken with her about it for "three, four years," that is, since right after the incident. One father told me that, although he and his wife had had "countless" conversations about it, he could count on one hand the number of times he had talked with his daughter about her assault.

Three fathers articulated their hesitance very well:

We actually have not spoken about it. I mean, she and her mom are like this [wraps middle finger around index finger], and I'm kind of like the third person out and that doesn't bother me. . . . I kid with her a lot and I don't know if I threw it to her as a joke or how I tried to open the conversation, I think I said I wanted to go break his legs. And she's like, "Well, you know" – and I guess it was just a little thing that she threw out there – is that she felt that they were going to blame her because she was underage. And I said, "No, at no point is this your fault." And that was it. I kind of kid with her about these things just to let her know how I feel, but I don't want to go in depth on it.

I do not remember a single time having a detailed conversation with our daughter about the facts and circumstances about what happened. So I believe I know all I know about what actually happened to her both times exclusively from my wife. I've never had a conversation with her where it's even come close to where she has asked if I perhaps blame her in whole or in part or blame society or how much blame do I put on the boy or what would I have done in those circumstances and how I view, if you will, the rightness or the wrongness of the situation. But because of what I've said in connection with other people in other situations, she knows largely how I feel about a lot of these things. Again, part of the oblique discussions. But as far as the specifics of how I feel about what actually happened to her, I have never had a conversation about that.

I have not [talked with her since she first told me] because I'm worried that if I bring it up, a) it could upset her and bring back bad memories, and b) she might feel again that I'm trying to blame her in some way or find out, infer, that some of her actions may have caused this to be or been a contributing factor. And I don't want to do either of those things.

One daughter told me that she understood her father's silence on the topic; she said, "the silence or lack of words from my dad hurt me the most because I know that that lack of the ability to say things just showed how it hurt him."

Why Dads Think Guys Do It

Few fathers speculated about what might have motivated the guy who assaulted their daughter. When the topic did come up, fathers talked about how things are different now than when they were younger. Their sense of the differences focused largely on increased alcohol consumption, increased drug use, and easy accessibility of graphic pornography, as well as a general decay of society. One father told me that it's a question he agonizes over: "When you look at it, it's something precious. No one has the right to take it or do the things that they do."

The search for a reason was sometimes coupled with a desire for punishment, as this father said:

I can't even imagine what would be going on in his head to do something like that. I honestly think the reason that the boys do it is because they think they can get away with it, and that the girls aren't going to follow through. And, I mean, literally somebody should do three to five years for that in prison. You see it all the time in the news – "It's really sad that these guys on the football team did this and they got thrown off the team." I think they just think it's just going to blow over and it's going to be fine. Well, they shouldn't be thrown off the football team – they should be thrown out of college and they should be thrown in prison, because that's where you belong when you do something like that. I don't understand where in society that it became okay for these boys to say, "Oh, well, they were drinking," and that's the excuse. Actually, there's not an excuse for it, no matter what. . . . I think the cops should go right into the classroom, they should put the handcuffs on the boys, and they should take them right to jail. But I don't think that happens. . . .You never would have guessed by knowing what we knew about this boy that he would have done that. . . . It makes you wonder.

How It Has Affected Dad's View of His Daughter and Their Relationship

Daughters often expressed fear that their fathers would view them differently if they knew they had been sexually assaulted. But that didn't seem to be the case, at least not with the fathers who spoke with me. Any sense of unease that the fathers felt was temporary, and the underlying esteem for their daughter came through strongly:

I recall being in a car with her and driving somewhere and kind of having a sense of uneasiness and quietness. But since then, I don't think it's changed things at all. We're back to our old joking, conversing self. She seems to be happier over the last couple of months. I know this has had an impact on her but with therapy, with yoga, she seems to have improved, and I see her smiling a lot and joking a lot. So I would say at this point in time, it's not affecting her and my relationship.

I don't think anything has changed with the relationship. I don't ask a lot of questions. My wife will ask a lot of questions. I figure our daughter will tell me what she wants to tell me. Maybe that's why she feels that there's a special bond, because I'm not gonna grill her and I'm not gonna tell her you have to do that [points to spot on table for emphasis]. Maybe I'm the easier of the two parents.

Not at all – I love the kid to pieces – it [the assault] has not affected my view one bit. [*face softens*] She's our pride and joy.

She and I need those [ways to connect] at times. We've connected on some wonderful things, but as time has gone on, as she grew up, they became fewer. So, strangely enough, it [more communication since the assault] has been a good by-product.

What Daughters Say about Their Fathers

When I asked the college girls to tell me a bit about their fathers, some smiled and went on to describe their dads with obvious fondness. Sometimes the father appeared to be perceived simply as part of the parental unit, but mostly, as would be appropriate for this age, the daughters saw or were beginning to see their fathers as individual people. Occasionally, the individual they saw was someone they wanted to escape; one described college as her chance to get away from a father who had been addicted to drugs and still drank heavily. Some described the relationship with their father as fractured, and often a sadness enveloped their words.

These four daughters expressed a range of emotions when talking about the relationship with their fathers:

I'm more logical and extroverted, like my dad, but I am also very perceptive and intuitive, like my mom . . . they're just so opposite, and I'm so close with them in such different ways. Like my dad and I, we'll drink a beer together and watch a football game, talk about random things. He gets very lighthearted – it's very fun. He used to take me to batting cages, bowling. I would always hang out with all of his teams. I always felt really involved in his life, and he was always proudest of me when I was running in track or playing volleyball, playing soccer, all of these things. So we always had sports to kind of connect us. —Sara

The way that I treat and I'm treated by guys I think is because of my relationship with my dad, which has been generally negative for most of my life. He's a very critical, criticizing person. His relationship with my mom was very negative. . . . I definitely feel like my dad doesn't really think a lot about the impact that his and my mom's relationship had on me or the impact that his role as my father had on me. He didn't really try to be a great father or anything. —Jocelyn

My dad and I, as close as we are in certain aspects, we don't really talk about the deeper aspects of life. We talk about politics occasionally because I just like to rile him up [*smiles*], but it's more at arm's length – it's never when it's personal to us. —Trish

My dad and I have grown apart a lot. My dad's a lot like me in the sense that he bottles things up a lot and he doesn't like to confront things. I mean, I think he's always afraid that I'll get hurt or I'm sensitive and that kind of thing. And so I feel like when I see him, when I talk to him, I just feel like there's so many things that he wants to say, but he just doesn't. I feel like after that incident, he's distanced himself. I mean, I know he's very busy, but he's always been busy. —Liz

Talking with Dad about the Incident

Daughters didn't find it easy to talk with their fathers about the assault. It wasn't necessarily because the father was harsh or cold, although it did sound as if a few of the fathers could be a bit tough. Mostly it seemed as if something personal simply was not a common topic of conversation, and being sexually assaulted is an intensely personal topic. For most daughters it was too far out of the range of normal conversation with their dad, and they chose to say nothing.

Sometimes strong, perhaps dimly recognized, emotions were a major obstacle or contributed to awkward dynamics, as implied in what these three daughters said:

As close as I am to my dad, I never told him. I think my dad would have found out the person's name, gone to the university, and assaulted him. My dad is that protective of me – only child, daughter, super close. He would have killed him. I'm 100 percent convinced. I could never tell my dad. I don't want him [the perpetrator] to die. I don't want my dad to go to jail forever. So, there's not really much of an option there. Plus, I think he would look at me totally differently. He knows that I'm not a virgin, but I think he thinks that I've only slept with two or three people. If he knew that I had one-night stands or slept with someone out of being upset, I think that I officially wouldn't be this good, innocent, perfect daughter that he's always [thought he] had. —Theresa

I guess I felt like he would be ashamed of me. I don't know why—he didn't do anything to give me that impression, I guess it's just our culture. We don't tell dads when that happens. I've talked a couple of times with him. I almost feel bad for my dad because he loves me so much, and I think it's really hard for him to see me in pain. —Catherine

I called my dad once when I was drunk. I was at a pregame with my friends, and I called him outside of the room. I told him that I wanted to do something about it [the assault]. I remember crying and saying, "It's not okay, I'm not okay, I can't believe that he's [the perpetrator is] okay, I don't want him to be okay." He was supportive. We talked for maybe four or five minutes, and then I went back inside and went to the party. —Abbie

And sometimes the father's reaction feels like it's too much for the daughter to handle. One young woman told me that she felt devastated after she learned that her dad cried when he learned the news.

But some fathers don't seem to have that soft spot, or perhaps they handle it very differently. One daughter relayed that she felt pressured to tell her father and wished she hadn't because "at the time, he was okay, but he'll frequently throw it in my face to be nasty."

They Try, But Fathers Don't Always Understand

Maybe girls don't talk with their fathers about being sexually assaulted because, despite their deep love for their child and their attempts to understand, some dads just don't comprehend what sexual assault means to a woman. Some do but some don't, as one mother described:

[When she talked with her father] she got very upset and felt unsafe. Even her own father, who really is a poster child for caring, understanding, loving, and has been super supportive of everything – it really threw her – even Dad is having trouble with this. . . . I tried to talk to him about it and realized very quickly that he was not gonna get it.

The fact that the assault has a sexual aspect seems to get in the way of clearer communication for both fathers and daughters. For many reasons, discussion about sex can be awkward. Intimations of sexuality also can elicit highly intimate revelations that fathers and daughters are reluctant to share, as this father relayed:

> I have sadness that I haven't had some of these very serious conversations with my daughter about these events, because I've had serious conversations with her about a lot of things. . . . I guess to a certain extent it's fear and protecting my own psyche that I don't want to view my daughter as a sex object or a sexually active person. But I know she is, and she knows I know she is, right? . . . It's the same thing almost as you don't wanna see your parents having sex, right?

A sexual assault can highlight generational differences in beliefs about appropriate roles for men and women or underscore invidious gender distinctions that can span the generations. One father described himself as "very chauvinistic, I suppose" when he talked about "the estrogen-based emotionalism of women, just like guys' testosterone-based emotionalism, can be very debilitating for women at times." Another father spoke about his daughter needing the protection of another man – "If you have a boyfriend on campus, the odds of getting abused are significantly less . . . even if she goes without her boyfriend, some of the other boys there will know, 'Oh, that's So-and-So's girlfriend'" – an idea that might simultaneously appeal to the young women and cause them to recoil.

One father told me how he lost his virginity and contrasted it to that of his daughter's experience:

> Times are different, I guess . . . but I lost my virginity when I was pretty plowed, and it was with someone who was also pretty plowed. We had been dating for a month and a half and we were moving very slowly. If it hadn't been for the fact that we were both pretty plowed, it might have been another month and a half, it might have been six. But it was – and to this day I truly believe it was – consensual. It was a wonderful thing to happen, and I ended up marrying her, so it was a good thing. But it wasn't for my daughter. [*His daughter had been drugged.*]

But some do get it, and they get it in ways that can be gratifying. One mother described a conversation with her husband that helped her see things differently:

So I finally told my husband. And his reaction was very unexpected from what I thought. He immediately sprung into action. For some reason he could see what it was clearer than I or our daughter could. I think both of us being women . . . went straight to shame. My husband, however, went straight to rape. —Mother

Based on my conversations with girls who had been sexually assaulted and fathers whose daughters had been sexually assaulted, a few commonalities emerged. It appears that if the mother is told, the father is told. Most fathers had secondhand knowledge, however: they learned about the assault from the mother rather than directly from the daughter. Perhaps out of respect for the boundary that the daughter has drawn, he responds in kind – circumspectly.

The predominant theme among fathers seemed to be one of caution. Fathers wanted their daughter to be vigilant, they had advised her about specific ways to look out for herself around men and at parties, and they approached her carefully after she had been assaulted.

Despite talk of how men's roles have changed, fathers and daughters alike tended to describe the role of the father as a fairly traditional one: his job was to maintain stability amid the turmoil. I would surmise that part of that function included providing support for the mother while she dealt directly with the daughter. Also consistent with sex role stereotypes, most fathers, even seemingly mild-mannered ones, reported that they wanted to beat up the guy who had hurt their daughter. In reviewing the transcripts of the conversations with the fathers, I was also struck by their focus on rape and the relief they experienced in the cases when they learned that the incident wasn't rape. Whether aware of it or not, they were responding to their concern about the physical, sexual act, not the emotional impact of the incident on their daughter.

After listening to the daughters, mothers, and fathers themselves, I was left with the perhaps mistaken impression that dads weren't necessarily expected to understand or communicate well or directly. Daughters didn't seem to expect much emotional support from their fathers, mothers explained and perhaps even defended their husbands' seeming inability to identify and express emotions aside from anger, and fathers stated that, not being a woman, there were limits on what they could understand. Perhaps recognizing and wanting to contain their anger, fathers often stayed on the sidelines.

I continue to wonder about the fathers who didn't talk with me. And I wonder even more about the fathers whose daughters never told them about being assaulted.

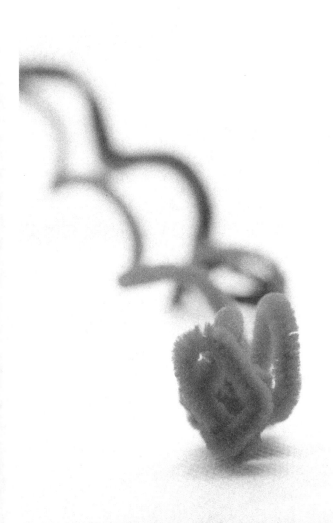

CHAPTER 7

Mothers

Mothers and daughters – it's a really special relationship – good, bad, and ugly. —Mother

Unless she doesn't have a mom, I would think that a daughter would want to speak to her mother before her father. —Mother

It really affected her [my mom] in more ways than I expected. I couldn't have predicted that. I don't really know what it's like to be a mother – to have to take care of someone and know that you can't always be there to protect them. It really, really affected her. She just wasn't herself for many months. —Kimberly

To echo the title of Sarah Knott's well-reviewed 2019 book on the history of maternity, "mother" is a verb.[1] The word refers to something you are but equally, if not more important, to something you do. Mother is the person in the family girls are mostly likely to turn to, and mothering is crucial to girls who have been sexually assaulted at college. Not surprisingly, this chapter contains more complex emotional content than the chapter about fathers. Please note that, unless attributed to someone else, quotes in this chapter are from mothers.

The mothers who spoke with me were busy. One heads a $100 million human services agency. Another is a psychotherapist. Two are teachers, another a nurse, another a physician. One works in construction, and another works with an international nonprofit organization. Another is working on a doctoral degree, another is a school counselor, and one is in real estate. Some were on their first career, others on their third, and some were at home. Their education varied considerably, ranging from a high school diploma to a graduate degree in business, religion, counseling, nursing, or medicine. Having multiple children was common. More than one had three kids in college at the same time.

A mother fills several roles in the lives of her children. The functions that seemed to be most salient for the mothers and daughters who spoke with me were anticipating and fixing problems and holding the family together. Even when the girl says she has a close relationship with her father, it's usually her mother she turns to for help and solace. I heard repeatedly that Mom is the go-to person in terms of concrete logistics as well as emotional caretaking when things go awry. More than one mother described living with her "antennae up" in an attempt to prevent problems in the first place, which requires a lot of energy and attention but can be preferable to doing cleanup. And a mother fills a special role not just with her daughter but also with the whole family. Mothers, fathers, and daughters described the mom as the glue that holds the family, and sometimes the daughter, together. That has a downside as well. Occasionally, the mother was described as someone who "takes on everyone else's things in the family . . . she'll find some fault with how she could have helped or how she could have prevented it or how she could have seen the signs," a prospect that generally was not reassuring to the daughter who had been sexually assaulted.

When it came to their daughters' assault, mothers took on myriad roles. Several described how they were the über caretaker and coordinator of emotions and actions within the family. As one mother said, "I saw my role as being the mediator, the compromiser, making sure that my husband and other daughter were okay, but also trying to guide them – she was so fragile that they had to keep their feelings to themselves." In other words, mothers were aware of how the information could affect others in the family and how their reactions, in turn, could affect the daughter. Sometimes they protected a family member. One kept the news from the girl's father during his serious illness, waiting to tell him when he had recovered to a point where she thought he could handle the information. Protectiveness was not unique to the mothers; many daughters described feeling protective of their mother, not wanting to make her sad or disappointed, to cause her worry or pain, or to somehow feel responsible for what happened.

Relationship with Daughter

Going off to college is another step in the ongoing process called separation and individuation, essentially the process of becoming one's own person. Your daughter might be long past the days when she was embarrassed to be seen with you or when your act of merely breathing could irritate her, but the process of the two of you separating from one another is still underway. Texting, keeping track of one another via Facebook or other social media, and having video and old-fashioned voice phone calls can bridge the sense of emotional distance associated with the physical distance of having left home.

Periods of conflict and estrangement are common in all relationships, including when a daughter discloses that she has been sexually assaulted. In the past you might have been a sturdy shoulder to cry on when she had a conflict with a friend or was rejected by a clique; watching her go through it might have been tough on you too. She might turn to you in a similar way now, but don't expect her to – it would be rare if she did. At this point in her maturity, she realizes that she doesn't have to, nor does she necessarily want to, tell you certain things. She might put some distance between the two of you; you might be the one who initiates it.

One mother told me that, after a while and a few glasses of wine one night, she realized she had to let go. Two mothers described their recognition of a separateness that hadn't been there before:

> I had to realize that I can't fix this for her . . . this is her journey and she has to handle it the way that's best for her. And so I kind of actually separated myself from her a little bit, because otherwise it would be much more difficult for me. . . . There's a part of me that always wants to fix it for my kids or to make it better, and this is something that I can't really do that with. . . . She knows that she can come to me with anything and that I'm always gonna be here for her.

We were super, super close. So to have this happen is kind of weird . . . it separated us in a way and there isn't really much that I can do to make her feel like I get it.

A heightened sense of separateness, artificiality even, can be antici-pated in the weeks and months after you learn about the incident. It needn't mean that whatever closeness you shared is gone; it just won't be there all the time. That's okay. It might be a good time to reflect on what you've taught her – intentionally or not – about some of the things she is struggling with now.

Mom on Men, Women, and Sex

Mothers teach their daughters about men and women. Sometimes it's a "sit down and listen to me" kind of teaching, but more often than not, daughters learn through routine conversations or simply by watching and absorbing what's going on around them. Without necessarily being aware of it, mothers impart knowledge about large societal matters as well as individual considerations.

As one daughter and two mothers relayed:

My mom always identified as a radical feminist. I'm an only child, so there were two women in the family versus my dad. She always pointed out inequalities to me, and I think much of the reason I am who I am is because she did [that]. . . . If she was always compliant and didn't teach me about these things, maybe I wouldn't be this passionate or this inter-ested in these issues. —Sara

I was a single mom for eight years. I never dated the whole time. My children didn't choose this. I'm going to be here for them. I did not have time to be looking for men. . . . I was focused on my kids. My ex-husband owes me over $70,000 in child support so don't tell me [men and] women are equal. —Mother

I blame myself a little bit, but I blame society too. I feel like we raise our girls to make sure other people are comfortable. She's always been a very high-achieving child. She got pleasure out of pleasing others and being good at things and not making people upset. And so [as the assault circumstances unfolded], she probably was like, "Oh, I feel a little uncomfortable, but I don't want to say anything." That is something that she's been working on since then – that you have to put yourself first, and you make choices about what you want to do and not worry, sometimes, about what other people are thinking. I don't know. It's complicated, very complicated. —Mother

What daughters said they learned from their mothers about men is not particularly flattering. Sometimes it was a step or two removed, such as when the mother's brothers disappeared when their parents were ill and needed help – "What's wrong with the men in our family?!" – leaving their sisters to manage a troubling situation. Occasionally a mother spoke to her daughter about difficulties with her husband, particularly when a divorce was in the offing, and was forthright about wanting something better for her daughter: "My mom was in a bad relationship with my dad, so it was very important to her that my sister and I be in good relationships and treat ourselves well."

Mothers typically imparted cautions about men in general. One daughter relayed her mother's rather harsh assessment:

> Mom was, "Men are like, well, men don't have brains. Men are rude and gross, so they're going to do stuff like this, and you just have to know better because as a woman you have to deal with this." . . . There's really no room to trust men, no room to trust a partner, or to hold them to a certain standard. —Lily

Even when mothers didn't give direct advice, they taught their daughters that they needed to protect themselves from men. These cautions seem to be handed down from generation to generation and, based on what the diverse group of girls and mothers told me, not limited to certain ethnic groups, cultures, or classes. In one instance, a mother directly warned her daughter about a boss who was paying special attention to her. The warning came with information about the mom: "When she was in school, the head of her lab had taken an interest in her and tried to make advances and ended up trying to kiss her or something like that – it'd been this whole thing for her. So she said, 'Just be really aware, be really cautious, these men can come after young women like you, and you just have to be really aware.'"

In addition, girls were told that men are not well versed in relation-ships and the language of emotions. And that men have a different position in the world. As one mother said, "Men have just a different experience. There's part of it [the experience of being female] that they just don't get." One mother generously attributed unwanted sexual touching and continued advances by a male friend to his not under-standing. As she told me:

> One of our close friends hit on me, he touched me in a way that wasn't appropriate. This is not something that should be happening in our society. And it's not like I am a va-va-voom type person that's asking for attention, I'm a very normal person. It's just so ingrained in our society that sometimes men think that it's a compliment to compliment a woman's physical appearance or to make innuendos or whatever. But again, it's so much a part of our society that sometimes I don't think that the guys really understand how prevalent it is – that every day at some point, you get somebody looking at you in a funny way. . . . [I want] to help men understand just how unsafe we feel. It's not a pleasant thing. It's not a compliment. You feel uncomfortable and unsafe. . . . I caught myself doing it with that family friend of ours, who suddenly was crossing boundaries. But I was like, "Hmm, he's such a good friend and I'm sure that's not what's happening." Until it got to a point where it was very clear that was what was happening. He didn't listen to me, so I had to finally go to the wife.

Some men might not get it, but the mothers and daughters do. Some, as one mother said, even compare notes: "My daughter and I laugh, we have the same feelings about certain people we know in our community. Like, 'That guy makes me feel uncomfortable, that one gives me bad jujus, or that's the one that holds you a little too long or rubs your back a little too much.' You've really gotta trust your gut."

Amid these cautions about predatory men and the need to protect oneself, what are girls taught by their mothers about sex and healthy sexual relationships? Sometimes not much. Several girls stated that they had not, and simply would not, talk with their mother about sex. On occasion, the mother might have been more comfortable with the topic than was the daughter. One mother spoke of sending her daughter to a church-run program about sex, a program for kids as they were reaching puberty that was about "feeling confident in your body and being proud of who you are and understanding the life-giving properties that you carry within you as a woman and your responsibility to grow up mature and sexually healthy. . . . [It was] supposed to demystify the whole process." But it backfired: "Somehow she heard it as if she did not control her urges, it was bad. I'm just horrified. She feels extremely guilty about her sexual feelings. I mean, this is sad, really sad stuff to me."

One mother likewise wanted her daughter to be comfortable being sexually active and told me what she conveyed following the assault:

> I said to her, "Here are my concerns. As an adult, I know that once you've slept with a man, it never goes away," that type of stuff. So you have to be thinking as you move forward, "Is this going to be something that's going to end up being damaging for me later or am I okay with this?" You obviously don't want to end up with a disease, but as long as you're okay with what you're doing, there's nothing wrong with taking your body back and using it as a way to have pleasure instead of [it being] something that's punishing you and that you're punishing yourself with.

Bodies were addressed in other ways, too. Although it was a sticking point in several mother-daughter relationships, their history of conversations about food and weight conveyed society's focus on appearance. Comments from two mothers capture some of the struggle around managing such expectations:

> I was raised that it's all about looks. I could walk into any room and every man in the room would look. And then when I gained weight, I had to learn to be a person that was not connected with my looks. And it was huge. Even today you go to one of our class reunions and people don't care if you're a good person, they don't care what you've done – it will be who's gained weight. It's vicious, it's just bizarre. I really think I screwed that child up about food. But I at least gave her a good sense of who she is, so I've got that going.

> I warn her about how she's dressing and the message she's sending. I tell her that in this country, people go out in very short minis, so just be one of them – but if you dress like that in another situation, people might think that you are inviting them to, well, I warn her. . . . She says I don't understand. She told me she feels she's not attractive, that nobody wants

her. [*By any standard, her daughter is a stunning young woman.*] . . . We walk around and many people comment, but she doesn't feel it in her.

Comfort with and in one's body can be severely disrupted following a sexual assault, as we'll see in later chapters.

The sense of one's body being a source of punishment after the assault seemed to be tied to disgrace and perhaps dishonor. Both mothers and daughters – albeit not all of them – expressed embarrassment, vague shame, and outright humiliation about how their bodies had been used. One mother, perhaps identifying with her daughter, was hesitant to tell her husband about the assault:

> To tell you the truth, there was a lot of shame on my part. I honestly felt that she was responsible for having gotten drunk and being in a state of mind where she could not be at all disciplined. I was so brokenhearted for her and, on the other hand, I felt ashamed. I wasn't sure how my husband would react. I didn't know how he would feel about her. I didn't want him to view her as a drunk girl who sleeps around.

And another spoke of how her daughter's sense of shame changed over time:

> Initially, she didn't want me to tell anyone because I think she felt shame. In fact, she told me specifically, "I don't want you to tell anybody what happened." Well, it was already too late because I had told my best friend – [I told my friend] don't tell my daughter I told you. My daughter has come completely the other way now. I think it shows that she's done some good work and she feels better about it.

It's reasonable to expect that a mother's opinions of men, women, physical appearance, sex, and how society functions around these issues can affect her daughter's views. Likewise, a mother having been sexually assaulted herself can both inform and color the daughter's perspective.

Mom's Experience

With sexual assault rates as high as they are, odds are that some of the mothers who spoke with me would have a history of being victimized.

They did, as did one of the fathers. In fact, this small group of parent volunteers tracked closely to what epidemiological studies show: about half of U.S. women have experienced some form of unwanted sexual contact, ranging from touching to penetration.[2] Some girls knew that their mothers had been assaulted. Others had their suspicions: "I was very certain that there was something in my mom's history. She had always told us, 'I don't trust any men, except your dad.' The way she hinted at it, it was very clear. She was like, 'I'll tell you when you're older, I'll tell you when you're older.'"

Others learned after disclosing their own assault, as this mother explained: "I had experiences like that when I was younger, a kid. I kind of understood how you can get into a situation like that. . . . I might've told her I've had similar experiences. I know that I have told her about some things, but not about everything." In other words, like their daughters, mothers often withheld some information. Personal privacy is important for both.

When the Daughter Already Knew
A few daughters were aware, prior to their own assault, that their mother had been sexually assaulted. Mom had talked about her assault – sometimes with explicit details, other times vaguely – and both daughters and mothers saw it as something that shaped their relationship. One girl relayed the details of her mother's assault and the subsequent effect it had on her:

> My mom was legitimately raped by her boyfriend in high school, and it essentially ruined her entire life from there. She was seventeen. She had been dating him for six months. He punched her in the face and fractured this bone [points]. She had choke marks, bruises everywhere. She was already really introverted, really insecure, and really sensitive and she always took it to be her fault. She couldn't tell, she didn't tell anyone. She just kept it all in and it ate at her. She said that she had been mugged and that this guy hit her in the face. It was right before she went off to college . . . she goes off to college and she's depressed and she attempted suicide twice. She's attempted suicide since I've been alive as well. . . . Last time it happened, I was fifteen. . . . She's been in and out of psychiatric treatment, she's been depressed, she's had cancer twice – a lot of things have happened to her. . . . As crazy

as she is, she's the best mom ever. I think she put all of the parenting she possibly could into forming me so that when she went off the deep end, I'd be able to take care of myself, which I kind of respect in a way.
—Kimberly

And a mother relayed how she handled the information with her daughter:

I was molested when I was young . . . I think she felt able to talk to me about some things because she knows I can relate on a certain level. . . . I am always worried because, well, when things happen to you in your life, you don't trust, and I don't trust well. . . . So I needed to explain to her early on when she was old enough to be able to comprehend – "Listen, I'm not trying to be overwhelming. I'm not trying to be overpowering as your mom. I'm afraid. And here's why I'm afraid. This bad thing has happened to me. Doesn't make me who I am. It shaped me to think and behave differently than I probably would have if it never happened. . . . Don't let my crazy seep on over into your crazy."

In both cases, the mother was aware that the experience could affect how she mothered her daughter.

When the Daughter Found Out After Her Own Disclosure

Some mothers disclosed their assault to their daughter for the first time after the girl had told them about her own assault at college. One mother told her daughter in the same conversation in which the girl recounted hers:

I never shared it with anybody. So sharing it with her thirty-five years later was kind of a personal moment. It was rough, I got all teary . . . just like I feel now. I was sitting there in my [hospital] scrubs and this guy has his hand down my bra. I felt the whole distancing thing, like you're not yourself anymore, you're just this object, and you don't know really what to do about what is happening to you. What I should have done is become very angry, I should have become irate, I should have called him a gazillion names. That's probably what she should have done and probably felt like doing. But instead, we both behaved the same way, we both let them proceed. Why is that? Why *is* that?!

Other mothers continued to keep the information to themselves, not sharing it with their daughters until long afterward. One mother said: "Eventually I told her I had once been assaulted. And she was very happy that I did." And one daughter noted that her mother, who had been assaulted and kept quiet at the time, was proud of her for not hiding.

Implications of Telling and Knowing

Whether the mother told or whether the daughter knew didn't seem to have a consistent effect on their relationship. I surmise that the diverse reactions and outcomes were related to the nature of their relationship and the timing of the disclosure. If they were testy with each other beforehand, knowing didn't necessarily make them feel warmer toward each other – it was just one more piece of information that went into an already difficult connection. If, while the daughter was disclosing her sexual assault, her mother blurted out her own, it usually wasn't well received. The daughter might understand the mother's bottled-up pain, but "if she had waited that long, couldn't she have waited a bit longer?!"

One girl said that knowing about her mother's sexual assault made it much harder to confide in her. She was distraught about the apparent effect it had:

> My mom has a history with that [trust and betrayal] too. No one believed her, that's the thing that hurt her the most. No one believed that her cousin tried to do something, and that lack of trust really destroyed my mom. Her own mother didn't believe her. . . . I felt that by telling her [that I had been sexually assaulted], not only had I opened up that wound again, I had made it deeper. —Jessica

For others it was a bond of sorts. As one mother said, "I think it's going to bring us closer because we've both experienced the same thing. . . . It'll just be in our back pockets – it's something that we kind of share, even though it's not a really great thing to have in common." When the mother identified too much with her daughter or wanted the daughter to identify with her, the girl drew back. As two girls told me:

My mom had this tendency of being, like, "He did this to hurt you, your stepfather did this to hurt me. . . . It was really hard for me to talk to people about his suicide, it also is hard for you to talk to people about this." It's hard for me to exactly put words to it, but it just felt like they were situations that didn't match . . . she tried to connect with me through her own experience. —Maddie

In some twisted way, my mom feels closer to me because this traumatizing thing happened to both of us. [*Do you feel closer to her?*] No, I don't at all. It was under totally different circumstances and we reacted to it totally differently. I think she also thinks that I harbor all this pain and all this inward trauma, when I really don't. . . . She's always wanted to see more of herself in me. —Trish

I was left with the impression that mothers and daughters could handle the dual disclosure if they had managed to establish a full sense of themselves as distinct from one another. If not, the fact that they each knew the other had been sexually assaulted was generally more fraught.

How Mom Coped

Mothers seemed to think that they should be able to "be there" for their daughter after she disclosed that she had been sexually assaulted. For some, doing so came easily. For others, it was a struggle. It might be an odd association, but as the mothers and daughters told me about their attempts to connect, I thought of breastfeeding. The idea that breastfeeding is a nearly instantaneous and automatic behavior holds true for some first-time mothers and their newborns; for many others, initial attempts result in frustration, disappointment, and even shame. The belief that I *should* be able to do it can get in the way of succeeding in doing it. In both situations, it can take a while for the mother and daughter to learn how to connect in a way that is satisfying to both.

Mothers reported searching inward at times, wondering if they could have done something that would have helped prevent their daughter's assault. Rumination on their responsibility was common among the mothers. As one said, "Mothers always go to bed guilty at night over one thing or another." A sense of guilt isn't universal by any stretch, but even extremely competent women in high-powered professions expressed doubt about how well they had parented.

For some, the uncertainty was linked to other things in their lives: a shaky marriage, a bout with depression, societal expectations of mothers and of daughters. Some calmed their fears by drawing strength from previous strains. One mother said, "I think I already had the confidence of [knowing] life really goes on even after you go through a very traumatizing thing."

Coping strategies, whether or not consciously chosen, varied widely. One mother put "the emotion away because if I don't, I can't deal with it. In crisis mode is usually when I am the calmest." Another complained that her daughter doesn't share enough with her at that same time as she said that she herself doesn't share with others; she didn't see the similarity.

Avoidance and other forms of self-protection were common. One mother told me that she takes care of herself by "just sort of hiding or taking it or waiting and hiding it, not exposing myself," which had helped her cope throughout her life but wasn't working well in terms of relating to her sexually assaulted daughter. Another talked about how she and her daughter navigate the obstacle the mother has put in the way:

> The issue is not forgotten, it's somewhere, but there's a very tight wall around it. . . . I ask myself, "How come we never talk about it?" And I know it's because of this wall that I've built around the issue. I think that I would talk to her about it, but I don't know if I can – even yesterday we said, "Let's not talk about it." . . . The wall works. I walk around happily. I don't talk, my colleagues don't know anything about me. . . . I open that wall only to pray, and I close it afterwards. But that's how I cope.

One of the girls relayed how her mother manages to move ahead by not looking back:

> My mom's father was really abusive and abused her often, and then he kicked my grandma and my mom and her sister and brother out of their house and said, "I want nothing to do with you all." So my mother grew up in poverty . . . in very bad conditions; they didn't

even have food sometimes. I think the way she's been able to get through life is by dealing with something once, then never going back to it or thinking about it. Because if she was to sit down and discuss all that's gone on in her life, I don't know whether she would be able to handle it. —Alicia

Likewise, another mother copes not only by not looking back but by erasing memories too:

One of the things I think that makes me a survivor . . . is that I just forget the really dark, ugly stuff. I think it makes me stay alive . . . it's a survival mechanism. . . . I'll be, like, "I don't remember that. I literally have no memory of that." It works well for me. I'm pretty damn happy.

Such coping styles, which might be easy to find fault with, clearly work for these women. We tend to keep doing what works. That said, when a new and challenging circumstance involves another person, particularly someone important to us, many of us will instead experience a lot of interpersonal discomfort. Turning to others can help.

Mother's Confidants

In a few cases, aside from her daughter, I was the only person the mother had spoken with about the assault. Some mothers were described, or described themselves, as a keeper of secrets. They had been told about the assault but agreed to keep it secret – or offered to or simply assumed they would. One mother was concerned, however, about the effect of secrets on the family: "I felt that it [the disclosure] was an important part of our bond as a family. . . . I mean, we've all got little secrets, of course. But I don't think anything big like that should be held private, because I think that it weakens the bond." Another mother was clear that having the entire family in the loop was good for the girl: "Her revealing it to all of us has helped her stay with us in a stronger sense than feeling apart from us." Mom was concerned about the family unit as well as the daughter who had been assaulted.

I found myself wishing that the parents could get together and talk with one another. I understood how they wanted to protect their daughter's privacy, but they often were left trying to figure out and deal with things by themselves. It can be difficult and lonely.

Mothers who hadn't talked with anyone else often cited reasons remarkably similar to those given by the girls who hadn't told their parents about being sexually assaulted – reasons that can be distilled down to silence feeling safer. The mothers who had kept it to themselves often encouraged their daughters to do the same:

> I'm very close to my own mom but I would never tell her. . . . I want to protect my daughter from judgment, the hard judgment of "Why didn't she say no?" [Note that the mother knew that the daughter had said no repeatedly during the incident.] Let's say they see her dress in a certain way – they'll think, "Oh, no wonder that happened." . . . So that's why I keep it to myself.

> My mom didn't want me to tell anybody about this, and she wasn't gonna tell any of her family members or anybody. She always told me that when I get married or start to have a relationship with a guy, don't ever tell him about this incident because it's very embarrassing, it's shameful. I could understand why she said that. —Hannah

When these mothers spoke with me, they described our conversation as a catharsis – "It was cleansing to give that away" – and I had the sense that they might consider talking with other adults. If they do, I anticipate that they will follow the path taken by a few mothers who identified someone who served as a "test case" for their decision to speak more openly. These test cases sometimes ended well, sometimes not. As one disappointed mother said, "I felt so let down, I decided I'm not going to tell anybody else because the one person who I thought would care didn't care." I'm not sure it's relevant, but the disappointed mother was the only one whose confidant was a male friend. All others turned to women.

For several mothers, the experience of telling someone that their daughter had been assaulted paralleled that of their daughters. The mothers thought carefully about whom to tell, often turning to a sister or close female friend. As is often true for the girl herself, how that first person responded influenced whether a mother told anyone else and who else they might have told.

One mother identified the three people she had told:

> I spoke to my sister because we're very close. And I have another good friend that, on vacation, I mentioned it to her and she cried. This is something that doesn't take a lot of words to share. I think that there are just some people who get it – that helps, that helps enormously. And my best friend from high school. I talked to her at length about all of this and we prayed together. . . . She is definitely always there for me.

Another was deliberate in her decision to speak with someone who wasn't a friend or relative:

> I knew I had to talk to somebody outside the family. So I called my daughter's academic coach one day – she loves my daughter – and said, "Got a minute?" I don't even know where the tears came from, I just started sobbing, and she's like, "What is the matter? I've never heard you like this, you're always so put together." I told her what happened, and I said, "You wouldn't even know her now, you wouldn't even know her. I don't know where my kid's gone. She's gone. She's not there."

The confidant occasionally was someone who could provide tangible help as well as emotional support for the mother, the daughter, or both. One girl described how living in a three-generation household was helpful; her grandmother was distraught at the news but, after a few days, took on the role of being strong for her daughter who, in turn, was strong for the girl. Workplace confidants were not common but did prove helpful for a few mothers. One had an administrative assistant who moved things off her calendar and kept information about what the daughter and family were going through private.

On the other end of the continuum were mothers and daughters who were willing to discuss the topic when it came up in conversation. They had usually checked out the possibility with each other and assessed their comfort level rather than waited until they were in a situation in which they had to make a choice. One mother saw telling others as a public service of sorts: "Talking and sharing your experience does hit home with people who've not experienced it themselves." The decision to talk openly did not necessarily correspond to the "severity" or type of assault.

Sometimes the mother took into confidence someone who, in hindsight, was not a good choice. This seemed to occur when the disclosure was driven by hard-to-sit-with feelings, and the reaction of the other person created its own craziness. A daughter and a mother captured this scenario well:

> The first person my mother told was my cousin, who's kind of an older sister to me. . . . My mom told me, "I'm so sorry, but I just told her everything about what happened and I'm really sorry and I know you might not have wanted me to tell her, but I told her because I didn't know what to do and I just told her everything." That cousin lectured me on why I should drop the case and about everything that happened. That bothered me. I felt violated because I told my mother in trust, and she goes and tells somebody everything without even asking me – she felt so emotionally weak that she couldn't even hold it. That really bothered me. —Stacey

> I had to tell my boss, and maybe I shouldn't have, but I shared with my boss that my daughter had been raped and that she was having these eating disorders and I needed to go [be with her]. And she asked, "Was it someone she knew?" "You know what? Does it fucking matter? Because if it was date rape, it maybe wasn't as bad? Or [you're asking] so you can put me on a level of how much you should feel sorry for me? Fuck off." What I have learned at a personal level about how people deal with rape is way more information than I ever wanted to be in possession of.

More formal sources of help can be of use too. One mother spoke with an employee assistance counselor at her workplace for a few sessions. Another spoke with a spiritual director with whom she meets monthly, and another with her daughter's coach. Others reached out to their daughter's psychotherapist, as one mother relayed: "My daughter's therapist was very helpful. She shared with me that she had had a similar experience happen to her when she was a young woman . . . she told me that she has had several clients who have had similar experiences."

Others sought services for themselves:

I knew I needed to say and feel and unload all kinds of things that were right, wrong, ugly, unattractive on every level. I was angry. And I can't honestly tell you who I was angry at. Was I angry at my daughter? Was I angry at myself? I told her to go [with him] – whose responsibility is that? Again, who takes the blame? I knew I had a lot of stuff inside. But it's not fair to react until you've sorted it out a little bit, so that you can talk about it. . . . I can't show her that I love her and I support her until I know what is going on inside me.

To release emotional and physical tension, one mother turned to massage therapy. She clearly valued the special context it provided her:

Physical touch is integral. I've had weekly massage – maybe that's how I got through this. I'd get on the table and I'd be crying . . . we would talk the entire time I was on the table. Now I just go in and I go to sleep because I'm fine. But I really think that [it] was my therapy – the physical piece and the ability to talk to somebody who didn't know my daughter. You can't tell your mother because she'll never look at your kid the same. [A massage therapist is] an outside person who can be indignant [along] with you, and [talking with them] is not going to screw up a daily relationship.

The mothers' decisions whether and with whom to talk seemed to be driven by a range of motivations that, like those of their daughters, changed over time: to seek support, to release tension, to gain understanding, to get help with problem solving, and to feel less alone. Even if you don't talk to them frequently, it can be comforting to have people in your life – a sister, a close woman friend, a therapist – who know. Two mothers had a sister whose daughter had also been assaulted; talking with them created a special bond. One mother, mindful of how she relates to others, said, "When people ask how things went for our daughter, I want to be honest. There are certain people that I have to be honest with." For most of us, there are people who are so important to us that we choose to be forthcoming.

No matter how old we get, many of us still think of our mothers as special beings – maybe not perfect, but as more than the person who raised us (as if that's not enough). In fact, it's probably because our existence depended mostly, if not exclusively, on her for the first few years of our lives that we sometimes mistakenly think of our mothers as all power-ful. We know in our heads that they aren't omnipotent or flawless, but in our heart of hearts we might want them to be. When Dad lets us down, it's a disappointment, sometimes a small one, sometimes a big one. When Mom lets us down, it can be devastating.

And as mothers we experience multiple intense feelings when our children are clear that we have let them down. One mother captured the outsized emotions of both girl and mother during an initial post-assault conversation when she said:

> [She told me,] "Well, if my friends can see that I was robbed, why doesn't my mother see? You're my mother, you're my *mother*!" I'm a sucky mother. I'm a terrible mother. That's how it felt. I guess this means I'm a really bad mother because my daughter called me after she was assaulted and I asked her what she was doing there, as if it was her fault, which is not what I meant. It just – I was just kind of like, "You can't put this all on him, honey," which is wrong.

Both the mothers and daughters who spoke with me seemed to hold the mothers to a pretty high standard. Girls wanted and expected a lot from their mothers, often immediately. Mothers seemed to think that they should have been able to incorporate shocking news and respond with grace and kindness that would somehow make everything better. The girls feared that they would disappoint their mothers and did not hesitate to let their mother know that she had disappointed them. Mothers returned to their perceived failings like a set of worry beads, replaying memories and wishing that they had handled things differ-ently, in the most extreme cases wishing that they were someone who they are not.

The negative interactions distressed both girls and mothers. But most seemed to soldier on. Even when things went poorly, they returned to each other – sometimes in sorrow, sometimes in anger. As one mother said, "I can take it. I can hear what she has to say about me and the mistakes that she feels I've made, and it's okay. It's not gonna kill me."

It takes a certain strength to reach out to others when distressed. Whether a sister, friend, therapist of some sort, or someone else, the mothers who activated their support networks well felt calmer and more centered. Caring can be complicated when it calls up old wounds or when one feels not up to the task. When mothers turn to a person with whom they feel safe, they often can be more available to their daughter as she deals with having been sexually assaulted. One mother conveyed a particularly poignant exchange with her daughter: "[I told her,] 'I'm on your side. Your happiness is the only thing that matters to me. Honestly. That's it.' When I said that to her, she was just, like, 'Really?!' I think that she knew that, but I don't think that she really comprehended the power of a mother's love." The simple, clear statement brought relief and reassurance.

The process can be less bumpy when the mother is mindful of her own needs and separateness from her daughter. One mother reminded me – and herself – that recovering from the trauma is her daughter's task and that excessive worry benefits no one: "It's a matter of her going through these experiences and kind of figuring it out on her own in a lot of ways. I guess that's the way it is for everybody. I know when I was her age, people would say things, but do you really listen? It's really learning through your mistakes. I worry about her a lot, and I've got to stop worrying about her because it's not good for me and it's not good for her – she doesn't like to know that I worry about her all the time."

Being mindful that it's hard for you too and that you need to take care of yourself as well as your daughter is important. Sometimes you might start to feel overwhelmed. If so, it's okay to say, "This feels awkward for me but if you want to talk about it, I'll try" or "I'd like to take a break for a bit. Does that work for you?" Letting your daughter know that it's not a one-and-done situation – you are willing to have several conversations – can relieve some pressure on both of you.

CHAPTER 8

Campus Resources

Parent support can be vitally important at such a critical time in a young person's life – when they face these true forks in the road, real crises, and moral and ethical lessons. It's a huge opportunity for parents to assist in a big way. —Mother

[It's important for parents] to recognize that maybe the most they can do is less than they would want to do: Maybe what my kid wants from me is to just be there and listen, while I might want to do a lot more, like show up at their door and stay with them. But I need to take my cues from them and really try and empower them to figure out what healing is going to look like for them. Personally, I think I would probably also get my own support – it's important and parents don't do that. —Campus staffer

We, as a school, are trying to be fair and thorough. And, as parents, I don't think we want fair. We want our kid to be safe and for there to be justice. —Campus staffer

Your daughter has been sexually assaulted and it's not the end. It's the beginning of another path on which she must make multiple decisions. She likely is feeling vulnerable in multiple ways, and physical security is a basic one. She considered college a safe place, an assumption that has been shattered or at least challenged on a very deep level; it will take a while to rebuild that sense of safety. Your impulse might be to pull her out of school, to bring her home (although home is not a safe place for a lot of women and girls, but that's another story), and it's an option but rarely one to exercise immediately.

College campuses have multiple people on staff who, following a sexual assault, can inform students of their options and serve as a sounding board. Most of these people are not responsible for determining guilt or innocence; they are responsible for responding in the moment to the needs of students. Some are similar to patient navigators in health care settings – they help students get the services they need and don't judge the choices they make about which to access. Others provide direct health care and other services. This set of campus staffers, as I refer to them in this chapter, are most relevant in the immediate aftermath of an assault but can be resources throughout your daughter's college days.

Most students do not use the resources available to them. In fact, in a 2019 survey of 181,752 students at thirty-three campuses, 70 percent of the female students who had "experienced penetration by physical force or inability to consent or stop what was happening" *did not contact any campus resource.* Their reasons? Nearly half said they could handle it themselves, about that many considered it not serious enough to contact programs or resources, and about two-fifths said they felt embarrassed, ashamed, or that it would be too emotionally difficult. The students who responded that it was "not serious enough" and "other reason" were asked an additional question; their top four reasons for not seeking help were they weren't injured, alcohol or other drugs were present, the incident happened in a context that began consensually, and because "events like this seem common."[1] The last reason speaks to a task that one of the campus staffers has taken on: "I focus on getting people to think about how normalized sexual violence and harassment are. . . . It becomes so normalized that when they have an experience that is sexual assault, they're not calling it that."

The campus resource and service providers who spoke with me – all quotes in this chapter are from them unless specified otherwise – are extraordinarily competent and compassionate people who are proud of the systems and structures they spent years creating, not always with the support of the university administration. (Just as students push university administrators for reforms, so do faculty and staff.) They represent a university's commitment and dedication to responding to campus sexual assault.

A lot of trust is placed in these people. They must balance their responsibilities as an agent of the institution with the needs of the student sitting in front of them, often in crisis. Altruism seemed to drive them, as this quote illustrates: "It's just really important work. It can be draining, it can be long hours, it can be odd hours, but if you weren't there, this eighteen-, nineteen-year-old student would be doing this all by themselves." They are aware of their dual role and its limits: "It's really hard for us, as an institution, to do this right. And we're not going get it right every time. But we care about and love your kid too – not like you do, but we do."

The functions and services they describe illustrate what one university is doing in 2020. There are many variants of these functions and structures at institutions of higher education across the country, so you should not expect to find the exact same systems at your daughter's school. The school's website is a good place to begin to explore resources that can be possible sources of support and assistance for your daughter: student services, health services, counseling center, Title IX office, chaplain's office, campus police, and more.

In might be reassuring to learn that, according to the 2019 survey of nearly two hundred thousand college students, about 82 percent of those who used such services found them to be helpful. A total of 85 percent reported feeling no pressure to proceed with a formal complaint; the remaining 15 percent were divided relatively evenly between feeling pressure to report and pressure not to report.[2]

Reporting

There's reporting and there's help seeking, and students tend to draw a pretty clear line between the two. And one does not substitute for the other. Let me explain.

In my experience, students tend to use the word "report" to mean officially notifying a campus authority (for example, campus police or the university's sexual assault investigative office) or the local police. Such notification is uncommon. Only about one in ten female undergraduates who have been the victim of a wide range of sexually assaultive acts say that they report the incident to campus police or local police.[3] That's actually higher than I thought it would be given that rape is the most underreported crime in the country.

Students typically are ambivalent about making an official report. Some fear social consequences from their peer group and friends of the perpetrator, and others are responding to pressure from their parents. As one of the campus resource providers said:

> I rarely hear "Oh, they're supporting me, telling me to do whatever feels right for me." I think the fear of reporting is that it is going to take over their life, that everyone's going to know about it, that it's going to be too exhausting, it's not worth it, don't even go that route. That's really hard for students because maybe they feel like it would be an important part of their healing process, but it's hard for them to go against what their parents think is best for them.

The struggle is internal as well, as one student told me:

> I was considering filing a big report like that. That just seemed like a lot, and I was in no mental state last semester to even think about that. Maybe in the future I might, but it was just too much last semester. . . . I'm just scared that he's going to hurt somebody again – he did last year, he did this year. —Sophia

It's important to recognize that your daughter's priorities might not correspond to what you think is important. You might want her to move on, to make her life easier, when she is finding her rudder. As one girl spoke, I wondered if her mother realized how she undermined her daughter's moral authority:

> I told my mother [after I filed a report at the university], and she was a weeping mess. She wasn't upset, but she was like, "Why are you getting involved with the police and complaining about this and everything? Why can't you just be quiet about it? Why are you taking this and making it a big deal? . . . What if he does something to you afterwards?" And she was so upset and so insistent that I withdraw the case that I did; I felt like there was, literally, no reasoning with my mother. . . . We argued, we fought. I [felt it was] the right thing to do. I should follow through with this if I started it. And now I'm leaving that girl [another girl the

perpetrator assaulted] by herself to fend off this person and fend off the system . . . it almost seems like I don't actually subscribe to whatever I said, right? My mom was, like, "Well, that's fine, but you don't want to ruin his life, and you shouldn't just get involved in all of these things. Just pretend it never happened." —Veronica

Oh, my.

Activating Campus Resources

Regardless of whether an official report is ever made, it's important that girls who have been sexually assaulted at college have help, that they are supported as they struggle with what happened and how to move forward. Moreover, it is important that schools know about assaults on and by their students; services cannot be provided if they don't know. One mother said her daughter didn't want to tell anyone in authority at school, but she insisted:

> I said, "Somebody at that school has to know. I can't send you back to that school without somebody knowing. We need help. . . . You're supposed to take your exams this week and you're not going to show up. They're going to give you zeroes unless we have a valid reason. We've got to tell somebody."

Students find out about these resources through new student orientation, workshops, trainings, brochures available at various locations across campus, the university website, and campus-specific apps that link to a variety of resources and services such as the library and student health. Word of mouth seems to be important too – students tell one another about their experience with a resource much like how they cue one another in about a compelling course or a boring professor. It is up to students whether they access any of the services.

Confidentiality and Privacy
Some resources on campus might be designated as confidential, whereas others are not. Those designated as confidential can provide support and guidance without an obligation to inform the Title IX coordinator on campus. Most of the campus staff members who spoke

with me were designated as confidential resources and protect student privacy and confidentiality in multiple ways. As one said:

> We preserve their confidentiality. . . . A student just got hit by a car, I call the dean's office and say the student has a medical emergency and will not be in class and will need some accommodation. Same thing for other circumstances – this student is having a personal emergency and will not be in class or will need some kind of academic adjustments. . . . They don't need any information other than what I say . . . we always tell the student it's up to them if they want to share more than that.

In addition, federal law – the Family Educational Rights and Privacy Act, known as FERPA – prohibits the disclosure of information, even to parents.[4] The restriction can create uncomfortable circumstances for both parents and university staff. As one staffer told me:

> Students come here and they have privacy rights because of FERPA. But Mom and Dad are paying the tuition and they want to know what's going on. . . . I have to say, "I'm sorry, I cannot share with you. You need to talk to your son or you need to talk to your daughter. I can't give you any information." It's not because I'm being disrespectful; it's because I'm prohibited by law from sharing with them.

If it's not clear which resources are and are not confidential at your daughter's school, ask.

Options and Interim Measures

When students access these campus resources, they are typically seeking information about options and what their decisions might mean for their future. The staff are ready to help them understand the alternatives and the services that are available; as I was told:

> I think people are looking for a little bit of direction – "I have been holding this absolute nightmare of a thing in my life, I don't know what to do with it." "Well, there are a couple things you can do: here's the police route, here's the counseling route, and more." I think they're looking for a place to dump it all emotionally . . . a safe, confidential space that sometimes is disconnected from their daily space.

One of the benefits of accessing campus resources is that staff can institute what are called "interim measures." The purpose of these temporary measures is to give students who come forward an opportunity to think about their options, including whether or not to file a formal complaint. Such measures – a no-contact directive, relocating one of the two people if they live in the same residence hall, a conditional attendance agreement, and a leave of absence – focus on reducing the potential for subsequent harm to the individual who came forward and on protecting others in the campus community.

Interim measures can be instituted pending the outcome of an investigation, and many students report feeling relief knowing, for example, that their perpetrator has been told to stay away from them and not contact them. Some are satisfied with what the interim measures accomplish and decide not to pursue things further in terms of the perpetrator. That does not mean that things are resolved for her though; as one campus service provider said, "They'll get a no-contact order and think they can just move on. . . . That's not a successful long-term solution, but it's the immediate solution."

Sometimes the campus staffer can be of help long after the immediate crisis has passed. As one of the staff members told me:

> A year and a half later, I remember sitting at my desk and getting a frantic phone call. This one young lady had just walked into a class that she had added at the last minute. And there he was, sitting in the front row. So she searched around, and there was another section of the course, but it was full. And so I called [the appropriate office] and said, "I need one exception. I need this young lady in this class. I need her in this class, so could you just add one more person?" [It worked.]

In the next section, we'll learn how parents can help or hinder their daughter as she decides how to move forward.

Partnering with Parents

The campus resource and service providers who spoke with me said that they almost always ask students whether they have told their parents. The advice one gives students would please many parents: "My thing is always be honest. . . . It's so hard to remember a lie. . . . And if you're capable and if you have a family where you can disclose, do it. The healing process goes so much smoother when you have your family supporting you."

They are mindful that the first-year students in particular have been away from their parents for only a short time. As one of the service providers said:

> I tell them, "Your parents don't feel that differently about you than they did the summer before you came [to college], and I guarantee you were leaning on them for all of the things that were coming up in your life. And now, all of a sudden that you're here, you think you're going to upset them if you call and tell them that you're having this issue? There's only a three-month difference. . . . They haven't flipped the switch that you're a full-blown adult yet, I guarantee it. They want to help you. They want to be with you." But again, I think that's dependent on the family.

They told me about preparing the girl to make that difficult initial call to her parents, sometimes even joining her on the phone if that's what she wants. I was told that a lot of kids are afraid of their parents – even at eighteen, twenty, or twenty-two years old, they're still afraid of their parents – and campus staff can provide support. How do parents react to such a call? Two campus resource providers conveyed their experience:

> The parents are usually pretty upset, and they want to know what the university's doing. And so we go through what the resources are and the options are for the student. And once they hear that, I'm surprised at how grateful they are. . . . Sometimes they're just not happy and what they're not happy about is the person [perpetrator] is still here. And sometimes at that point, the parents say, "From now on, I'll be the one to talk to you, I don't want you to talk to my daughter anymore." Stuff like that. But most of the time, they're grateful.

> If they start to make this huge deal of it while we're on the phone, we can kind of help to say, "This isn't the biggest of your concerns. There are bigger things that we need to be focusing on and not what led to this crime."

That "bigger thing" is how to help your daughter when she is in crisis. And as you might anticipate, they had some ideas about that.

Parents Being Helpful

Campus resource and service providers sometimes know more about your child and what happened than you ever will. They said that parents are most helpful when they trust their daughter and, whatever choices she makes, support her.

Parents might be concerned that their daughter doesn't have enough life experience to make decisions about how to handle circumstances such as this. When I posed that idea, the staff members who spoke with me invariably rejected it as well as the idea that they or the parents should tell the student what to do.

One of the university staffers drew upon her prior experience:

> There might be a perception that people don't know what they need for themselves, but when a trauma such as an assault has happened, I feel like all of that goes out the window. When someone's power and control is taken away, the only thing that matters is regaining it. When I worked for community agencies, most of the victims were older and they were in the same place emotionally. So whether you're eighteen or sixty-eight, all you're trying to do is regain normalcy, to put the pieces back together . . . it's a little offensive when people don't think that an eighteen-year-old could make those decisions for themselves. They might not have a lot of life experience, but trust and believe them when they say, "I need this to feel better."

While one of the campus resource and service providers responded to my question about what advice he would offer to parents, an image came to mind of someone using a thick crayon and drawing a box to indicate its boundaries:

> Do your job and don't do someone else's job. Meaning, your job is to be a mom or a dad. Love them, raise them, parent, support, provide. That's your job. You're not their lawyer. Even if you are a lawyer, you're not their lawyer. You're not their doctor. You're not their therapist. You're not their advocate on campus. You're not their avenger. The temptation is to be all those things for your kid when there are people who your child potentially has asked to be those things. We

don't need you to be the cop. We have cops here who are investigating. You don't have to investigate. . . . Your calling in this moment is to be a mother or father or guardian or grandparent. And, again, be that for them. If they need help identifying a lawyer, then help them identify a lawyer. If they need you to be the heavy and call the school, then go and be the heavy. But if they just want you to cry with them, then cry with them. And that's torture because you want to fix it. When they got boo-boos, you patched up their boo-boo when they were a kid. And when a teacher was mean when they were growing up, you wanted to go down to the school and tell off the teacher. Same thing here, but I just feel that it's doing further violence if we don't respect the boundary that a kid has asked us to . . . that has its limits, but I think we have to try.

They also welcomed the opportunity to assist parents: "Be supportive, that's what she needs right now . . . and call us if you have questions" and "Parents have come in and talked [to me] . . . it's pretty amazing when the parent acknowledges and recognizes that they might be in over their head a little bit. They want to do it right."

Parents Being Unhelpful
The ways in which parents were described as being unhelpful focused on interactions with their daughter and with university staff. I was routinely told by this group of staff members that one of the least helpful things a parent can do is to take charge and make decisions for the student. Part of the healing is to regain a sense of control that was lost, was taken away; it is important for the student to regain and retain control moving forward. Being supportive and caring without being overly intrusive or trying to take over was described as key. One of the campus resource and service providers noted that it can be hard for parents who are "kind of living this event vicariously through the student just like they would live a good event through them."

It's important to keep your cool. You might be really angry, convinced that the university is responsible, and it would be good to find a way to manage all that without taking it out on your daughter or the staff who are trying to help her. Three staffers conveyed difficult interactions with parents of girls who had been sexually assaulted:

The parents were so distrusting of the institution and they were so angry on the phone. The student and the parents were combative the whole time, and I could see how unhelpful it was for the student. The student couldn't think clearly and ask the right questions because there was so much tension and anger towards one another and towards the person they were making the report to. There was tension because the parents thought you should not be making this report, institutions don't take this seriously, this is just going to be bad for you. It was really hard to hear.

The parent contacts I've had have been very hard, difficult conversations. . . . It's been really frustrating to have to be patient with a parent who's not patient with their student and not patient with you. I'm not the police, so I can't investigate . . . I want to help you help your child who you are definitely concerned about. I hear your concern and I empathize with that concern, but there's a limit to what we can do because if your student doesn't want that, then I can't provide that for them. I can't make them go to the police, I can't make them go to counseling, I can't make them go to any services. I think that for a parent to hear me say that, they get pissed off and I get it. They're processing their own hurt and their own frustration and their own anger, but it becomes less helpful, it does more harm than good.

I've had students come in and the first thing they say is "I'm really sorry for the way my mom talked to you on the phone." That shouldn't be their first statement to me. Because then the kid feels like they need to come in and advocate for their parent – "My parents are really not that bad, they're just hurting right now." And I get it, they don't have to explain that to me. But then they feel responsible for being diplomatic when my concern is only for their well-being and their experience.

Put succinctly, if you are being confrontational with your daughter who has just disclosed to you that she was sexually assaulted, or even if you're simply being confrontational or combative around her, she may be less likely to seek the support she needs and can get on campus. The school might be culpable in some way, just as society might be, but it will be to your advantage to proceed with some caution so she can get the help she needs.

Health Services

Student health services – for both physical and mental health – are ubiquitous on college campuses. If a student who has been sexually assaulted seeks help on campus, it is typically for health care. What services is your daughter's college likely to provide?

Physical Health and Sexual Assault Exams

Most student health services have a gynecologist on staff or another health care provider designated to provide basic gynecological care, as well as to see women who've had "unwanted, coerced, unplanned, or unhappy sexual experiences – the whole gamut," as one service provider told me. She also said that emergency contraception (widely known as Plan B) used to be a common request, but, now that it's available over the counter (albeit at a price that is steep for most college students), the most frequent request is to be tested for sexually transmitted infections after unprotected sex. She's aware of the important function she fills for such girls, all of whom she asks if the sex was consensual: "most women who've been sexually assaulted never go for help, never tell anyone, never report it in any way. However, they do want to make sure they don't get pregnant and don't get an infection."

Student health services can provide ongoing care, which is especially important when the initial visit has been difficult. For some girls, a post-assault exam is their first gynecological exam. An experience conveyed by one of the girls who spoke with me brought home how difficult it can be:

> I had to be put on pain medication for the soreness. I didn't tell them about the assault because I was just really embarrassed. When they did the cultures of inside of my vagina, they said it really looks like what they look for in rape kits, the tissues inside of you are not looking right, they are very torn. I just tried to put it away and not think about it.
> —Theresa

A student health center might conduct sexual assault exams, but it would be rare. It's more common for those to be conducted at designated hospital emergency departments or special service locales. The gold standard is for a SANE nurse (Sexual Assault Nurse Examiner) to gather forensic evidence through internal and external examinations that involve, among other things, painting the area with toluidine blue dye so that damage not visually apparent can be more readily observed. (Note that currently available techniques do a better job of identifying such injury on lighter than darker skin, which has important criminal justice implications.[5]) Medications are provided to prevent pregnancy and sexually transmitted infections, including HIV. Follow-up care is offered and can include linking to needed services. When called upon, the examiner can provide court testimony.

Having such an exam after being sexually assaulted is not easy, and victims sometimes wait hours to be seen. But the exam has important implications in terms of moving forward with the criminal justice system. A decision about whether to proceed with a police report does not need to be made when an exam is conducted. Victims of sexual assault can have the exam and make up their minds later, but the crucial information will have been collected. By law, such exams are free.

Mental Health and Psychological Services

Many college girls who have been sexually assaulted will benefit from some sort of psychological help. The on-campus mental health service center is the choice of many.

As with all counseling and psychotherapy, the fit between the person seeking care and the caregiver is important. The campus resource providers who spoke with me were very familiar with the mental health services at their school and could suggest the name of a specific therapist, which is much more personal and helpful than simply saying, "Go to the counseling center." Universities often have multiple counselors who care for victims of campus sexual assault and who have expertise in posttraumatic stress disorder: "A specially trained group of mental health service providers was formed to meet the need of students coming in who have disclosed an assault. . . . We have met consistently for four years – we read literature and discuss it, we read theory and discuss it – so that we're all approaching the issue and how we work with students in a consistent way." Your daughter will not be the first sexual assault victim they have seen.

Regular individual counseling appointments can be supplemented by support groups, which can be particularly helpful in reducing the girl's sense of isolation and stigma. And of course, emergency services are available as students navigate the aftershocks of the assault. One girl told me how her mother activated resources for her:

> One night I was just in a very bad, bad space and I called my mom. . . . I was just crying intensely and saying, "I don't want to be here." And she was like, "What do you mean, you don't want to be here? You don't want to be at school? Or you don't want to be here at all?" She said I wouldn't answer the question, so she was nervous. She emergency-called [the college's counseling service] and that was the first night that I went. —Emily

As with all psychotherapy, privacy and confidentiality are essential. The student is the client and, having turned eighteen, is legally an adult. As such, the student must provide written consent for the therapist to talk with a parent.

Another way that college counseling and psychological services protect privacy is that students can seek services without their parents being notified. Unlike private practice psychotherapy, mental health services on most campuses do not come with an hourly bill; the general fees that students pay each semester include psychotherapy as well as the library and many other services and facilities. Some colleges and universities limit the number of sessions each student can have, so it's important to find out whether your daughter's school is one of them. Another way to protect the girl's privacy is for her to seek mental health care off campus. The school's resource providers can help identify local clinicians who are experienced in caring for sexual assault victims and are familiar with campus procedures.

Justice Systems

The two primary ways by which victims of campus sexual assault can formally seek redress are the traditional criminal justice system and the system of policies and procedures that the college or university has established. Title IX regulations require that such structures be in place; how schools interpret and implement the regulations vary. Students sometimes don't tell their parents as they go through an internal (campus) investigation but, according to one staff member, they almost always do when deciding whether to pursue it criminally.

Although institutions of higher education can be rightly criticized for not allocating sufficient resources to address campus sexual assault, they likely invest far more per student than the government invests per person or per woman regarding sexual assault. A friend of mine who prosecuted sexual assault cases in a district attorney's office expressed frustration regarding the large number of cases, the limited time for review, the inconsistent investigations, and the rape kits that sit untested. In other words, it's not like *Law & Order: Special Victims Unit*, which for more than two decades has shown heartrending stories with rapid investigation and resolution. In reality, she said, victims can wait two or more years for their day in court, assuming the case gets to court. Many opt out of the system by then.

The two systems, as one campus service provider told me, are alike "in that there's an investigation and then a factual determination of responsibility [in the college system] or guilt [in criminal court]." They're also quite different in several ways. The burden of proof, for example, is higher in criminal court (beyond a reasonable doubt) than campus hearings (clear and convincing, that is, "highly and substantially more likely to be true than untrue"[6]). ("Clear and convincing" was implemented as the federal standard in August 2020; prior to that, campus sexual assault determinations were judged on the same standard as all other Title IX civil rights cases: the preponderance of the evidence, that is, more than 50 percent likely.) Criminal court can take years, whereas campus policies typically specify a period of weeks or months, although resolution often takes longer. Criminal court could potentially result in jail time, whereas campus procedures do not. Finally, a criminal trial is a matter of public record, whereas universities are extremely protective of the confidentiality of investigations and their outcomes.

The first step in the criminal justice system is to make a police report, a process that can be intimidating. Campus police sometimes take an initial statement and pass it along to the local law enforcement agency. After that, there is an investigation by detectives or other officers whose responsibility includes sexual assault cases. If the officers believe that the reported act meets the state's statutory language for what constitutes one or more forms of sexual assault, the law enforcement agency takes the information to the district attorney's office, where a determination is made whether to file charges. A common misperception is that the victim determines whether to press charges; that's not how it works. Only the district attorney (or, in certain instances, the city attorney) makes that decision. Some district attorneys will not go forward with a case unless the victim is willing to testify, a criterion they do not apply to other cases. (Think, for example, of how many cases would go to trial if murder victims were required to testify.) Others are hesitant to "take a case" if the two parties know each other or if alcohol was involved, two circumstances that are common in campus sexual assault. Thus not only is it rare for campus sexual assault incidents to be reported to law enforcement, it is also rare for charges to be filed when incidents are reported. Few campus sexual assault incidents ever make it to court, let alone result in conviction.

Some of the girls and parents who spoke with me initially wanted criminal justice involvement. In every case, after the initial interview with officers and the passage of time, they decided not to pursue it. The reasons included that it really wasn't going to accomplish anything, it was going to be too hard, the girl didn't want to have to relive it, it was better to move on, and her healing was more important than trying to hold the perpetrator accountable. In sum, girls saw not making a police report or not following through when one was made as a way to protect themselves from the risk of further harm. Some parents agreed, but others pressed the view that it isn't fair and their daughter shouldn't let him get away with it.

Participation in the campus system that was established to deal with sexual assault was far more common.

Campus Processes

When a student is thought to have cheated, plagiarized, or committed some other act of academic dishonesty, it is typically handled by the school's office of student conduct. Sexual assault, a violation of the code of student conduct, is very different from plagiarism, and many institutions of higher education have developed a separate office to handle potential violations. The office often is charged with protecting the larger campus community as well as addressing specific cases.

Students turn to campus sexual assault procedures because they are trying to get something they haven't been able to obtain elsewhere. In my experience, there are two things they most often seek: the perpetrator to admit that what he did was terrible and an apology.

The process begins when a student files a report and ends whenever agreement between the two parties is reached in a series of steps. Sometimes one or the other simply gives up when the outcome is not what they want. As one of the campus resource providers relayed, "I have spent a lot of time telling students just because this person wasn't found responsible, just because this person isn't guilty, it doesn't mean that your experience didn't happen."

With that sobering thought, let's turn to how one university handles such reports. It is important to note that all aspects of the process are confidential. There is no gag order for the two people involved, but there is one for everyone else.

Investigation and Determination

When a student files a report, the university moves relatively quickly, usually within days or weeks, with the goal of reaching an agreed-upon resolution in the timeline set forth in their policy. The process can be delayed by scheduling difficulties as well as the complexity of the case. One of the staff described the role:

> My role is to investigate any complaints made against enrolled students and faculty about sexual violence, relationship violence, and stalking. I liken my position to a pseudo-detective and pseudo-judge because that's what I'm doing: I'm doing investigations and then making determinations as to whether a respondent has violated university policy. We use the terms complainant and respondent because it's an administrative proceeding; in a criminal proceeding, we call them victims and defendants. This is not criminal court. Our procedures are extremely different than criminal court. I think there is less pressure and stress on both the complainant and respondent in the administrative proceedings than there would be in criminal [proceedings].

Staff designated to deal with sexual assault cases begin, as in criminal court, with a presumption of innocence. Staff described themselves as treating both parties with respect. In addition, both students involved are offered a list of specially trained individuals from across campus who are willing to serve as an advisor through the process.

One of the staff members was firm in believing that an advisor is integral:

> I liken it to going to the doctor and getting five pieces of bad news. If you go by yourself, you go home and you remember two of them because it was just so startling. But if you bring your friend to take notes, they can remind you [later] because you're in the moment, you're not liking what you're hearing, and you're kinda reeling. And then, when you have quiet time, you can go over [things with the other person], "Well, this is exactly what the doctor said, and here are your options."

While students consult with their advisors, staff designated to deal with these matters gather information. Depending on the case, such information can include verbal and written statements, ID card swipes to gain access to a building, security camera video, and relevant text messages (it seems that students rarely delete their texts and sometimes send incriminating messages). After weighing the evidence, the staff member makes a factual determination and recommends no further action or a range of sanctions for the perpetrator. The purpose of sanctions is to hold students accountable for their actions and to protect the campus community.

Sanctions handed down in past cases are taken into account when determining what sanctions, if any, should be imposed. In addition, sanctions imposed by the investigative officer are tailored to the individual. A staffer said that:

> Sanctions range from probation, suspension, to expulsion. In addition to sanctions, we're trying to have the respondent learn from his or her mistakes, so we put in an educational aspect, which could be education regarding consent, sexual violence, relationship violence, alcohol, drugs. We could refer them to the office of alcohol and other drug initiatives because that is . . . giving them support and helping them along . . . counseling and psychological services are always, or nearly always, part of the sanction because that's supportive of the student.

Although expulsion is among the possible sanctions, it is rare.

The investigative officer provides a written report to the students and asks if they agree with the information it provides and the recommended sanctions. You might be surprised to learn that they often do. When the parties don't agree, the investigative officer attempts to help them find common ground within the parameters set by the office. That usually works too. But in the rare cases in which agreement cannot be reached, students can request a hearing.

Hearing

Some parents learn about their daughter's sexual assault after campus authorities have been engaged, an investigation has been made, and a hearing is about to be scheduled. She may have handled things by herself to this point – in fact, perceived them as a kind of litmus test, "I'm kind of an adult, right?" – but, concerned that the hearing might be an ordeal, she reaches out then for support.

A hearing follows the procedures that are spelled out in the university's sexual misconduct policies and procedures that are posted on its website. Before the hearing begins, a panel of three faculty members and a faculty hearing officer, who volunteered to serve on hearings and underwent special training, review written statements provided by both parties, the sexual assault investigator's report, and any other supporting documents that have been provided. The materials are new to the faculty but already known to the others. During the hearing, each student tells the panel about the incident and responds to questions from the panel and from the other student. The students do not meet face-to-face but, along with their advisor, can view the testimony via video link from separate rooms. The sexual assault investigative officer and others thought to be relevant (for example, a friend who was told shortly after the incident) are asked to speak and respond to questions. At the conclusion of the hearing, the faculty panel – with no others present – discusses the case, considers the sanctions recommended by the investigative officer, reviews sanctions imposed in prior cases (identifying information is redacted to protect confidentiality), and determines whether it concurs with the recommended sanctions and, if not, develops new ones.

If new sanctions – more lenient or more severe – are recommended, they take precedence over those made by the investigative officer. A written report is submitted to the hearing officer, who distributes it to the parties involved. If either one does not accept the terms, they have the option to appeal again, this time to a specially designated individual who has not been part of the proceedings. That person reviews all written materials and makes their own decision regarding what is a fair and appropriate sanction. If different sanctions are imposed, they take precedence over previously issued ones. The advisor chosen by the student is available for guidance and can help draft statements and responses throughout the entire process.

Some parents engage the services of a lawyer to advise the student during the hearing process. There are several views on whether doing so is a good idea. Attorneys themselves, including law faculty, have pushed for the inclusion of attorneys, while others believe that doing so will bring into campus procedures the adversarial framework of our court systems. One law school colleague told me that, given their training, lawyers seem unable to consider a scenario in which truth, or a close approximation of it, is the goal. He went on to share his unvarnished opinion that attorneys simply can't imagine a situation in which they are not necessary. The people who spoke with me did not share that assessment.

One mother said that their family considered hiring a lawyer and decided that it wasn't worth it because "these guys make money on hours instead of on justice." When I asked a campus resource person whether it would be useful for students to get an attorney, the response was quick and to the point:

> My answer is no because our advisors here are phenomenal, they know the process like the back of their hand. . . . What I see is somebody hiring an attorney who is a criminal attorney. And they know criminal law, but they haven't read our policies, they haven't read about consent, they're not in a position to give good advice. . . . [*I wonder if the presence of an attorney on either side changes the dynamic.*] I think it does. I think, more so, it's the perception. I've heard students complain that this process favors the rich because rich respondents can get attorneys, and that's intimidating to complainants. And what I envision is that respondents, far more so than complainants, would retain attorneys. But I'll tell you, the ones I've seen have not impressed me.

On the other hand, friends of mine, attorneys themselves, found it useful to hire a lawyer when an incident involving their victimized daughter went to a hearing. They sought and obtained the services of someone whose practice consisted primarily of such cases. A cottage industry has developed in legal circles to address the needs and perceived needs of complainants, respondents, and institutions of higher education. Searching online for a "campus sexual assault attorney near me" yields a surprising number of options.

The experience of participating in a hearing is stressful and satisfaction with the process and its outcome varies. Three parents who spoke with me reflected on their perceptions:

> She was anticipating it to be very stressful. . . . I think it wound up being just passable for her – she wasn't thrilled with the outcome, but she was so glad it was over. I asked her whether she wanted to go further with this. And she said absolutely not. —Mother

> Sadly enough, he all but admitted that he did it. He was removed from the school and wasn't allowed to finish his last semester of classes. He wasn't allowed to go back until she graduated. But the day she left, he was allowed to go back to school, finish out his classes, and get his degree. . . . To me it looks like just saying, "Well, a bad situation happened. And so we're just going to give you a short punishment here, and then we're going to let you carry on." And I don't think that should be the result of that. —Father

> Upon reflection, we can see how key the hearing was to her healing and development of self-esteem in the aftermath. Actually having to face her abuser and having a forum to stand up for herself was a great gift that allowed her to change the victim narrative and empower herself. —Mother

A daughter offered yet another perspective: "Did I feel like I had struck a blow for justice? No."

If either student is not satisfied with the outcome of the multistep campus process, they can turn to civil court for remedy. Lawsuits have been filed in civil court against the university handling the case and the person who filed the report. One of the staff members acknowledged current societal tensions: "I think there are two movements going on in the United States: the #MeToo movement with let's start by believing victims, and the backlash of respondents who are saying it's completely untrue and are suing, which could have a chilling effect on complainants being afraid they're going to be sued."

Complicating Circumstances

As if it's not enough to deal with having been sexually assaulted, some students' experiences are complicated by additional concerns. In her conversation with me, one girl divulged that she was brought to the United States when she was very young and does not have a path to become a legal citizen. Knowing that she couldn't tell others about her legal status without putting her family at risk gave her years of practice hiding important information. She said, "This [the assault] is something that I can deal with on my own, because it's the way that I've been used to doing things." She did not access any campus services after being raped.

Religious and Cultural Considerations

For others, having been sexually assaulted brings religious and cultural considerations to the fore. There obviously are distinct ethnic, national, and cultural aspects related to beliefs about dating, alcohol consumption, sexual activity, and other matters that might have been part of the incident. Sexually assaulted students who turn to one of the relevant cultural centers on campus often are seeking someone who understands the identity intersections that can add a layer of complexity to what happened.

One of the staff relayed how some sexually assaulted students ask big questions: "Why would a good God let this happen to me? I've been good, I believe in God, why didn't God protect me?" The chaplain's office itself might provide a comforting connection to religious and familial history. As one put it:

Sometimes being in a religious space can feel like God is close. . . . Back when they were a kid, they used to feel good in church and Sunday School, they used to pray with their parents. And praying with the chaplain or seeing the religious signifiers around the office sometimes, I think, can help them feel safe again. . . . When things feel chaotic, they can get a taste of the constant again. . . . A solace that they are going to get through it – there's something bigger than them, this is temporary.

Reaching for religion after having been sexually assaulted can be likened to the spike in church attendance after national tragedies such as hurricanes, earthquakes, and mass shootings: "It's not so much like I believe in God again after this tragedy . . . it's like this feels right, and it feels like I'm safe again."

Study Abroad

Study abroad was not safe for some of the girls who spoke with me. Three of the twenty girls who spoke with me had been sexually assaulted while on study abroad – two students from the United States who were studying abroad and one student who came to the United States to study – and another had what might be described as a close call. In none of the cases was the perpetrator a stranger. Students might unwittingly put themselves in circumstances that are riskier than they would in the United States because they don't understand local norms – "He invited me to this party. I didn't realize I was going to be staying at his house!" There's a larger context as well: views of women, of Americans, and of American college girls are pretty negative in some places, and of course, women's rights, laws, and legal systems vary substantially around the globe.

Many students participate in one-year, one-semester, or summer study abroad programs or in faculty-led short courses outside the United States. Colleges and universities design online and in-person predeparture orientations to introduce students to a country's culture and customs, nonverbal communication, what students might expect being a minority in a particular country, and information about gender expectations and sexual assault. The "goal is to inform, not frighten." But sometimes it's not enough.

The best advice I can offer if your daughter is sexually assaulted on a study abroad program is to immediately reach out to the university. Even if you have traveled to the same country your daughter is studying in, the university has far more knowledge, connections, and resources that they can bring to bear. Unfortunately, they also have experience; your daughter is not the first of their students who has been sexually assaulted on study abroad. Things can get dicey quickly. One mother recounted her daughter's harrowing experience:

> She decided to go to the police and press charges, and the U.S. Embassy actually escorted her to [the] police. . . . The police didn't believe her. They were like, "Well, where's the evidence? . . . There's no crime here." But when they found out that she had an incorrect visa, they were going to throw her in jail. People sit in jail there for weeks. . . . It's like you might never see them ever again. The embassy people actually scooted her out – when the police weren't looking, they scooped her up, put her in their car, and drove her out of there. —Mother

The time of day or night that you learn about the assault is not relevant; call the school's police department or security office then and there. They are open twenty-four hours a day and can reach out to others at the university who are responsible for helping you determine whether your daughter is safe to stay there and other such decisions you will immediately face. The time difference, cultural differences, and sometimes government limits on certain forms of electronic communication that are common in the United States (and concern about the privacy afforded by the ones the government does allow) complicate things. She is engaged in a university-sponsored activity; use the resources that are available to you. Everyone's initial focus will be on the concrete decisions that need to be made; the psychological component will become more salient when she is safe, perhaps back in the States.

Problems with Campus Administrators

Even in the best of circumstances and just as you will have with your daughter, you can expect a few rough spots when dealing with your daughter's school. This is normal. But some college and university practices really do need to be cleaned up. Institutional betrayal – "the role of institutions in traumatic experiences and psychological distress following these experiences"[7] – complicates an already difficult time. The Title IX complaints filed against hundreds of U.S. colleges and universities by victims of campus sexual assault are a testament to students' efforts to hold their schools accountable and to improve policies and practices for subsequent students. Some parents are inclined to seek legal advice in such circumstances, which is certainly one avenue. Another option is to seek the counsel of parents who've encountered similar problems; I'm thinking specifically of Parents Take Action to End Rape on Campus, a grassroots, volunteer organization led by parents of victims and survivors of campus sexual assault. They are available for consultation and offer a wealth of knowledge based on firsthand experience.

Not all colleges and universities respond to campus sexual assault as badly as those that make the news. Some are doing a pretty decent job. Maybe none are doing a great job, but some are doing an okay job. What ends up in the media are the horrible cases, and the effects can be chilling: girls who have been victimized and their parents become wary of seeking help.

It's important to remember that parents don't have to be everything. You serve an important role and can do things that might make it easier – or harder – for your daughter, but you can't do it all. She likely has turned to her friends and found support, and you can encourage her to continue to do so.

You also can encourage her to use the multiple resources that colleges and universities have available for victims of campus sexual assault. Few assaulted students take advantage of these services, even though confidentiality and respect for privacy are standard and every bit of help they would get is covered by the general fee levied by the university. (Or nearly every bit. Check with your daughter's school.) In addition to being able to provide physical and mental health services throughout her college years, your daughter's school can do things that can make her day-to-day life easier and safer.

Colleges and universities have staff who can be a sounding board as your daughter sorts out what she needs and wants. I cannot overstate the importance of these people and the knowledge and experience they can bring. Even if your daughter has helped a friend who was sexually assaulted, she doesn't know what all the options are for herself and, like most of us when in crisis, can't be expected to think as clearly and be as decisive as she normally would.

If your daughter is among the relatively few victims of campus sexual assault who choose to make an official report and ask the university to investigate, you can find out about the school's policies and procedures to have a sense of the process. Although the investigations seem to take a long time, they are almost always faster and can be more thorough than if the student had gone to the police. Additional resources and supports are offered to students going through an investigation. Some parents of victims become angry when they learn that the university provides support to the perpetrator as well as the victim. But as one of the staff members said, "There are two persons involved, and those two people are our students. Both students are entitled to the support and resources that we offer during the process." There often are no "winners" in this process, and justice – however defined – can feel elusive.

What should not be elusive is your support for your daughter as she figures out how best to move forward. At this point, she won't know how the multiple aspects of the trauma will reverberate in the coming weeks and months and beyond. Nor will you. Do what you can to help her regain a sense of control and retain her autonomy so she can meet the challenges that are ahead.

CHAPTER 9

Struggling and Problem Solving

It impacted me for so long. My entire last semester was consumed with this. It impacted every facet of my life: academics and friendships and extracurriculars. Nothing else has been so impactful like that. —Jenny

I was trying to understand why she was doing what she was doing . . . to give her the grace to figure out what she needed to figure out and – as long as she was healthy, as long as she wasn't doing something to harm herself – to let her have the time she needed to try to work it out. —Mother

I think the hardest thing is that your child disappears. . . . The kid you knew – the kid I sent to college, that I dropped at their doorstep, was no longer there. She was a mess. She was emotional, couldn't focus, couldn't concentrate . . . she couldn't control it. She wanted to fight with you, she wanted to argue with you, she was snapping and nasty. And so, people started pulling away, her roommate started pulling away. She was a mess . . . several months of this up and down. —Mother

I'd say the most common answer to the question of "What do you want to happen next?" is "I want to forget about this, I just want to move on with my life." I say, "That's fine. Yet it's not often possible because when you bury feelings, you tend to bury them alive. You might want

to consider that you might need to process this more. Let me know."
—College staffer

A sexual assault is stressful. And stress affects every part of our being. Discussions about stress usually include talk of "resilience," a term that has been used in multiple fields and means to bounce back, to return to original shape, to "absorb or avoid damage without suffering complete failure."[1] Your daughter, who has been sexually assaulted, will likely not suffer "complete failure," but she will not bounce back to her original form either. What has happened cannot be undone. It is unrealistic to think that she will return to how and who she was before being sexually assaulted. She will change and grow. But *how* will she change? *What* will happen?

I'll offer an image that might be relevant for the coming stretch of time: "Compare the results of throwing a rock and a live bird. Mechanical linear models are excellent for understanding where the rock will end up, but useless for predicting the trajectory of a bird – even though both are subject to the same laws of physics."[2] I like the image in part because birds do the improbable: they walk on seemingly fragile legs, unfold wings, hoist their full weight into the air, and soar. We humans sometimes soar despite apparent frailties too. You know your daughter and have some general ideas about where and how she will land. You might spin worrisome possibilities in your mind and you might be right. Or not. Your daughter has agency, she makes choices, and, as such, there is unpredictability. You too have choice.

No matter how good your parenting skills might be, in the weeks and months ahead, you probably will need to expand your repertoire. One mother relayed a conversation with her daughter's longtime therapist; the therapist advised the mother to tell the daughter what she (the mother) wanted. The mother's response? "I'm not really that kind of parent. . . . There are parents that are very, very controlling and they would literally say, 'I don't want you to do that,' but I just didn't ever want to be the parent who told my kids how to live their life." My sense is that the therapist was trying to get the mother to step up, to offer her opinion, to throw her daughter a lifeline. The mother demurred, seeming to confuse being upfront with being authoritarian. Is the mother really that timid? I don't know. She may have been so terrified of saying or doing the wrong thing that she simply hung back even when someone who knew her daughter well told her that the girl needed something different, something more. The daughter likely felt very alone when her mother didn't respond. It won't be easy at times, but you have parented your daughter for nearly two decades; helping her deal with having been sexually assaulted means that you need to be willing to get out of your comfort zone and try something new if that's what she needs from you.

At the same time, your daughter will find solace in the ordinary activities of your family: watching a movie together, having phone calls about mundane topics, just hanging out, and sharing favorite foods. Talking can be good, sitting together in silence is good at other times, and, as one mom said, "Sometimes she just wanted the dog; she would hold the dog and cry."

In the days and weeks after the assault, the miles between you at home and your daughter at college may feel like too many. Communicating via phone can bridge the gap. Video interaction is even better because it provides an additional channel of communication. As one mother told me, "Watching their face and their body language becomes very important . . . it was telling me what she wasn't telling me. It was telling me how angry she was, how traumatized she was. When I saw the catatonic look on her face, she was numb; it was so bad that she couldn't allow herself to feel it."

There are occasions when it's important to be in the same physical space and to have time for a conversation that can meander and loop back on itself. Such talks can result in greater understanding and a closer connection. It's not always possible, but being physically together can be important for both of you.

Mutually agreed-upon visits can be useful for all. Visits that aren't agreed upon can be dreadful. Who wants to hear, as one mother did, "I know why you're here. You need to buy a ticket, you need to leave, you are not staying here"? And yet some mothers risked just that:

> Me showing up was, like, "If you don't do something, I'm going to harass the crap out of you until you do – in a nice way, but I am your mother. . . . Just like I don't get to tell you [how to react], you don't get to tell me how to react as a mom. This is information that I also have to

deal with. . . . I will listen to you, I will try to react to what you're saying to me, but you don't get to tell me how I'm going to be your mother." She sent me packing, but she did get help when I got back. —Mother

And when travel isn't possible, consider making a request: "I miss you extra these days and wish we could be together. I don't have much of a sense of what your life is like right now. Could you text me each day for a while? You don't need to say anything if you don't want to – just send a picture of something you're doing. I'll do the same if you want." Keep the connection alive.

Your daughter's goal is to become a survivor. You need to help her call upon her strength and move forward from the victimization as best she can. "Recover" is a word that is sometimes used to describe the process, but it is generally avoided given its connotation to sexual assault being something to "get over" and return to "normal." The experience of being sexually assaulted changes a person. It's a journey that she – and you – must now take.

As you embark on this journey, in addition to having a good sense of your daughter as a person, it will help if you are aware of your beliefs about sexual assault victims and victimization in the abstract. Many of us knowingly or unknowingly subscribe to a "just world" perspective ("just" as in fair) in which we expect that good things will happen to good people, and that if bad things happen, the person must have done something to bring it upon themselves or otherwise been somehow responsible for what occurred. If when your daughter told you about the assault you focused on her behavior far more than his, you will be wise to pay attention to how your belief system affects how you interact with her.

It will also be useful to pay attention to your general expectations about how someone who has been victimized "should" behave as she tries to come to terms with having been sexually assaulted. You, your friends and family, police, judges, and juries all have expectations about how sexual assault victims should act, what emotions they should express when and with what intensity, and so on. If you give priority to your assumptions about victims, you may well miss the girl you want most to help.

This chapter will address some of the things you might be called upon to help her navigate. It isn't what you *will* encounter but what you *might* encounter. Although it will be painful to see her suffer, pressuring her to "get over it" quickly won't work. It will be months and maybe even a few years before she gets her feet under her again.

Getting through the Day

The most basic thing your daughter will deal with is navigating her day-to-day life at college. So let's start with the fundamentals: sleeping and eating. We know a lot about the importance of sleep: inadequate sleep is associated with difficulty concentrating and irritability; when chronic, it can also be associated with mood disorders, weight gain, and multiple health problems. Your daughter's sleep is likely to be disrupted in one way or another. As we prepare for sleep, our psychological defenses fade. As anxiety that has been held at bay during the day comes crashing in, she might delay or avoid going to sleep. Or she might fall asleep with relative ease only to awaken early in the morning, which can be a sign of depression. Encouraging her to pay attention to her sleep and to practice good sleep habits (establishing a routine, not using electronic devices shortly before going to bed that emit blue light from their screens, and having a quiet, relaxing room) can be helpful. Consuming alcohol can interfere with the dream phase, the part of the sleep cycle that is associated with mental and emotional restoration. And it's important to learn if some of her dreams are nightmares, filled with images of the perpetrator.

If she was sexually assaulted in her own bed, buy her new sheets – or all new bedding if you can afford it – and be sure to let her pick them out; she needs choice and control about a physical setting in which she had none. Offer a gift certificate to go toward redecorating her room and encourage her to enlist a few friends who could help with the task. Help her do it if you're able and if she wants your help.

If she wants to move after being sexually assaulted in her own home away from home, find out how you can help with that. Asking the university to relocate her to another residence hall is a reasonable request. And if she's in an apartment, the lease can be broken or, depending on the terms of the lease, the apartment can be sublet to someone else and she can find another to rent or sublet. Asking the school to help identify options is a reasonable request. It is fine for her to leave the space where she was assaulted rather than stay and be reminded of the assault in all sorts of ways that she might not even be able to identify. She will deal with many things in the aftermath of having been sexually assaulted; spending precious psychic energy on becoming comfortable in the physical space where she was assaulted needn't be a priority.

Eating, like sleep, is a priority. It is important that your daughter eat regularly and at least somewhat healthily. And that should be your focus – "How's your eating these days?" – not her weight. Despite increasing acceptance of a variety of body types, society continues to hold out certain shapes and sizes as being preferable to others. And if her weight has been a topic of tense conversation in the past, tread lightly. Shame is unfortunately relatively common among sexual assault victims, and she does not need any additional sense of shame about her body.

Moreover, being sexually assaulted can disrupt a girl's connection with her body. She lost control of her own body – something so very basic – and it can damage her sense of self-determination. Physical movement can do more than help dispel some of the tension she carries (more on this later in the chapter), but suffice it to say for now that running, swimming, yoga, karate, working out, or whatever she chooses can be very beneficial. Encourage physical movement through exercise to help her stay connected with her body; massage or other bodywork might be too intense or too intimate at first.

These fundamental actions are ways you can encourage her to take care of herself. With adequate rest and nutrition, she will be able to better navigate each day.

Dealing with Others

A college boy she knows is the person who most likely assaulted her, and she probably will see him again on campus. And to be fearful of seeing him again. Girls who have been sexually assaulted at college manage the anxiety through avoidance and hyperalertness: they stay away from places where they might run into him and scan groups of students to be sure he's not among them. Coping extends to places as well as persons; some take circuitous routes to class so that they don't have to walk by the apartment or fraternity house where it happened. Talking with her about what she might do if and when she runs into him on campus or at a party can help her consider options and plan a course of action.

Lifelong friendships are formed during college, and, as noted before, female friends are typically the first and most common individuals to whom a girl who has been sexually assaulted turns. Such friends can be vitally important in her daily life on campus. Parents can help their daughter by supporting these friendships, encouraging her to connect even when she might feel like pulling away. Her sense of trust is particularly threatened when her perpetrator was someone she thought of as a friend; if he hurt her like that, what can be expected of others? Moreover, her friends likely know things about her and the assault that you don't and, as such, can be of help in ways that you aren't; it isn't helpful to express disappointment or feel threatened by these facts. Do extend the privacy that an adult deserves; let her know that she can talk with you about one aspect of what she is going through without having to open up. In addition to buttressing supportive relationships, it is helpful to *reduce* her exposure to difficult ones. A bad roommate can make your daughter's life exponentially harder; help change this situation if she wants.

The reactions of peers are sometimes a considerable additional source of stress. I heard from college support staff as well as parents and girls themselves that peers typically rush to the defense of the perpetrator. This was particularly the case when the perpetrator was a member of an all-male group; fraternity members and sports teams would question her veracity and motives, blame her, and minimize whatever they heard. Abandonment and blame by those who were considered friends can be devastating, especially when extricating herself from the group means a major change in her social network and a drop in perceived social status. At the same time, I was told of sorority girls who, learning that several of their members had been victimized by the same guy, banded together and told a fraternity that if they pledged him, the entire sorority would not socialize with the fraternity. There's something to the idea of strength in numbers.

She will have sensitivities and might have to deal with what is commonly known as "triggers." An example of a sensitivity is when a girl who was sexually assaulted feels uncomfortable meeting with a professor who bears a faint resemblance to the perpetrator. A trigger, by contrast, is generally considered some sort of stimulus that recalls the assault unbidden; the association of the trigger with the assault might not even be conscious, at least not the first few times it is experienced. For example, she might unexpectedly smell the same cologne worn by the guy who raped her and psychologically go back to the intense feelings she had while being assaulted. One of the campus support staff told me that "you might not be able to stop from going back there, but you can manage how long you stay there. You can manage coming out of that." Techniques such as pinching the palm of her hand and being aware of the sensation can help her feel grounded when triggered. In other words, triggers are more than simple distress. They can be experienced as flashbacks and might be inevitable, but they can be identified and managed.

Your daughter has likely already thought about each of these as well as other matters related to her daily life. So if and when you bring up the topic, you probably won't hear, "Gee, I never thought of that." Directly yet gently inquiring about how her day-to-day life is going – and then listening to what she has to say and letting her guide the conversation – is important. Sometimes asking questions can lay the groundwork for contemplating action. Recognizing that the need for safety and soothing is central, one college support staff member recommended that girls who have been sexually assaulted at college create a safety plan: "Who are you gonna talk to? Where do you feel safest on campus? What do you like to do when you're feeling down that loves and honors your body, your mind, your soul? Do those things. What's your favorite food to eat? Eat that." Your kind acknowledgment that the incident has seeped into her everyday life can be comforting; it indicates that you understand a bit.

Risk Taking

Without prompting, many of the girls who spoke with me said that they had changed their behavior after they were assaulted. Some described themselves as becoming far more cautious, others as becoming reckless, and others as bouncing between the two extremes. Parents, also without prompting, offered examples of how their daughters had increased their risk taking; they were less concerned when she circumscribed her actions, which might be beneficial in the short term but have long-term consequences.

The same internal process motivates seemingly opposite behaviors: reasserting control. It is important to respect the goal and to respect the behavior, unless it becomes destructive. As one university staff member advised:

> Let them steer until it looks like they're potentially self-harming or self-destructing consciously or subconsciously. Then, I think, you have to cross the line. If they say, "I just want to let you all know I got the ball rolling, I'll let you know when I need you," respect that. You don't want to be a further violation on someone's boundary. As torturous as it will be . . . if they say, "I got it," respect that until they don't got it. —College staffer

I'll highlight here a few examples of behaviors that can be or can become self-destructive. Some aren't "bad" in and of themselves but can be considered risky given the potential for further harm.

Continued Communication with the Perpetrator

Continuing to communicate with the perpetrator can be expected if the assault occurred in the context of an acquaintanceship, friendship, or more intimate relationship – that is, in the vast majority of campus sexual assaults. Some girls were confused, trying to sort out what had happened – *How could someone I trust and care about have done that?* – and talking with him was an attempt to make sense of it. Sometimes she continued to see him – she cared for him, after all – anticipating that he would come to understand. Continued contact was a way to seek closure in one form or another. The hoped-for outcome was pretty straightforward: the girls wanted him to acknowledge that what he had done was wrong and had caused harm and for him to apologize. It might have been salutary but rarely did any get something so pure and complete.

Several told me some version of what one girl said:

> I was telling him [several weeks after the incident] that it wasn't okay and he kind of started sort of crying and was, like, "I know it wasn't okay, I'm really sorry." He texted me the next morning and was, like,

"Now that we're sober, can we talk about this?" So I went over to his room and he sort of tried to talk his way out of it. . . . First he said, "I don't remember anything." And I said, "You do, because you apologized to me." Then he was, like, "Well, I didn't hear you say stop." . . . Then he was like, "I realize what I did was really wrong, I'm so sorry. . . . Why didn't you tell me you went to the Women's Center?" He was relieved that I didn't want to go to the student conduct office. Later that day, he texted me and was like, "Thank you for not wanting to turn this into a larger issue. I'm so sorry for what I did. I hope you're successful in moving on and finding someone better." I didn't respond to that. —Jocelyn

The girls rarely got what they sought, and their reactions to such conversations generally weren't positive: terribly wounded, "gaslighted," angry, disgusted ("He's clueless, a complete idiot."), disappointed, and dismayed. In each case the recurring theme was betrayal. They were often left to reconcile the conflicting thoughts and emotions alone.

When the perpetrator was an acquaintance rather than a friend or partner, it was easier for her to turn away. It was less complicated, except when he perceived her distance as "playing hard to get" and called and texted, sometimes for months afterward, even when she did not reply.

Rewriting the Script

I indicated that some behavior seemed to be one extreme or the other following the assault; sex and sexual activity was the clearest example. A substantial portion of campus sexual assaults begin with consensual activity that, at some point, she does not want and her "No" is disregarded. Some of the girls protected their ability to say "No" by swearing off sex, saying that they couldn't imagine being intimate with anyone for a long, long time. Others dealt with the damage with a phase of what they later described to me either as a "do-over" attempt (they put themselves in situations similar to what they experienced in the assault, hoping it would turn out differently) or as being reckless and uncaring. Some reported being physically intimate with lots (whatever their definition of "lots" was) of partners. They treated their bodies and partners as the perpetrator had treated them, as an object. They weren't all that concerned about their behavior at the time and seemed to find their balance after a few months or a semester and stopped. I didn't have the sense that their subsequent sexual activity was related to the type of assault – many had some form of penetrative assault – or whether they had had sex before they were penetrated by the perpetrator.

Information about such sexual activity can be terribly upsetting to parents, and, anticipating the distress, daughters generally didn't share it with them. One girl who spoke with me, however, trusted and felt comfortable enough with her mother to share the information. Her mother struck me as kind and compassionate as she described her daughter's sexual activity after the assault:

> She slept with a couple of guys in there. I've learned over time [and I said to her], "It's a way of taking back your own body. The first time you had sex, you didn't get to have that decision. This is you saying, 'You know what? This is my body. I *do* get to decide.' It's your way of saying 'Sex isn't dirty and cheap and all that stuff. I get to decide.' . . . That's not abnormal and there's nothing wrong with it. And as long as you don't get a disease and as long as you're okay with what happened, it's fine. It might be something you eventually want to talk about with a counselor or whatever." —Mother

Excessive Drinking

Much has been made of the association between alcohol and campus sexual assault. Alcohol can be a social lubricant for awkward, shy, stressed, and anxious people of all ages, perhaps even more so for young people who are more comfortable with virtual than in-person communication. It also can be an effective tool used by someone bent on harm – he gets her drunk or drugs her so that he can assault her in her incapacitated state. Other drugs are sometimes involved, but alcohol is the most common by far.

Rarely acknowledged is something relayed by several of the girls who spoke with me: problematic drinking that begins after a sexual assault. As they described it, their excessive alcohol consumption seemed to be part of a general "I don't care anymore" perspective that was evident for varying lengths of time. The girls typically said that they realized at the time that their increased drinking could put them at risk for additional bad experiences, but it just didn't matter then; drinking was part of their coping. As one of the girls relayed, she thought drinking would help her accomplish her goals:

Drinking had never been a big part of my relationships . . . [but after the assault] I think there were a few ways that I was sort of trying to establish control over the situation. Like, first of all, it's so counterintuitive, but by drinking so much it made me think, "Oh, well, I wanted to do this and I'm just a crazy, vapid, party girl and I deserved for this to happen and I wanted it to," which isn't at all true. But I think I felt that if I convinced myself of that or convinced other people, it made me feel better because I didn't want to feel like I lived in a world where someone who didn't deserve that would have that happen to them. . . . I was drinking just way too much. Especially after I joined a sorority, I was, like, I just want to be the happy girl that I was. Maybe if I'm really happy and really cool, it won't matter that this happened, and no one will know that I have this underlying problem. —Leah

On rare occasions, excessive drinking was more than a temporary behavior. The same girl reported that, at one point, she realized that things had become serious:

I wanted everything to be simple. I wanted to feel empty. And I was blacking out a lot. I never ever thought I would use drugs. I was president of my class in high school. I was behaving really destructively . . . I was putting myself in situations where I was really drunk and sort of trusting people to not hurt me or take advantage of me. And, at fraternities, that doesn't seem to go your way. My friends ended up calling my parents and saying that they were really, really concerned for my safety and how much I was drinking. I guess they didn't get the response they wanted from my parents, so they called the school. So, last year, I met with student intervention services and decided that I wanted to take a medical leave. I went to an inpatient center for drug and alcohol abuse. I was there for thirty days . . . I spent a lot of time talking about it [the assault]. I would say 70 percent of the girls in my unit had a really similar situation happen. I'm feeling really good now. On Saturday I'm going to have eleven months of sobriety.

She described her parents as having put the assault "way, way in the back [of their minds]. . . . I think the narrative that they like to say is that our daughter was partying too much and had to leave school, which I think they do maybe to protect themselves." I wonder what it's like for her to know that her parents would rather present themselves as having a daughter with drinking problems than one who had been sexually assaulted.

Because of the multiple vulnerabilities and negative potential outcomes, keeping tabs on your daughter's drinking subsequent to the assault is important. Admittedly, it can be awkward to address, especially if your primary communication with her has been "Don't drink!" I would usually avoid such an arrangement, but if it's a topic that simply cannot be broached with your daughter because of your reaction when you learned that she had been drinking prior to being assaulted or because cultural expectations would preclude the needed honesty or any other compelling reason, it might be useful to engage one of her siblings or close friends. They could be asked to alert you if her drinking seems to start becoming a problem; for this to work, you need to be able to define "becoming a problem" and to choose someone in whom you have confidence. You might want to be up front with your daughter and say that you know this is a sensitive topic for the two of you to address and that you've asked her older sister in whom she confides, for example, to let you know if the drinking becomes troublesome. An "I'm here but not in your face" kind of approach might work well. Or not. You need to know your daughter, her trust in the person you chose, and your trust in them to have a modicum of confidence that it will be useful. If there comes a time when you must intervene, it might be difficult, but I think people want someone to lovingly tell them the truth at a certain point.

What Was Asleep Awakens

Sexual assault, like other major stressors, can stimulate underlying conditions and reactivate prior troubles. Difficulties as diverse as eating disorders, drug misuse, and attention deficit and hyperactivity disorder (ADHD) that had been successfully managed sometimes resurfaced. One girl with ADHD, for example, found herself unable to employ the executive function skills (cognitive skills to plan, prioritize, and carry out tasks) she had developed years earlier and had to go back on medication.

Previously existing and familial vulnerabilities sometimes come to the fore following an assault. The girl whose alcohol misuse I described had a grandfather (her father's father) who was an alcoholic and had died young; it was understandably difficult for her father to deal with her drinking. When diagnosed with bipolar disorder after her assault, another girl learned that it "runs in the family." When these familial issues are manifested in a daughter following her assault, parental anguish can be intense. To be of best help to their daughter – or at least to reduce the chance of compounding problems – it would be wise for parents in this situation to seek professional help themselves to sort out and address the cross-generational issues. A parent's sense of responsibility for yet another thing over which they have limited or no control can be a heavy burden.

Prior traumas can provide a template for dealing with having been sexually assaulted. One of the girls who spoke with me had a father who was incarcerated, another had a stepfather who had committed suicide, and another survived an incident in which a swimming companion drowned. These examples were all volunteered; I suspect I would have learned of more traumas had I asked directly. The point is one made in a previous chapter: girls who are sexually assaulted while at college rarely are blank slates when it comes to trauma; their psyches have been written upon and will shape their response to the current trauma.

Psychotherapy

Your daughter will change after having been sexually assaulted. Trauma specialists, whose expertise is in helping people come to terms with horrible things that have happened to them, refer to the changes as posttraumatic growth.

Several of the girls who spoke with me struggled to understand why the assault continued to influence them several months later, hoping, it seemed, to minimize the impact. As one girl said, "I was doubting that people believed me and then I sort of was internalizing it – like, 'Well, why is it a big deal? Why has it affected me?' It was a few minutes of my life. It shouldn't be that big of a deal." To help make sense of the complex thoughts and emotions, many of the girls considered psychotherapy.

Choosing Therapy

Some had been in counseling previously and saw it as a logical choice. Some were able to work with the same therapist, which was beneficial: the therapist already had some sense of the girl, and the girl felt more comfortable opening up. Those who hadn't been in therapy sometimes went at the urging of friends and university support staff, less often at the suggestion of a parent. Others were hesitant, not knowing what it would be like, but went anyway, sometimes only for a session or two. And others were resistant, perhaps due to the stigma associated with mental health problems, and rejected the idea outright.

Parents might not be as familiar or comfortable with psychotherapy as are their offspring. One or both parents might doubt the relevance of counseling. If that's the case, I'll pose a question: If your daughter were physically injured in the assault, would you encourage her to forgo medical care? If you answered, "No, I'd want her to get medical care, but I don't want her to get psychological care," you'd be wise to consider what's driving your reaction. Mental health care is valuable, not because there is anything "wrong" with her but because something truly terrible happened to her, and therapy can accelerate and strengthen posttraumatic growth.

Alternatively, if you are missing or denying the fact that much of the harm to a victim of sexual assault is psychological and emotional, you are not helping your daughter as much as you could. (My guess is that you understand to some degree, however, otherwise she probably wouldn't have told you in the first place.) How she deals with having been sexually assaulted should not be viewed as a test of her character or psychological strength; the assault is a trauma that care from trained professionals can help alleviate.

As with any trauma, it's advisable to get care sooner rather than later. Just as a bone can grow crookedly as it begins to repair itself with new growth after a break that has not been properly set, one's psyche can begin to crystallize in unhelpful ways if needed care is not obtained in short order. If that is the case, the subsequent "crooked" growth can certainly be addressed, but it often means a longer course of treatment because it too must be addressed along with the "real" issue.

The school's counseling and psychological services center, funded through the general fees the university levies each academic term, is a reasonable place to turn for services. Given the ubiquity of campus sexual assault and the distress it causes, you can be assured that your daughter will not be an anomaly; the therapists there have seen many students who have been sexually assaulted. You or your daughter might prefer, for a host of reasons, to seek care from someone in private practice. The student counseling center and the local rape crisis agency can be good sources for referrals.

When it comes to finding a therapist, I strongly encourage you to work with someone who is trained in trauma treatment; experience is more important than the educational degree. Therapeutic approaches to trauma can be distilled into two broad categories, which is an oversimplification, of course, but perhaps useful. Based on learning theories, some treatments seek to alleviate anxiety and avoidance by focusing on cognitions (that is, thought patterns) and/or by asking a victim to mentally return to the scene repeatedly and to describe each moment in detail in an attempt to reduce the emotional charge of the incident (that is, desensitization). It sounds painful to me, but revisiting the incident is a part of healing and can be done without being retraumatizing when one feels safe. More recently, a different set of approaches has emerged in which victims are encouraged to stay connected to their body and the physical manifestations of their trauma response. Such thinking is captured in Bessel van der Kolk's widely heralded book *The Body Keeps the Score*.[3] I recommend it. He uses vivid examples to elucidate how healing from trauma involves the brain, mind, and body and documents multiple movement-based interventions. A good physical workup can rule out underlying health issues that might be affecting her mood or concentration or otherwise impeding her ability to cope.

As with any health care, feeling safe and at ease with the caregiver is important. If she does not feel comfortable with the therapist, it's okay for your daughter to switch to another. It's much better to let go of a specific therapist than to abandon therapy itself.

Common Themes
Regardless of the type of therapy, the academic degree of the counselor, and the setting in which the counselor works, certain themes are common for those who have been sexually assaulted and are likely to emerge in your daughter's therapy.

Self-blame is one such theme. Even when it's clear that the perpetrator is ultimately responsible, victims of sexual assault can be full of self-recrimination. Saying, "It's not your fault" doesn't have much traction when paired with comments and questions about her drinking and other behaviors. She has internalized societal judgments and can torture herself with questions about what she did wrong from start to finish. Nonetheless, blaming oneself is a way to maintain the view that the world is fair. One of the college support staff put it simply: "You want to believe that this can't happen in a normal world unless you did something to make it happen."

Self-blame typically takes one of two forms: characterological or behavioral. Characterological self-blame is when she feels responsible for the assault because of who she is: I am too trusting, I am a bad judge of people, I am not good enough to have a guy treat me well. By contrast, behavioral self-blame is when she focuses on her actions: I didn't pay attention to feeling uneasy with him earlier in the evening, I drank too much, I should have been more definite about what I did and didn't want. Characterological self-blame is associated with depression and a lowered sense of worth, whereas behavioral self-blame is associated with a sense of agency and the possibility of self-protection. One mother described a conversation in which she tried to refocus her daughter: "I said to her, 'You can't take the blame here for what happened. Maybe poor choice for drinking. . . . There are consequences for everything we do, good and bad. But I don't really see how that particular thing said, 'Okay, gee, I had a couple of drinks so I should be raped.'"

Shame is common as well. As noted previously, most campus sexual assaults begin with some form of consensual activity. Maybe it included activities that she had not engaged in before, and she was interested and excited until she wasn't and wanted to stop. She can feel that she participated, to some degree, in her own assault at the same time as feel demeaned by the perpetrator who disregarded her humanity. Moreover, although the sex positivity movement has gotten traction, for her entire life your daughter has been exposed to ambivalent, at best, messages about women's sexuality. Thus feeling guilty about and ashamed of her own sexuality often partners with doubt, self-blame, and shame about the assault.

Anger at the perpetrator is healthy. It might take a while to get to it if it's hidden under layers of anger at herself, her friend who was to have kept an eye on things at the party, at her parents for how they reacted, or at the university for its failure to protect. All of those might be legitimate targets of her anger, but they are not substitutes for clear expressions of anger at the perpetrator, regardless of whether she expresses it directly to him.

Grieving can be expected. She has experienced multiple losses – perhaps the loss of her virginity, which she had been "saving," the loss of her sense of safety, the loss of her sense of invulnerability, the loss of her confidence that her parents would always "get" her. So many losses to identify and mourn.

Strengthening one's internal compass is a key benefit of good therapy. Rather than rely on external rules – there always will be circumstances for which a rule has not been specified, and the behavior of her perpetrator may well have been one of them – she will learn more about how to be true to herself and to pay attention to and trust her own judgment rather than look to "rules." In other words, in posttraumatic growth, she will mature in certain ways that she might not otherwise have at this time. As one girl said, "This has been the most I've ever had to do with my life. I feel very grown up now."

You can encourage and support the idea of therapy but not force it. As noted in chapter 8, if she is eighteen or more years old, you cannot force your daughter into therapy. (A caveat: Adults can be involuntarily committed to treatment after a competency hearing in which they are deemed to be a risk – typically defined as an imminent risk – to themselves or others. It's an intentionally high standard in order to protect civil liberty.) She might delay entering into therapy or cancel sessions once she has started, but it can be a most valuable path when there is a good fit between her and the therapist.

Need for Intervention

Strong support with a light touch will be best most of the time. But not always. When intervention is necessary, it's important to call upon all available resources; you will learn about additional options and make better decisions than if you try to go it alone.

Suicidal Tendencies

If your daughter's coping becomes self-destructive or harmful to others, you might need to intervene. The most extreme of such circumstances is if she becomes suicidal. Wanting to end the pain but not being able to can be excruciating. And when the future seems bleak, hope can fade. It is essential to pay attention to your daughter's words and moods, especially if she is an impulsive person. An important study comes to mind: of 153 thirteen- to thirty-four-year-olds who made a nearly lethal suicide attempt, one-fourth attempted suicide within *five* minutes of first thinking of it.[4] Compared to other attempters, those who make an impulsive attempt were more likely to think they would be discovered and less likely to think they would die. To that end, it's important to remember that even when an attempt is very severe, death is not necessarily the desired or expected outcome. And there is hope. People who make a suicide attempt so serious that they require hospitalization rarely go on to kill themselves.[5] Over 90 percent will find a way to go on and will end up dying of the same things that you and I are likely to die of: cancer, heart disease, or stroke.

Thinking about how you might be helpful if your daughter does become suicidal, I'll turn to comments from a woman whose daughter was very distressed. She spoke with her daughter's therapist about signs and symptoms to watch for. And when her daughter was prescribed psychiatric medication, she literally took away the pills. She told her daughter:

> "If I have to drive here every two or three days, I'll do it. But I'm not leaving you with a bottle of pills." She was upset that I would think that she would do that. I said, "I don't think that you'll do it. But a lot of people don't think that they'll do it. I just want to make sure that you're safe. You want to be here [at college], I'm going to let you be here, but I'm not going to let you have thirty sleeping pills." —Mother

The daughter complained to the psychiatrist, who reached out to the mother:

> He said, "Are you concerned?, I'm not seeing it." And I said, "I'm just worried. It's a parent that's worried. I don't know what is going on completely inside of her, do you?, no one ever does. . . . I'm just trying to take reasonable precautions." —Mother

And during a particularly difficult stretch, the mother took additional steps by ensuring that her daughter's roommate, sister, or a friend was always nearby:

> I was afraid to let her stay alone. She kept saying to me, "I'm not going to kill myself, Mom." And I just said, "That's not a chance I'm taking." She said, "Do you think I'm crazy?" I said, "No, I don't. But I think your mind is going right now, and it's better to be with somebody and not alone."

The daughter came through it with the help of psychotherapy, a lot of yoga and running, and a strong and supportive network of friends and family. She focused on creating a good future for herself and went on to gain entrance into a very competitive academic program, land prestigious internships, and launch a career she values with a company that holds her in high regard.

Leave from School

A leave from school can be helpful under certain circumstances. Such circumstances include, but are not limited to, when she is not able to concentrate long enough to complete an assigned reading or other homework, stops going to class, stops socializing, and doesn't get out of bed, that is, when she is troubled to the extent that she isn't able to function at school. Falling behind in coursework and failing classes will compound existing difficulties. It's okay to take a break; her place at college is assured and she can return. Calling it "a leave" rather than "dropping out for a while" seems to be less stigmatizing and underscores that it's a choice and that it's temporary.

Taking a leave from school will disrupt friendships, completion of her degree, and plans for the future. Thus it's not surprising that among the few girls who spoke with me who had taken a leave for one or more academic terms, the idea of taking a break from school and returning to the parental home initially was not appealing. As one girl said:

> It was an adjustment. I felt so useless most of the time. I wanted to be doing work, and that was weird because you're obviously not in a good headspace. You really did need to sit around, but I wanted to do something, it's just who I am as a person. But, looking back on it, I needed it

so much, just to be home with my mom and to be taken care of and for therapy to be my biggest focus. —Abbie

For others, school provided needed structure, and a leave would have been counterproductive. After her daughter had been brutally raped, one mother suggested that she take a leave, but the daughter had other plans. As the mother told me, it didn't mean it was easy:

> For about a week, she couldn't even fathom that [she could go on]. And then all of a sudden, she came down with a suitcase. I said, "What are you doing?" She said, "Take me back to school. I'm going back." I said, "You're not ready." She said, "I'm going back." I said, "But you're not sleeping." She said, "Mom, I can't let him win. I can't let him destroy my life. And if I sit here any longer, that's what's going to happen." I think that was a turning point for her. . . . She was still having a hard time concentrating, a hard time finding that compartment where she could put it and get through her day. The next month was terrible. The month after that was bad. . . . I think the real turning point took about two or three months.

To minimize the disruptions associated with taking and returning from a leave, it is essential to seek advice from and coordinate with staff at the college or university. Because students take leaves for all sorts of reasons each year – to recover from a car crash, to work on a political campaign, to help care for an ill family member, to earn money for tuition – campus personnel are familiar with administrative policies and can help ease the transition back into, as well as out of, an academic term.

Sometimes a leave is not enough and your daughter will choose to transfer to another school. Transferring can be disruptive in multiple ways, but if the goal is to complete her degree and returning to her current school seems untenable, it's a good option. Three of the twenty girls who spoke with me had transferred to their current university after being sexually assaulted at another school.

A girl who has been sexually assaulted carries awareness of the assault with her every day and takes actions to make herself feel safer. From the outside, it might not look like there was much harm, but there was. Some of her thoughts, emotions, and behaviors might not make sense to others or might seem to be an overreaction, but that isn't what it's like from the inside. You can expect a bit of a roller coaster; she will be more sensitive than perhaps you've ever seen her. And she might be hyperalert to the thoughts and feelings of those around her, including you; it's as if she's become an emotional tuning fork. If you keep in mind that her reality is not your reality and that you need to pay attention to and respect her reality, the coming months will be easier.

Despite initial frustration, one mother eventually accepted how her daughter handled the year after having been sexually assaulted. She compared her daughter's coping to her own:

> When I was going through stuff [with my divorce] I'd be, like, "Okay, everybody's healthy, nobody has cancer, nobody's dying, we're okay, we're going to be fine, we're going to get through this, there are so many worse things." That's how I would plug my way through it, and part of me is angry at her for not doing the same thing. Maybe she will eventually and maybe she won't, and she has the right not to. She's a different person. She doesn't have my personality. And God help – I hope she never does, because I had to go through a hell of a lot of stuff to get to this. So if she hurts, let her hurt. —Mother

Even when you extend (at least from your perspective) steadfast support, there will be difficult conversations, and your daughter will be downright hostile to you at times. A friend told me that she wanted her daughter to be able to look back and know that her parents had really been there for her. She said that to her daughter. Her daughter's response? "Mom, it isn't all about you." Ouch. Needing parents at the same time as wanting to be independent of them is tough.

New and unpleasant, albeit usually temporary, dynamics can emerge. If, for example, parents have been unhelpful, their daughter might be so irritated and so hurt that she leaves them to twist in the wind for a while. As they have the opportunity to feel what it was like to be on the receiving end of what she felt, she can experience this to be gratifying, relieving, or empowering in the short term. One mother said that she and her daughter had an entire year of difficulty: "I felt like I was constantly being misunderstood by her. No matter what I said, it was upsetting her, rubbing her the wrong way. It was reminding her that I judged her in her time of terror. I judged her as being somewhat responsible for this situation." It wasn't pleasant for the mother by any stretch, but her daughter was trying to reclaim her dignity and, yes, get back at her mother some. Tender spots will be hit; you know how to push each other's buttons. She might get angry at you if you express feelings that she's not yet ready or willing to feel. Hang in there.

We each bump into our limits, and sometimes the limits are tangible. One mother told me that her daughter "became obsessed with money and whether we could afford things after the rape. Again, it was a control issue: 'I don't have enough control over my world, and if we had more money, then I wouldn't have to worry about this.' I wish I had money that we could just give her . . . the poor kid has to worry about twenty-five bucks. I wish I could change that for her . . . maybe someday." It's hard not to be enough for your child and fortunate that there are many others who can and will step up to help her.

She will continue to need you. One mother reflected on the process in this way: "It's like when my husband died. At first, everybody's all there to help and support you, but then after weeks pass, months pass, everybody's kind of moved on and you're kind of still stuck there." One mother was surprised and gratified by her daughter's assessment long after the crisis had passed:

She said, "Your encouragement, your quiet presence, just that steady [presence] helped me more than anything, Mom." It was a long time ago and I don't think I did anything. I *didn't* do anything. And she said, "But you did. You gave me help finding some resources when I couldn't think clearly." —Mother

Sometimes showing up is the bravest and most important thing you can do.[6] Over time, you might begin to laugh again – not a rueful laugh, but a happy laugh.

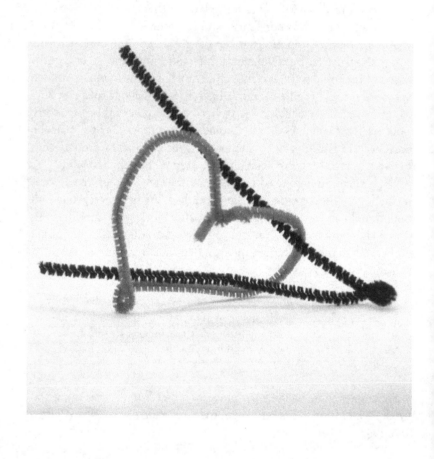

CHAPTER 10

Look to Where You Want to Go

Victims, especially in matters like these, rarely heal for many years, if ever. I think society tends to forget that. "Yeah, buck up, you get better, go seek professional help, get through that, move on with your life." Easy for you to say. —Father

You can't dwell on it because you can't change the past. You just can't change the past. Three years from now, something could pop up from this. I don't know [if it will], but you know what? – I'll deal with it when it comes. —Father

You go through all these phases, and then eventually you're like, "It happened, it's over." Seeing how my mom's assault affected her in such a negative way for so long made me realize that I cannot let that be me, I could not let that ruin my life. And then it just sort of gives you the realization that with any bad thing that happens, that's how you have to take it, you just can't let it ruin your life. You have to take a deep breath and just go forward. —Julia

A sexual assault leaves jet trails. It will be part of your daughter's life, your life, and your family's life to some extent from here on. Paradoxically, it will be, as one mother said, "hard stuff to remember and hard stuff to forget." Memories of specific facts (for example, which semester) seemed to fade for parents, but recollections of emotional components were etched deeply. In taking stock when they spoke with me, many parents told me some version of "Right now, we seem to be at a cruising altitude, and that seems to be how we're dealing with the effects"; "It's still there in residual ways"; and "It's part of our family history now."

In terms of getting through the initial post-assault period, I'm reminded of a story relayed by Bill Alexander upon his retirement as the longtime director of the Counseling and Psychological Services for students at the University of Pennsylvania. He wrote about learning to ride a motorcycle (bear with me – it's relevant):

> As part of the training, there is an interesting problem presented. You are riding comfortably in the middle lane of a big highway. In front of you is a large flatbed truck carrying refrigerators. Suddenly, without warning, one of the refrigerators falls off the truck and crashes in the center lane in front of you. What are you to do?
>
> The answer is: DO NOT look at the refrigerator. If you look at the refrigerator, you will hit the refrigerator. Look to one side or the other. You will go wherever you look. You will not hit the refrigerator. Look where you want to go.
>
> Don't think that you are pretending the refrigerator is not there. Trust me, you will always be aware of the refrigerator. It is very compelling. . . . There will be lots of time to . . . fully explore and understand the problem. . . . But for now, look where you want to go![1]

So where *do* you want to go? What do you imagine for what's ahead?

Hope for the Future

After telling me what the past months and sometimes years had been like, it was apparent that most parents and daughters had gone through some serious ups and downs. Wondering what they anticipated the future to hold, I half expected parents to respond with some version of continued struggle. Instead many parents focused on a positive future. One parent paused, reflected a bit, then said, "the end result that I want for my daughter and for the rest of my family and for myself, ultimately, is some level of peace and a lot of understanding and awareness." I often heard about hopes and dreams. Two responses struck me as particularly poignant:

> I just want to see her go up the aisle someday and be married and be happy. There's not a time I don't go to church or that I don't pray that I can see them with grandkids, because when you're in your sixties and they're still in college [*trails off*]. I just hope I don't go before they get to where I'd like to see them be. —Father

> I anticipate that she's going to have a guesthouse for me to live in and that my husband and I are going to help raise her children someday. I mean, that's really my picture – going from daughter to daughter to daughter spoiling our grandchildren and enjoying them. —Mother

Those warm and maybe even wistful hopes had not been dashed by what had been done to their daughter, nor by how much she struggled with its aftereffects, nor by how much their own lives had been disrupted. They wanted a bright future filled with loving relationships.

Daughter's Future Intimate Relationships

In addition to being concerned about their daughter and their connection with her, parents worried about the impact of the incident on her intimate relationships in the future. Their apprehensions are not unfounded, and many of their daughters share them. One girl told me, "I just want things to be normal. . . . It's the same as if I said I broke a bone when I was twelve, that's just a fact about me. . . . It's not something that should affect a relationship." Given the nature of the assault, though, it's likely to be much more than "just a fact" about her. She will need to grapple with if and when to tell a potential partner, and she and her partner together will need to be aware of when and how "the fact" affects their ability to connect with each other in multiple ways.

She may not be in a relationship for a long time, or she may be in a series of relationships. As one mother said, "The line is long but it moves fast." Pay attention to the message: she's not interested in a committed relationship. You might think that her being in a long-term relationship is a sign that she's "over" the assault, but that's not necessarily the case. And the kind of relationship she's in matters. As one parent told me, "I've always said that your relationships with men should bring out the best in you. And if you ever feel that you're being subjugated or you're being dragged down or in any way put down . . . it's not just the sexuality part of it." One father said, "I believe in my heart of hearts that she was a virgin when she was raped, I believe that was her first experience with physical intimacy, and that sucks, that really sucks." It will take a while for her to want to connect. You might be eager for them, but hold off a long time with comments about grandchildren.

Advice to Parents

I asked many who spoke with me about what advice they would give to others. A few demurred and one outright rejected the idea that she could hazard a guess as to what would be useful to others. But most had definite ideas. One said, "I would tell a parent, deep breaths. Try to think like you're two years down the road thinking about this retrospectively for a moment. Just disengage your emotional reactions as best you can and listen and connect and try to put yourself into your daughter's shoes." The assumption, confirmed by the daughters, was that a certain perspective was important: to be respectful, not intrusive, and to ask about and offer help that she says she'd find useful.

What you say might not register sometimes, but how you say it always matters. Silence can be important too. When you use words, it can help to be a bit tentative. It also can help to reach out without expecting anything. One girl described her sister's light touch: "She's, like, 'Oh, here's something that I thought about, just so you know.' I think that's nice because it gives support without demanding a response." She went on to tell me how she enjoyed getting letters from her folks; letters kept lines of communication open, slowed things down, and demonstrated special thought and caring in a time of text and email messages.

It helps to pay attention to what she conveys nonverbally, as well as with her words. As one mother said, "I'm a big talker, I like to think I have the answers, but I had to listen to her to give me the answers, even when they weren't spoken. I had to learn to watch her body language. I've watched her patterns of behavior now so closely, more closely than

I ever did before. . . . I understand her more, and what she's not telling me."

Recognize what you do have to offer. You can help in ways big and small, for example, by distracting her from the pain by helping her keep busy or engaging in other, seemingly insignificant actions. And don't underestimate the importance of showing up, of just being there. As one mother said, "She tells me that I helped her a lot, and I don't believe that I did. I think she helped herself. I was just a sounding board, but it helped just being her sounding board."

So do you talk about it? Do you bring it up? Parents said that they don't necessarily talk about the assault often, but they do talk about it from time to time, even years later. The topic comes up in movies, the news, in all sorts of ways. If you are thinking about sexual assault or something related to her assault and want to bring it up, ask your daughter if she's open to hearing it. It might be helpful for her to know that as much as it might be on her mind, it's on yours too. And you can ask what it was like for her when you brought it up. If she doesn't want to listen – then or ever – she will tell you, perhaps emphatically. Her interest in hearing from you will not be static; she will be receptive sometimes and not others. She might bring something up with you and then not again for a long time. She might open up to you partway and close again. That's okay. If you are respectful of her choices, you will leave the door open for future conversations.

What happened outside the family with the perpetrator is one thing; it's another to invite him in for a lengthy stay in your family's dynamics. You might wish he'd gotten more of what you thought should happen to him, you might hope he understood how much he hurt your daughter, and you might have lots of hopes and wishes about him or against him. Focusing on him takes a lot of mental energy, energy that you might decide is best put elsewhere. He's not part of your family, and he's not welcome. Your daughter is. Always.

Prevention

Parents who spoke with me had several concrete suggestions about how to reduce campus sexual assault. One idea was to punish colleges and universities by withholding federal funding such as financial aid and research support, closely supervising "absolutely every party that happens on or near campus" and arresting every student engaged in underage drinking. Another thought centered on including men and boys in conversations about campus sexual assault so that it becomes more than a "women's issue." And a third set of ideas emphasized awareness and providing more explicit rules for girls, as if the parents could have or should have done more to prepare their daughters for what was cast as a nearly inevitable circumstance.

A few parents said that nothing could be done. One mother underscored the cost of doing nothing: "I really hope that our culture changes because this can't go on for women . . . my daughter is a casualty. When she went to college, she saw nothing but beauty. She had an untainted, innocent view of life, and it crashed in on her at her most intimate, vulnerable part, her sexuality . . . I know she's scarred."

Some thought big thoughts, asserting that there will be less sexual assault only when we change the way we think. It's a daunting task. As one college staff member told me, "It's bigger than any one university. If I thought about how big the problem really is – hundreds of years of oppression, hundreds of years of violence, of a culture that says it's okay for us to do these things to one another – it's enough to make you not want to get out of bed in the morning." Another college service provider said, "There's never an end. It's crazy that this just keeps happening and happening, and there's never not someone who doesn't need to be seen. It's mind-blowing." New York senator Kirsten Gillibrand succinctly brought the issue into focus: "The price of a college education should not include a one-in-five chance of being sexually assaulted."[2]

So what might we do?

Values, Not Rules

Mothers and fathers instill lots of rules in their children. Daughters are instructed specifically how to avoid being sexually assaulted. Sometimes the rules run counter to life on a college campus and sometimes the rules don't fit. Moreover, there will never be enough rules for all the circumstances that any of us will encounter. If you've emphasized following rules, what is she to do in a situation for which no rule has been specified? Thus the focus on rules – and parents' anger and a daughter's guilt and fear of disappointing them when she didn't follow the rules and was harmed – is a bit misplaced. Of course rules are important, but they're not the point.

I think of teaching my son about money. He easily grasped the importance of not overdrawing a bank account, paying a credit card bill on time, and reviewing a balance statement. The underlying, larger concepts with which we all grapple – how much money is enough, how to decide if something is worth spending money on, and so on – are not as easy. But it was important that we have such conversations; they prompted him to consider and define his values. For him to develop and be aware of the value system that underlies his judgments and drives his actions is far more important than any rule. It's an imperfect analogy, to be sure, but it seems that we'd be better off emphasizing values and underlying concepts than inculcating rules.

Sex. One arena in which students must make decisions over and over again is their sexuality. If they were fortunate to have a unit on human sexuality in their high school health class, they may have learned a bit about biology and the mechanics of reproduction but little to nothing about the associated powerful feelings, intimacy, pleasure, or, aside from condoms, safety. Perhaps it's no wonder that high school and college students turn to one another and online for information and guidance. Is it okay to have sex when you've had so much to drink that you aren't likely to remember it? How can desires and limits be expressed clearly? These are the sorts of questions that we, as adults, must muster the guts to talk about with our girls and our boys. Getting an "A" on a test on the parts of the reproductive system isn't enough.

Alcohol. Alcohol is common, expected even, at most campus parties. When young people have been told that sex is wrong, bad, or even forbidden but want to be sexually active to some degree, alcohol is a way to ease those inhibitions. The majority of campus sexual assaults involve alcohol consumption (by the perpetrator, the victim, or both) and consensual sexual activity. Sometimes alcohol is weaponized: a person bent on harm uses alcohol as a way to incapacitate a potential victim.

Colleges and universities have yet to figure out how best to handle alcohol use and misuse among their students. Banning alcohol on campus isn't likely to work; smart, creative kids will find another way, and problem drinking will go underground, farther out of reach of supervision and enforcement. Lowering the legal drinking age to eighteen would make drinking lawful for most college students, but it wouldn't address binge drinking or other problematic use. It might be worth posing scenarios: "During your first weeks on campus, you'll likely be both nervous and excited and want to fit in with people you're meeting. How does alcohol fit in the picture for you?" Or revising some of that rule-based advice to include things such as "Be sure to eat before you go to a party." (On an empty stomach, alcohol is absorbed more quickly into the bloodstream.) Or "Keeping up with someone else's drinking might seem innocuous, but you both could end up doing something you wouldn't otherwise do or want."

Drinking to excess is not a harmless social exercise. If students drink heavily, they will have great difficulty discerning the intention and desires of each other.

Does this mean that girls are responsible for being sexually assaulted if they have been drinking? No. Maybe someday we will go beyond the dichotomous thinking often evidenced in discussions about alcohol and campus sexual assault.

Rethinking Gender Roles and Expectations

Increased acknowledgment of individuals who identify as nonbinary, transgender, and gender nonconforming is shaking up expectations of men and women. One mother expressed intense frustration with the vulnerability of women in society when she said:

> Well, the whole thing is unfair. I mean this whole "Well, you were drinking, what'd you expect?" She expected a hangover, that's what she expected, a hangover. Why is it that because we have a vagina that can be penetrated that we have to worry about whether or not we're going to be a victim? I mean, what kind of fucked-up world do we live in that that's even an issue?

Good questions. One of the college service providers had an answer: "Boys don't come to college and suddenly have these appalling, predatory attitudes toward girls. It happens in eighth grade or at that age when they're taught that they're supposed to be as sexual as possible. In college they refer to the number of girls they've had sex with as a 'body count.'" I'm probably not the only person for whom sports scorekeeping comes to mind. Do boys and men understand how damaging sexual assault can be? I'm not so sure. The college staffer went on to address how girls, as well as boys, are raised:

> I don't know what the expression "Boys will be boys" means. But it's never about being responsible and trustworthy and all those good adjectives. We still teach our girls to be nice, and I think that's a really bad idea. Kindness is very important. Being nice, big mistake. Because what it does is prevent girls from saying, "Leave me alone." It keeps girls from trusting their gut, from saying, "I feel very uncomfortable in this situation." I think that by the time they go to college, there's nothing you can do. Oh, sure, you can sit and tell your daughter, "Don't get drunk." Well, save your oxygen because it's too late to talk to her about that. I really feel that the future of the world is based on teaching boys what it means to be a man. —Campus staffer

We continue to value girls for being attractive and polite, for not making waves. Her body is something for others to judge. She is taught to be attentive to the feelings, reactions, and needs of others to a degree that she easily overrides her own gut, if she is even able to recognize its signals by the time she gets to college. No wonder that, when faced with an ambiguous situation and a guy intent on his own purposes, a girl feels unsure and hesitates. In addition to changing some of what manhood means, it's time to start raising girls to become women, not girls grown older.

Community

Defining "them" as different from "us" can be an attempt to maintain belief in a just and fair world. Thinking of campus sexual assault in terms of *those* boys or *those* girls or *that* school or *those* people might make you feel safer as a parent, but it's a false sense of security. Sexual assault occurs on campuses of all sorts across the country.

An effort to claim sexual assault as a problem of the *community* as well as individual people is evidenced in the widespread implementation of bystander intervention programs in colleges and universities as well as high schools. In such programming, students are encouraged to expand their sense of responsibility to others and learn how to spot and disrupt a potentially harmful circumstance. The training invariably brings up questions about individual choice. A university service provider relayed this story about her attempt at bystander education:

> I did a thing at my synagogue a few months ago. They'll never invite me back. But I wanted to talk about bystander issues. This was with the fourteen- and fifteen-year-olds. Bystander issues are a big deal for Jews because of the people who were sent to concentration camps while bystanders did nothing, so it was reasonable to start with that. Then I moved to a different scenario – a woman in a hijab is sitting on a bus, a skinhead is verbally attacking her, and you're sitting next to her. What would you do? What could you do? Then we talked about school bullying and sending around naked pictures; they're getting quieter and quieter. Then I said, "Okay, you're at a party, some kids are drinking. You're not, but some kids are drinking. And you see a really drunk boy going up the stairs with a really drunk girl. What do you do?" They all said, "Nothing. He's not pulling her up the stairs, she's going at her own free will, it's okay." So I said, "All right. What if she's your sister?" "Well, that's different." "Okay. Why is it different? What if it's your best friend? What if it's just someone you know in school? What if it's a stranger?" So we talked about how you define your community, and I'm trying to make a case for the bigger your definition, the better our world. At the end, I said, "What if she's passed out on the bed, and you find out he's had sex with her? Are there any repercussions for him?" "No," they replied. I said, "Well, actually, what he did was against the law." And they were stunned, they were stunned. —Campus staffer

We are part of the community that denies sexual assault on our campuses. And we bear responsibility. Jennifer Hirsch and Shamus Khan, in their book about campus sexual assault, offered an incisive analysis:

> We do not deny the problems of certain expressions of masculinity. But just as explanations that are purely psychological (sociopathic perpetrators) are incomplete, so too are ones that are entirely cultural (toxic masculinity). We are all responsible. Most of us have never committed assault. But all of us have allowed social conditions to persist in which many young people come of age without a language to talk about their sexual desires, overcome with shame, unaccustomed to considering how their relative social power may silence a peer, highly attentive to their personal wants but deaf to those of others, or socialized to feel unable to tell someone "no" or to give a clear and unambiguous "yes." Without

question, individuals bear responsibility for their own actions; the exercise of the responsibility to respect others' bodily autonomy can be seen in the many instances in which one person said no or otherwise managed to convey that they were not into what was happening, and the other person noticed and stopped.[3]

In other words, it's on us. Us, as in the adults who have done what we've thought is our best to raise our children. We may have done our best in many ways, but looking more broadly there are some things we have neglected.

Taking Action

So how can these big ideas be put into action in the short term? Quite a few college girls provide a good example. They are finding their internal compass and relying less on rules set by others, they are reevaluating the explicit and subtle things they've been taught about gender and gender roles, and they are finding strength as they redefine and create community. There are a lot of girls who are sexually assaulted while in college, and they help one another. They provide a shoulder to lean on, a safe place to vent their fury, accompaniment to a rape exam, and guidance in seeking helpful adults on and off campus. Many of the girls were helped and supported by female friends who themselves had been assaulted, and they in turn helped others when they were victimized. We can be proud and grateful that they create a knowledgeable and knowing community for one another but must lament the fact that the network is needed.

Social action can be one way to further process what was done to her. Parents might learn that their daughter who previously hadn't paid attention to such things has begun to take part in marches, make speeches, write, and organize about sexual assault on campus. The parents who spoke with me seemed forthright in their opinions and reactions to their daughters' activism:

I know once my daughter started to heal, she became very active at college and hosted events for women who have been, who have had, other women who have had this problem. [*Three years later, "rape" was still a hard word for him to say.*] . . . She became an activist. I think that was very critical to her healing process. It made me a little bit nervous when she started to do that. But the more I thought about it, the better I felt about it. —Father

She wants to be a change agent more than she wants sympathy or empathy for herself. She wants to do something about it. She feels so wronged by it that, unlike me, who didn't even warn anybody else [after being groped by a man in authority at work], she wants to take out the bullhorn and really speak out about it. —Mother

Standing up for others can be a way of standing up for oneself, the person she was and the person she has become.

Parents, on the other hand, typically struggled with the situation alone. Many did not turn to others, offer help to others, create community, or consider social action. Yet they were frustrated. When I asked one mother if she had looked for resources for parents, she responded with disgust: "In our state there were over 11,000 backlogged rape kits that they didn't have the funding to test. Again, women don't matter. So if you don't even have anything for the rape victim, of course there's nothing for the parents." And one father said, "Something has to change, otherwise it will go on like this forever." One thing that might create change is greater involvement of parents.

Parental involvement can take many forms, and one concrete example is connecting with other parents in similar circumstances. In chapter 8, I wrote about Parents Take Action, an adjunct to the organization End Rape on Campus. The small, core group of mothers and fathers whose daughters have been sexually assaulted at college can be a wonderful resource for parents as they navigate systems at institutions of higher education and figure out how to be of best help to their own daughters. They occasionally host webinars and are available for one-on-one conversations. When you've settled into a good place and are comfortable sharing what you've learned – and your daughter is okay with you speaking about something that is intimately about her – becoming involved in Parents Take Action would be a unique way to help other parents.

The Culture of Respect Collaborative, a project of NASPA, currently works directly with more than 120 colleges and universities to create change on campuses. Their signature tools include a blueprint for change and a core evaluation guide. You can join their efforts to improve campus culture by volunteering to serve on committees at your daughter's school. If that feels too close, there are many other colleges and universities that would welcome the participation of a knowledge-able, caring parent. Parents and alumni are often overlooked when universities appoint committees.

If you want to take action but a focus on campus sexual assault stirs up too much for you for now, consider contacting a local rape crisis agency, women's law center, women's rights organization, or other such group. They often welcome the participation of community members in a variety of capacities: to give talks to interested groups, to meet with policy makers regarding pending legislation, to help raise funds for their work, and more. And if you have a younger daughter or son, you might invite them to become active in these organizations as well.

Speaking of funding, another way to have impact is to include these nonprofit organizations on your list of donations. If your daughter's school is anything like most institutions of higher education these days, you probably get semiregular solicitations from it. One mother relayed how she drew attention to the issue at the university her daughter attended: "Last year, I gave a large donation and I could specify where I wanted it to go. 'Educational programs for prevention of sexual assault' was not one of the categories, but there was an 'Other.' And I put that in as the other – that I wanted it go to educational programs to prevent the sexual assault of students." If you do something like that and want to be sure that you don't end up funding something the school already does, you might want to further specify that the donation be used to expand or enhance existing services.

Several years ago, college girls who had been sexually assaulted began to identify themselves publicly when they spoke out. In doing so, they claimed their experience and asserted their personhood: sexual assault is more than an abstraction, it happened to me. Then the #MeToo movement gained traction and dozens of celebrities were fol-lowed by thousands who spoke up and spoke out. I wish for something similar for parents who, wanting to protect their daughters' privacy, often grapple with the circumstances in great isolation; it takes a toll on them. Being part of a knowing community can reduce one's sense of isolation and vulnerability.

You can help create community. Returning to Bill Alexander's parable about motorcycles and refrigerators, "If you're feeling a little empty, feed someone else. If you're feeling unprepared, show a friend how. If you fear you are faking it, support someone honestly. You get the idea."

After listening to daughters, mothers, fathers, and university staff, if I was challenged to put everything into three or four words, it might be "Listen and love." Or maybe "Take the long view," a perspective that keeps immediate needs and ongoing issues in the larger frame of past and future life together. Regardless of a family's dynamics and the specific situation they face, being receptive to one another and having hope are likely to lead to a better outcome for everyone.

The parental task is to be close but not too close and far but not too far. And to have the sensitivity to know when closeness is needed, when distance is needed, and the flexibility to move back and forth. You will likely spend a tremendous amount of energy thinking about what's going to help your daughter. You don't have to be perfect. As obvious as this seems, it can be important to say it aloud during particularly trying times. What you need to be is good enough.

As parents, we learn over the years that our children figure out their own way to be, to get through disappointments and horrible hardships, and it's done with more grace in some instances than others. Occasionally, the best a parent can do is to just hold on. During particularly difficult stretches, some parents who spoke with me found solace in their faith in God, others held on to their faith in the good in their daughter, and others drew upon knowing that they have a solid foundation with their daughter and that she knows that they love her. As we spoke about the role of parents, one college service provider told me, "When the people she seeks validation from the most validate her in deep and transformative ways, she feels like 'I can do this.' . . . When that doesn't happen, it's devastating. But when it does, the healing process just takes flight in ways that it doesn't otherwise." Knowing that her parents' love is fierce and will continue can be crucial: "Just knowing that they're always there is huge; it's all I need."

Being human, we inevitably cause harm, even when we don't intend to. So forgiveness helps. I'm not talking about the polite, automatic kind of forgiveness or an apology offered to relieve feelings of guilt but one that involves a powerful process of accountability to oneself and others. Daughters might ruminate on thoughts such as "Maybe I shouldn't have been there or maybe I shouldn't have done that," and eventual resolution might take some form of "But I didn't know, and I goofed up." Parents may well follow a similar path, troubling themselves about how they could have responded differently to their daughter's disclosure of the assault, how they missed the signs of her distress, and maybe how they held her accountable for the actions of someone else. Their resolution might take a similar form: "I didn't know; I have learned."

Moreover, it might take a while as the hurts are sorted out and tender spots heal, but tears in your relationship with your daughter can be mended. You will need to forgive one another for the hostile things that were said, the acidic thoughts that were left unsaid, and the resentments held onto long past any useful purpose. A generosity of spirit toward oneself and one another goes a long way.

Simply continuing to parent and having the opportunity to see how your daughter works to right herself can imbue a confidence that might not have been there in those first few days, weeks, and months. In closing, I call upon two conversations to illustrate some of the many kinds of change and growth you will witness; they document a daughter's increased understanding about who she is in relation to others in the family and clarity about her future:

> My father is very much about victim blaming . . . and when I free myself of the control of that kind of language – "Oh my God, you're my dad how could you be saying that about me?" – I say, "Okay, fine, that's just something he believes, it doesn't mean I believe that, it doesn't mean I believe that about myself." When I take a different approach, then I'm able to also not fight that battle and not exhaust myself. —Jenny

> It's shaped a lot of who she is and what she does. And sometimes we talk about it, and I say to her, "Now listen. I wish with my whole being, and if I could go back and sacrifice anything to change it, I would, I would. But I can't. And the reality is it happened. But look at where it's taken you. Look at the journey that it's put you on. Because now you have a direction and you know that you want . . . to advocate for women, to

do women's rights, and be a voice for them. You're strong, you have a strength that's incredible. And now you have knowledge." —Mother

You too will grow. Perhaps in ways you could not imagine.

Notes

Introduction

1. David Cantor et al., *Report on the AAU Campus Climate Survey on Sexual Assault and Misconduct* (Rockville, MD: Westat, January 17, 2020), Table 44, https://www.aau.edu/sites/default/files/AAU-Files/Key-Issues/Campus-Safety/Revised%20Aggregate%20report%20%20and%20appendices%201-7_(01-16 -2020_FINAL).pdf.

2. Cantor et al., *Report on the AAU Campus Climate Survey on Sexual Assault and Misconduct* (2020), Table 13.

3. Charlotte Pierce-Baker, *Surviving the Silence: Black Women's Stories of Rape* (New York: Norton, 2004). Lisa Factora-Borchers, ed., *Dear Sister: Letters from Survivors of Sexual Violence* (Chico, CA: AK Press, 2014).

Chapter 1

1. American College Health Association, *American College Health Association-National College Health Assessment II: Undergraduate Student Reference Group Data Report Spring 2019* (Silver Spring, MD: American College Health Association, 2019), https://www.acha.org/documents/ncha/NCHA -II_SPRING_2019_UNDERGRADUATE_REFERENCE_GROUP_DATA_ REPORT.pdf.

2. Robert P. Gallagher, *National Survey of College Counseling Centers 2014*, Monograph Series no. 9V (The International Association of Counseling Services, 2014), http://d-scholarship.pitt.edu/28178/1/survey_2014.pdf.

3. Peter LeViness et al., *The Association for University and College Counseling Center Directors Annual Survey. Reporting Period: July 1, 2017 through June 30, 2018*, https://www.aucccd.org/assets/documents/Survey/2018%20AUCCCD%20Survey-Public-June%2012-FINAL.pdf.

4. Scott Jaschik, "Anxiety, Depression, Waiting Lists," *Inside Higher Ed*, July 5, 2016, https://www.insidehighered.com/news/2016/07/05/survey-counseling-center-directors-finds-anxiety-and-depression-are-top-issues.

5. Substance Abuse and Mental Health Services Administration (SAMHSA), *2015 National Survey on Drug Use and Health (NSDUH): Detailed Tables*, Table 6.84B: Tobacco Product and Alcohol Use in Past Month among Persons Aged 18 to 22, by College Enrollment Status: Percentages, 2014 and 2015 (Rockville, MD: Substance Abuse and Mental Health Services Administration Center for Behavioral Health Statistics and Quality, September 8, 2016), https://www.samhsa.gov/data/sites/default/files/NSDUH-DetTabs-2015/NSDUH-DetTabs-2015/NSDUH-DetTabs-2015.pdf.

6. SAMHSA, *2015 National Survey on Drug Use and Health (NSDUH)*, Table 6.84B.

7. American College Health Association, *American College Health Association-National College Health Assessment II*.

8. Sigmund J. Kharasch et al., "Drinking to Toxicity: College Students Referred for Emergency Medical Evaluation," *Addiction Science and Clinical Practice* 11, no. 1 (2016): 11.

9. American College Health Association, *American College Health Association-National College Health Assessment II*.

10. Jennifer S. Hirsch and Shamus Khan, *Sexual Citizens: A Landmark Study of Sex, Power, and Assault on Campus* (New York: W. W. Norton, 2020), xx.

11. American College Health Association, *American College Health Association-National College Health Assessment II*.

12. Melissa A. Lewis et al., "What Is Hooking Up? Examining Definitions of Hooking Up in Relation to Behavior and Normative Perceptions," *Journal of Sex Research* 50, no. 8 (2013): 757–66.

13. Lisa Wade, *American Hookup: The New Culture of Sex on Campus* (New York: Norton, 2017).

14. Peggy Orenstein, *Girls & Sex: Navigating the Complicated New Landscape* (New York: HarperCollins, 2016).

15. American College Health Association, *American College Health Association-National College Health Assessment II*.

16. Onesick mind, "I Remove the Condom Without Them Knowing During 'Stealth' Sex," June 24, 2012, https://perma.cc/453V-PPQJ.

17. Alexandra Brodsky, "'Rape-Adjacent': Imagining Legal Responses to Nonconsensual Condom Removal," *Columbia Journal of Gender and Law* 32, no. 2 (2017): 183–210.

18. Elliot Rodger, "My Twisted World: The Story of Elliot Rodger," News Documents, "The Manifesto of Elliot Rodger," *New York Times*, May 25, 2014, https://www.nytimes.com/interactive/2014/05/25/us/shooting-document.html.

19. Kyle Borowski, "Judge Bars Brown from Suspending Student Found Guilty of Sexual Assault," *Brown Daily Herald*, June 1, 2016, http://www.brown dailyherald.com/2016/06/01/judge-bars-brown-from-suspending-student-found -guilty-of-sexual-assault/.

20. Eran Shor and Kimberly Seida, "'Harder and Harder'? Is Mainstream Pornography Becoming Increasingly Violent and Do Viewers Prefer Violent Content?" *Journal of Sex Research* 56 (2019): 16–28.

21. Marleen J. Klaassen and Jochen Peter, "Gender (In)Equality in Internet Pornography: A Content Analysis of Popular Pornographic Internet Videos," *Journal of Sex Research* 52 (2015): 721–35.

22. Paul J. Wright, Robert S. Tokunaga, and Ashley Kraus, "A Meta-Analysis of Pornography Consumption and Actual Acts of Sexual Aggression in General Population Studies," *Journal of Communication* 66, no. 1 (February 2016): 183–205.

23. Maggie Jones, "What Teen-Agers Are Learning from Online Porn," *New York Times Magazine*, February 7, 2018, https://www.nytimes.com/2018/02/07/ magazine/teenagers-learning-online-porn-literacy-sex-education.html.

24. Anna Orso, "N.J. Judge Cited Good Grades and Eagle Scout Status of Teen Accused of Sexual Assault," *Philadelphia Inquirer*, July 3, 2019, https:// www.inquirer.com/news/new-jersey-judge-accused-teenager-sexual-assault -eagle-scout-good-grades-good-family-juvenile-court-20190703.html.

25. Lauren F. Cardoso et al., "Recent and Emerging Technologies: Implications for Women's Safety," *Technology in Society* 58 (2019): article 101108.

26. *Trends in College Pricing 2019*, College Board, Trends in Higher Education, 2019, https://research.collegeboard.org/pdf/trends-college-pricing-2019 -full-report.pdf.

27. Raj Chetty et al., "Mobility Report Cards: The Role of Colleges in Intergenerational Mobility," National Bureau of Economic Research Working Paper no. 23618 (July 2017).

28. Jeremy Redford and Kathleen Mulvaney Hoyer, *First-Generation and Continuing-Generation College Students: A Comparison of High School and Postsecondary Experiences* (U.S. Department of Education: Stats in Brief,

September 2017 NCES 2018–009), https://nces.ed.gov/pubs2018/2018009.pdf.

29. Sara Goldrick-Rab et al., *Still Hungry and Homeless in College* (Madison: Wisconsin HOPE Lab, April 2018), https://hope4college.com/wp-content/uploads/2018/09/Wisconsin-HOPE-Lab-Still-Hungry-and-Homeless.pdf.

30. Suzanna M. Martinez et al., "No Food for Thought: Food Insecurity Is Related to Poor Mental Health and Lower Academic Performance among Students in California's Public University System," *Journal of Health Psychology* (June 1, 2018): 1359105318783028, doi: 10.1177/1359105318783028.

31. National Center for Education Statistics, *Digest of Education Statistics: 2018*, Table 302.20: Percentage of Recent High School Completers Enrolled in College, by Race/Ethnicity: 1960 through 2018 (Washington, DC: U.S. Department of Education National Center for Education Statistics, 2019), https://nces.ed.gov/programs/digest/d19/tables/dt19_302.20.asp?current=yes.

32. Mary J. Fischer, "Does Campus Diversity Promote Friendship Diversity? A Look at Interracial Friendships in College," *Social Science Quarterly* 89, no. 3 (2008): 631–55.

33. Stephanie F. Rose and Michael W. Firmin, "African-American Students on a Predominantly White University Campus: Qualitative Research Findings." *Psychological Studies* 58, no. 1 (March 2013): 58–65.

34. Danielle Paquette, "Why Frat Bros Can Throw Parties but Sorority Sisters Aren't Allowed To," *Washington Post*, January 22, 2016, https://www.washingtonpost.com/news/wonk/wp/2016/01/22/why-frats-can-throw-parties-but-sororities-cant/.

35. David Cantor et al., *Report on the AAU Campus Climate Survey on Sexual Assault and Misconduct* (Rockville, MD: Westat, January 17, 2020).

36. Emilie Buchwald, Pamela Fletcher, and Martha Roth, eds., *Transforming a Rape Culture* (Minneapolis, MN: Milkweed Editions, 1993/2005).

37. Dan Spinelli, "Flyers Cover Campus with Suggestive Email, Saying, 'This Is What Rape Culture Looks Like,'" *Daily Pennsylvanian* (Philadelphia, PA), September 6, 2016, https://www.thedp.com/article/2016/09/rape-culture-flyers.

38. Rebecca Solnit, "Younger Feminists Have Shifted My Understanding," *The Guardian*, February 29, 2020, https://www.theguardian.com/world/2020/feb/29/rebecca-solnit-younger-feminists-shift-understanding-give-new-tools.

39. Brian Arao and Kristi Clemens, "From Safe Spaces to Brave Spaces: A New Way to Frame Dialogue around Diversity and Social Justice," in *The Art of Effective Facilitation: Reflections from Social Justice Educators*, ed. Lisa M. Landreman (Sterling, VA: Stylus, 2013), 135–50.

40. T. Rees Shapiro, "Expelled for Sex Assault, Young Men Are Filing More Lawsuits to Clear Their Names," *Washington Post*, April 28, 2017, https://www.washingtonpost.com/local/education/expelled-for-sex-assault-young-men-are-filing-more-lawsuits-to-clear-their-names/2017/04/27/c2cfb1d2-0d89-11e7-9b0d-d27c98455440_story.html?tid=ss_tw&utm_term=.a90429a6ba3b.

Chapter 2

1. Susan Brownmiller, *Against Our Will: Men, Women, and Rape* (New York: Bantam, 1975).

2. Brownmiller, *Against Our Will*.

3. Sexual Assault Support Center, "The History of Rape Laws," https://prezi.com/fo9lruzwgovn/the-history-of-rape-laws/.

4. Crystal N. Feimster, "'What If I Am a Woman': Black Women's Campaigns for Sexual Justice and Citizenship," in *The World the Civil War Made*, ed. Gregory P. Downs and Kate Masur (Chapel Hill: University of North Carolina Press, 2015).

5. Estelle B. Freedman, *Redefining Rape: Sexual Violence in the Era of Suffrage and Segregation* (Cambridge, MA: Harvard University Press, 2013).

6. "First Ban on Smacking Children," last updated January 9, 2020, https://sweden.se/society/smacking-banned-since-1979/.

7. Clifford Kirkpatrick and Eugene Kanin, "Male Sex Aggression on a University Campus," *American Sociological Review* 22, no. 1 (February 1957): 52–58.

8. Eugene J. Kanin and Stanley R. Parcell, "Sexual Aggression: A Second Look at the Offended Female," *Archives of Sexual Behavior* 6, no. 1 (January 1977): 67–76.

9. Mary P. Koss, Christine A. Gidycz, and Nadine Wisniewski, "The Scope of Rape: Incidence and Prevalence of Sexual Aggression and Victimization in a National Sample of Higher Education Students," *Journal of Consulting and Clinical Psychology* 55, no. 2 (1987): 162–70.

10. Clery Center, *Summary of the Jeanne Clery Act: A Compliance and Reporting Overview*, https://clerycenter.org/policy-resources/the-clery-act/.

11. Diana E. Russell, "The Prevalence and Incidence of Forcible Rape of Females," *Victimology* 7 (1983): 81–93; Susan B. Sorenson et al., "The Prevalence of Adult Sexual Assault: The Los Angeles Epidemiologic Catchment Area Project," *American Journal of Epidemiology* 126, no. 6 (December 1987): 1154–64; Idee Winfield et al., "Sexual Assault and Psychiatric Disorders among a Community Sample of Women," *American Journal of Psychiatry* 147, no. 3 (1990): 335–41.

12. Douglas Linder, *The McMartin Preschool Abuse Trial* (2007), https://papers.ssrn.com/sol3/papers.cfm?abstract_id=1030559.

13. Susan Estrich, *Real Rape: How the Legal System Victimizes Women Who Say No* (Cambridge, MA: Harvard University Press, 1988).

14. Mary P. Koss and Christine A. Gidycz, "Sexual Experiences Survey: Reliability and Validity," *Journal of Consulting and Clinical Psychology* 53 (1985): 422–23.

15. Sapana D. Donde et al., "If It Wasn't Rape, Was It Sexual Assault? Comparing Rape and Sexual Assault Acknowledgment in College Women Who Have Experienced Rape," *Violence Against Women* 24, no. 2 (January 2018): 1718–38.

16. Koss, Gidycz, and Wisniewski, "The Scope of Rape."

17. Koss, Gidycz, and Wisniewski, "The Scope of Rape," 169.

18. Neil M. Malamuth, Scott Haber, and Seymour Feshbach, "Testing Hypotheses Regarding Rape: Exposure to Sexual Violence, Sex Differences, and the 'Normality' of Rapists," *Journal of Research in Personality* 14, no. 1 (1980): 121–37, 121.

19. Neil M. Malamuth, "The Attraction to Sexual Aggression Scale, Part Two," *Journal of Sex Research* 26, no. 3 (1989): 324–54.

20. Bonnie S. Fisher, Francis T. Cullen, and Michael G. Turner, *The Sexual Victimization of College Women*, NCJ 182369 (Washington, DC: National Institute of Justice, Bureau of Justice Statistics, December 2000).

21. Fisher, Cullen, and Turner, *The Sexual Victimization of College Women*, iii.

22. Fisher, Cullen, and Turner, *The Sexual Victimization of College Women*.

23. Martha R. Burt, "Cultural Myths and Supports for Rape," *Journal of Personality and Social Psychology* 38, no. 2 (1980): 217–30.

24. Brittney Cooper, *Eloquent Rage: A Black Feminist Discovers Her Superpower* (New York: Macmillan, 2018). Rebecca Traister, *Good and Mad: The Revolutionary Power of Women's Anger* (New York: Simon and Schuster, 2018).

25. Mike Jones, "Because of His Past, Jameis Winston Can't Afford More Transgressions," *USA Today*, June 22, 2018, https://www.usatoday.com/story/sports/nfl/columnist/mike-jones/2018/06/22/because-his-past-jameis-winston-cant-afford-more-transgressions/725825002/; Harry Zahn, "Brock Turner Released from Jail After Serving Half His Sentence," *PBS NewsHour*, September 2, 2016, https://www.pbs.org/newshour/nation/brock-turner-released-jail-serving-half-sentence.

26. Katie J. M. Baker, "Here's the Powerful Letter the Stanford Victim Read to Her Attacker," *BuzzFeed*, June 3, 2016, https://www.buzzfeednews.com/

article/katiejmbaker/heres-the-powerful-letter-the-stanford-victim-read-to -her-ra; Chanel Miller, *Know My Name: A Memoir* (New York: Viking, 2019).

27. U.S. Department of Education, Office for Civil Rights, *Pending Cases Currently Under Investigation at Elementary-Secondary and Post-Secondary Schools as of July 31, 2020 7:30am Search*, https://www2.ed.gov/about/offices/ list/ocr/docs/investigations/open-investigations/tix.html.

28. It's On Us, "It's On Us: Sexual Assault PSA," YouTube video, 0:32, posted by "It's On Us," September 18, 2014, https://www.youtube.com/ watch?v=wNMZo31LziM.

29. It's On Us, "It's On Us to Stop Sexual Assault" (pledge), Civic Nation, https://www.itsonus.org/.

30. Ann L. Coker et al., "Evaluation of the Green Dot Bystander Intervention to Reduce Interpersonal Violence among College Students Across Three Campuses," *Violence Against Women* 21, no. 12 (December 2015): 1507–27.

31. David Lisak and Paul M. Miller, "Repeat Rape and Multiple Offending among Undetected Rapists," *Violence and Victims* 17, no. 1 (2002): 73–84; Kevin M. Swartout et al., "Trajectory Analysis of the Campus Serial Rapist Assumption," *JAMA Pediatrics* 169, no. 12 (December 2015): 1148–54; John D. Foubert, Angela Clark-Taylor, and Andrew F. Wall, "Is Campus Rape Primarily a Serial or One-Time Problem? Evidence from a Multicampus Study," *Violence Against Women* 26, no. 3–4 (March 2020): 296–311.

32. Tom Bartlett, "AAU's Planned Sexual-Assault Survey Draws Backlash from Some Researchers," *Chronicle of Higher Education*, November 18, 2014; Michael Stratford, "AAU Pushes Climate Surveys," *Inside Higher Ed*, November 19, 2014.

33. David Cantor et al., *Report on the AAU Campus Climate Survey on Sexual Assault and Sexual Misconduct* (Rockville, MD: Westat, September 21, 2015).

34. Cantor et al., *Report on the AAU Campus Climate Survey on Sexual Assault and Sexual Misconduct* (2015), Table 13.

35. Christopher Krebs et al., "The Sexual Assault of Undergraduate Women at Historically Black Colleges and Universities (HBCUs)," *Journal of Interpersonal Violence* 26, no. 18 (May 2011): 3640–66.

36. Cantor et al., *Report on the AAU Campus Climate Survey on Sexual Assault and Sexual Misconduct* (2015), ix.

37. Cantor et al., *Report on the AAU Campus Climate Survey on Sexual Assault and Sexual Misconduct* (2015), iv.

38. David Cantor et al., *Report on the AAU Campus Climate Survey on Sexual Assault and Misconduct* (Rockville, MD: Westat, January 17, 2020), https://www.aau.edu/sites/default/files/AAU-Files/Key-Issues/Campus-Safety/

Revised%20Aggregate%20report%20%20and%20appendices%201-7_(01-16
-2020_FINAL).pdf.

39. Susan B. Sorenson, Manisha Joshi, and Elizabeth Sivitz, "Knowing a Sexual Assault Victim or Perpetrator: A Stratified Random Sample of Under-graduates at One University," *Journal of Interpersonal Violence* 29, no. 3 (2014): 394–416.

40. Emmeline May and Blue Seat Studios, "Tea Consent," YouTube video, 2:50, posted by Emmeline May and Blue Seat Studios, May 12, 2015, https://www.youtube.com/watch?v=oQbei5JGiT8.

41. CollegeHumor, "What If Bears Killed One in Five People?" YouTube video, 2:25, posted by "CollegeHumor," November 5, 2015, https://www.you tube.com/watch?v=LNVFPkmZTQ4.

42. American Association of Universities, "Combating Sexual Assault and Misconduct," (Washington, DC: American Association of Universities, 2017), 3.

43. American Association of Universities, "Combating Sexual Assault and Misconduct."

44. U.S. Department of Education, Office for Civil Rights, "Nondiscrimination on the Basis of Sex in Education Programs or Activities Receiving Federal Financial Assistance," *Federal Register* 83, no. 230 (November 29, 2018): 61462–61499, 61462.

45. Greta Anderson, "U.S. Publishes New Regulations on Campus Sexual Assault," *Chronicle of Higher Education*, May 7, 2020.

46. Jennifer S. Hirsch and Shamus Khan, *Sexual Citizens: A Landmark Study of Sex, Power, and Assault on Campus* (New York: W. W. Norton, 2020). Quote from book jacket.

Chapter 3

1. Clifford Kirkpatrick and Eugene Kanin, "Male Sex Aggression on a University Campus," *American Sociological Review* 22, no. 1 (1957): 52–58.

2. Sharon G. Smith and Sarah L. Cook, "Disclosing Sexual Assault to Parents: The Influence of Parental Messages About Sex," *Violence Against Women* 14, no. 11 (2008): 1326–48.

3. Gretchen Livingston, "Fewer than Half of U.S. Kids Today Live in a 'Traditional' Family," *Pew Research Center: Fact Tank*, December 22, 2014, http://www.pewresearch.org/fact-tank/2014/12/22/less-than-half-of-u-s-kids-today-live-in-a-traditional-family.

Chapter 4

1. Harriet Harvey, *Stories Parents Seldom Hear: College Students Write About Their Lives and Families* (New York: Delacorte Press, 1982).

2. Roxane Gay, ed., *Not That Bad: Dispatches from Rape Culture* (New York: HarperCollins, 2018).

3. Hans Selye, *The Stress of Life* (New York: McGraw-Hill, 1956).

Chapter 5

1. Robin Warshaw, *I Never Called It Rape: The Ms. Report on Recognizing, Fighting, and Surviving Date and Acquaintance Rape* (New York: HarperCollins, 1988); Mary P. Koss, "The Hidden Rape Victim: Personality, Attitudinal, and Situational Characteristics," *Psychology of Women Quarterly* 2, no. 9 (1985): 193–212.

2. Melvin J. Lerner, *The Belief in a Just World: A Fundamental Delusion* (New York: Springer, 1980).

Chapter 6

1. Gretchen Livingston, "Fewer than Half of U.S. Kids Today Live in a 'Traditional' Family," *Pew Research Center: Fact Tank*, December 22, 2014, http://www.pewresearch.org/fact-tank/2014/12/22/less-than-half-of-u-s-kids-today-live-in-a-traditional-family.

Chapter 7

1. Sarah Knott, *Mother Is a Verb: An Unconventional History* (New York: Sarah Crichton Books, 2019).

2. Michele C. Black et al., *The National Intimate Partner and Sexual Violence Survey (NISVS): 2010 Summary Report* (Atlanta, GA: National Center for Injury Prevention and Control, Centers for Disease Control and Prevention, 2011), https://www.cdc.gov/violenceprevention/pdf/NISVS_Report2010-a.pdf.

Chapter 8

1. David Cantor et al., *Report on the AAU Campus Climate Survey on Sexual Assault and Misconduct* (Rockville, MD: Westat, January 17, 2020), Table 44,

https://www.aau.edu/sites/default/files/AAU-Files/Key-Issues/Campus-Safety/
Revised%20Aggregate%20report%20%20and%20appendices%201-7_(01-16
-2020_FINAL).pdf.

2. Cantor et al., *Report on the AAU Campus Climate Survey on Sexual Assault
and Misconduct* (2020).

3. Cantor et al., *Report on the AAU Campus Climate Survey on Sexual Assault
and Misconduct* (2020).

4. U.S. Department of Education, Family Educational Rights and Privacy
Act (FERPA), https://www2.ed.gov/policy/gen/guid/fpco/ferpa/index.html.

5. Marilyn S. Sommers et al., "Understanding Rates of Genital-Anal Injury:
Role of Skin Color and Skin Biomechanics," *Journal of Forensic and Legal Medicine* 66 (August 2019): 120–28.

6. Legal Information Institute, Cornell Law School, *Clear and Convincing
Evidence*, https://www.law.cornell.edu/wex/clear_and_convincing_evidence.

7. Carly P. Smith and Jennifer J. Freyd, "Institutional Betrayal," *American
Psychologist* 69, no. 6 (2014): 575–87.

Chapter 9

1. Dimitris Gritzalis, Marianthi Theocharidou, and George Stergiopoulos,
eds., *Critical Infrastructure Security and Resilience: Theories, Methods, Tools and
Technologies* (New York: Springer, 2015), 256.

2. P. Plsek, "Why Won't the NHS Do as It's Told," plenary address, NHS
Conference, July 2001.

3. Bessel van der Kolk, *The Body Keeps the Score: Brain, Mind and Body in the
Healing of Trauma* (New York: Viking, 2014).

4. Thomas R. Simon et al., "Characteristics of Impulsive Suicide Attempts
and Attempters," *Suicide and Life-Threatening Behavior* 32, no. 1 (Suppl.)
(2001): 49–59.

5. John Michael Bostwick and V. Shane Pankratz, "Affective Disorders and
Suicide Risk: A Reexamination," *American Journal of Psychiatry* 157, no. 12
(2000): 1924–32.

6. Brené Brown, *Daring Greatly: How the Courage to Be Vulnerable Transforms the Way We Live, Love, Parent, and Lead* (New York: Avery, 2012).

Chapter 10

1. William Alexander, "Look Ahead to Where You Want to Be," *Daily Pennsylvanian*, March 21, 2018, http://www.thedp.com/article/2018/03/guest -column-bill-alexander-caps-upenn-mental-health-philadelphia.

2. Amelia Thomson-DeVeaux, "A New Form of Justice for Rape Survivors," *National Journal*, May 2, 2015, http://www.nationaljournal.com/magazine/ sexualassaultcollegecampuses20150501 2/12.

3. Jennifer S. Hirsch and Shamus Khan, *Sexual Citizens: A Landmark Study of Sex, Power, and Assault on Campus* (New York: W. W. Norton & Co., 2020).

Bibliography

Alexander, William. "Look Ahead to Where You Want to Be." *Daily Pennsylvanian* (Philadelphia, PA), March 21, 2018. http://www.thedp.com/article/2018/03/guest-column-bill-alexander-caps-upenn-mental-health-philadelphia.

American Association of Universities. *Combating Sexual Assault and Misconduct.* Washington, DC: American Association of Universities, 2017. https://www.aau.edu/sites/default/files/AAU-Images/Key-Issues/Campus-Safety/AAU%20Climate%20Activities%20Full%20Report.pdf.

American College Health Association. *American College Health Association-National College Health Assessment II: Undergraduate Student Reference Group Data Report Spring 2019.* Silver Spring, MD: American College Health Association, 2019. https://www.acha.org/documents/ncha/NCHA-II_SPRING_2019_UNDERGRADUATE_REFERENCE_GROUP_DATA_REPORT.pdf.

Anderson, Greta. "U.S. Publishes New Regulations on Campus Sexual Assault." *Chronicle of Higher Education,* May 7, 2020. https://www.insidehighered.com/news/2020/05/07/education-department-releases-final-title-ix-regulations#.Xz3GsdX5dJ8.link.

Arao, Brian, and Kristi Clemens. "From Safe Spaces to Brave Spaces: A New Way to Frame Dialogue around Diversity and Social Justice." In *The Art of Effective Facilitation: Reflections from Social Justice Educators,* edited by Lisa M. Landreman, 135–50. Sterling, VA: Stylus, 2013.

Baker, Katie J. M. "Here's the Powerful Letter the Stanford Victim Read to Her Attacker." *BuzzFeed*, June 3, 2016. https://www.buzzfeednews.com/article/katiejmbaker/heres-the-powerful-letter-the-stanford-victim-read-to-her-ra.

Bartlett, Tom. "AAU's Planned Sexual-Assault Survey Draws Backlash from Some Researchers." *Chronicle of Higher Education*, November 18, 2014. https://www.chronicle.com/article/aaus-planned-sexual-assault-survey-draws-backlash-from-some-researchers/.

Black, Michele C., Kathleen C. Basile, Matthew J. Breiding, Sharon G. Smith, Mikel L. Walters, Melissa T. Merrick, Jieru Chen, and Mark R. Stevens. *The National Intimate Partner and Sexual Violence Survey (NISVS): 2010 Summary Report*. Atlanta, GA: National Center for Injury Prevention and Control, Centers for Disease Control and Prevention, 2011. https://www.cdc.gov/violenceprevention/pdf/NISVS_Report2010-a.pdf.

Borowski, Kyle. "Judge Bars Brown from Suspending Student Found Guilty of Sexual Assault." *Brown Daily Herald* (Providence, RI), June 1, 2016. http://www.browndailyherald.com/2016/06/01/judge-bars-brown-from-suspending-student-found-guilty-of-sexual-assault/.

Bostwick, John Michael, and V. Shane Pankratz. "Affective Disorders and Suicide Risk: A Reexamination." *American Journal of Psychiatry* 157, no. 12 (2000): 1924–32.

Bridges, Ana J., Robert Wosnitzer, Erica Scharrer, Chyng Sun, and Rachael Liberman. "Aggression and Sexual Behavior in Best-Selling Pornography Videos: A Content Analysis Update." *Violence Against Women* 16, no. 10 (2010): 1065–85.

Brodsky, Alexandra. "'Rape-Adjacent': Imagining Legal Responses to Non-consensual Condom Removal." *Columbia Journal of Gender and Law* 32, no. 2 (2017): 183–210.

Brown, Brené. *Daring Greatly: How the Courage to Be Vulnerable Transforms the Way We Live, Love, Parent, and Lead*. New York: Avery, 2012.

Brownmiller, Susan. *Against Our Will: Men, Women, and Rape*. New York: Bantam, 1975.

Buchwald, Emilie, Pamela Fletcher, and Martha Roth, eds. *Transforming a Rape Culture*. Minneapolis, MN: Milkweed Editions, 1993/2005.

Burt, Martha R. "Cultural Myths and Supports for Rape." *Journal of Personality and Social Psychology* 38, no. 2 (1980): 217–30.

Cantor, David, Bonnie Fisher, Susan Chibnall, et al. *Report on the AAU Campus Climate Survey on Sexual Assault and Misconduct*. Rockville, MD: Westat, January 17, 2020. https://www.aau.edu/sites/default/files/AAU-

Files/Key-Issues/Campus-Safety/Revised%20Aggregate%20report%20%20 and%20appendices%201-7_(01-16-2020_FINAL).pdf.

Cantor, David, Bonnie Fisher, Susan Chibnall, Reanne Townsend, Hyunshik Lee, Carol Bruce, and Gail Thomas. *Report on the AAU Campus Climate Survey on Sexual Assault and Sexual Misconduct.* Rockville, MD: Westat, September 21, 2015. https://www.aau.edu/sites/default/files/%40%20Files/ Climate%20Survey/AAU_Campus_Climate_Survey_12_14_15.pdf.

Cardoso, Lauren F., Susan B. Sorenson, Olivia Webb, and Sara Sanders. "Recent and Emerging Technologies: Implications for Women's Safety." *Technology in Society* 58 (2019): article 101108.

Chetty, Raj, John N. Friedman, Emmanuel Saez, Nicholas Turner, and Danny Yagan. "Mobility Report Cards: The Role of Colleges in Intergenerational Mobility." National Bureau of Economic Research Working Paper no. 23618 (July 2017). https://www.nber.org/papers/w23618.pdf.

Clery Center. *Summary of the Jeanne Clery Act: A Compliance and Reporting Overview.* https://clerycenter.org/policy-resources/the-clery-act/.

Coker, Ann L., Bonnie S. Fisher, Heather M. Bush, Suzanne C. Swan, Corrine M. Williams, Emily R. Clear, and Sarah DeGue. "Evaluation of the Green Dot Bystander Intervention to Reduce Interpersonal Violence among College Students across Three Campuses." *Violence Against Women* 21, no. 12 (2015): 1507–27.

CollegeHumor. "What If Bears Killed One in Five People?" YouTube video, 2:25. Posted by "CollegeHumor," November 5, 2015. https://www.youtube .com/watch?v=LNVFPkmZTQ4.

Cooper, Brittney. *Eloquent Rage: A Black Feminist Discovers Her Superpower.* New York: Macmillan, 2018.

Donde, Sapana D., Sally K. A. Ragsdale, Mary P. Koss, and Alyssa N. Zucker. "If It Wasn't Rape, Was It Sexual Assault? Comparing Rape and Sexual Assault Acknowledgment in College Women Who Have Experienced Rape." *Violence Against Women* 24, no. 2 (2018): 1718–38.

Estrich, Susan. *Real Rape: How the Legal System Victimizes Women Who Say No.* Cambridge, MA: Harvard University Press, 1988.

Factora-Borchers, Lisa, ed. *Dear Sister: Letters from Survivors of Sexual Violence.* Chico, CA: AK Press, 2014.

Feimster, Crystal N. "'What If I Am a Woman': Black Women's Campaigns for Sexual Justice and Citizenship." In *The World the Civil War Made*, edited by Gregory P. Downs and Kate Masur, 249–68. Chapel Hill: University of North Carolina Press, 2015.

"First Ban on Smacking Children." Last updated January 9, 2020. https://swe-den.se/society/smacking-banned-since-1979/.

Fischer, Mary J. "Does Campus Diversity Promote Friendship Diversity? A Look at Interracial Friendships in College." *Social Science Quarterly* 89, no. 3 (2008): 631–55.

Fisher, Bonnie S., Francis T. Cullen, and Michael G. Turner. *The Sexual Victimization of College Women.* NCJ 182369. Washington, DC: National Institute of Justice, Bureau of Justice Statistics, December 2000.

Foubert, John D., Angela Clark-Taylor, and Andrew F. Wall. "Is Campus Rape Primarily a Serial or One-Time Problem? Evidence from a Multicampus Study." *Violence Against Women* 26, no. 3–4 (2020): 296–311.

Freedman, Estelle B. *Redefining Rape: Sexual Violence in the Era of Suffrage and Segregation.* Cambridge, MA: Harvard University Press, 2013.

Gallagher, Robert P. *National Survey of College Counseling Centers 2014.* Monograph Series no. 9V. The International Association of Counseling Services, 2014. http://d-scholarship.pitt.edu/28178/1/survey_2014.pdf.

Gay, Roxane, ed. *Not That Bad: Dispatches from Rape Culture.* New York: HarperCollins, 2018.

Goldrick-Rab, Sara, Jed Richardson, Joel Schneider, Anthony Hernandez, and Clare Cady. *Still Hungry and Homeless in College.* Madison: Wisconsin HOPE Lab, April 2018. https://hope4college.com/wp-content/uploads/2018/09/Wisconsin-HOPE-Lab-Still-Hungry-and-Homeless.pdf.

Gritzalis, Dimitris, Marianthi Theocharidou, George Stergiopoulos, eds. *Critical Infrastructure Security and Resilience: Theories, Methods, Tools and Technologies.* New York: Springer, 2015.

Harvey, Harriet. *Stories Parents Seldom Hear: College Students Write About Their Lives and Families.* New York: Delacorte, 1982.

Hirsch, Jennifer S., and Shamus Khan. *Sexual Citizens: A Landmark Study of Sex, Power, and Assault on Campus.* New York: W. W. Norton & Co., 2020.

It's On Us. "It's On Us: Sexual Assault PSA." YouTube video, 0:32. Posted by "It's On Us," September 18, 2014. https://www.youtube.com/watch?v=wNMZo31LziM.

———. "It's On Us to Stop Sexual Assault" (pledge). Civic Nation. https://www.itsonus.org/.

Jaschik, Scott. "Anxiety, Depression, Waiting Lists." *Inside Higher Ed,* July 5, 2016. https://www.insidehighered.com/news/2016/07/05/survey-counseling-center-directors-finds-anxiety-and-depression-are-top-issues.

Jones, Maggie. "What Teen-Agers Are Learning from Online Porn." *New York Times Magazine,* February 7, 2018. https://www.nytimes.com/2018/02/07/magazine/teenagers-learning-online-porn-literacy-sex-education.html.

Jones, Mike. "Because of His Past, Jameis Winston Can't Afford More Transgressions." *USA Today,* June 22, 2018. https://www.usatoday.com/

story/sports/nfl/columnist/mike-jones/2018/06/22/because-his-past-jameis-winston-cant-afford-more-transgressions/725825002/.

Kanin, Eugene J., and Stanley R. Parcell. "Sexual Aggression: A Second Look at the Offended Female." *Archives of Sexual Behavior* 6, no. 1 (1977): 67–76.

Kharasch, Sigmund J., David R. McBride, Richard Saitz, and Ward P. Myers. "Drinking to Toxicity: College Students Referred for Emergency Medical Evaluation." *Addiction Science and Clinical Practice* 11, no. 1 (2016): 11.

Kirkpatrick, Clifford, and Eugene Kanin. "Male Sex Aggression on a University Campus." *American Sociological Review* 22, no. 1 (1957): 52–58. https://www.jstor.org/stable/2088765.

Klaassen, Marleen J., and Jochen Peter. "Gender (In)Equality in Internet Pornography: A Content Analysis of Popular Pornographic Internet Videos." *Journal of Sex Research* 52 (2015): 721–35.

Knott, Sarah. *Mother Is a Verb: An Unconventional History.* New York: Sarah Crichton Books, 2019.

Koss, Mary P. "The Hidden Rape Victim: Personality, Attitudinal, and Situational Characteristics." *Psychology of Women Quarterly* 2, no. 9 (1985): 193–212.

Koss, Mary P., and Christine A. Gidycz. "Sexual Experiences Survey: Reliability and Validity." *Journal of Consulting and Clinical Psychology* 53 (1985): 422–23.

Koss, Mary P., Christine A. Gidycz, and Nadine Wisniewski. "The Scope of Rape: Incidence and Prevalence of Sexual Aggression and Victimization in a National Sample of Higher Education Students." *Journal of Consulting and Clinical Psychology* 55, no. 2 (1987): 162–70.

Krebs, Christopher, Kelle Barrick, Christine H. Lindquist, Carmen Crosby, Chimi Boyd, and Yolanda Bogan. "The Sexual Assault of Undergraduate Women at Historically Black Colleges and Universities (HBCUs)." *Journal of Interpersonal Violence* 26, no. 18 (May 2011): 3640–66.

Legal Information Institute, Cornell Law School. *Clear and Convincing Evidence.* https://www.law.cornell.edu/wex/clear_and_convincing_evidence.

Lerner, Melvin J. *The Belief in a Just World: A Fundamental Delusion.* New York: Springer, 1980.

LeViness, Peter, Carolyn Bershad, Kim Gorman, Lynn Braun, and Trish Murray. *The Association for University and College Counseling Center Directors Annual Survey. Reporting Period: July 1, 2017 through June 30, 2018.* https://www.aucccd.org/assets/documents/Survey/2018%20AUCCCD%20Survey-Public-June%2012-FINAL.pdf.

Lewis, Melissa A., David C. Atkins, Jessica A. Blayney, David V. Dent, and Debra L. Kaysen. "What Is Hooking Up? Examining Definitions of Hooking Up in Relation to Behavior and Normative Perceptions." *Journal of Sex Research* 50, no. 8 (2013): 757–66.

Linder, Douglas. *The McMartin Preschool Abuse Trial* (2007). https://papers .ssrn.com/sol3/papers.cfm?abstract_id=1030559.

Lisak, David, and Paul M. Miller. "Repeat Rape and Multiple Offending among Undetected Rapists." *Violence and Victims* 17, no. 1 (2002): 73–84.

Livingston, Gretchen. "Fewer than Half of U.S. Kids Today Live in a 'Traditional' Family." *Pew Research Center: Fact Tank*, December 22, 2014. http://www.pewresearch.org/fact-tank/2014/12/22/less-than-half-of-u-s-kids-today-live-in-a-traditional-family.

Malamuth, Neil M. "The Attraction to Sexual Aggression Scale, Part Two." *Journal of Sex Research* 26, no. 3 (1989): 324–54.

Malamuth, Neil M., Scott Haber, and Seymour Feshbach. "Testing Hypotheses Regarding Rape: Exposure to Sexual Violence, Sex Differences, and the 'Normality' of Rapists." *Journal of Research in Personality* 14, no. 1 (1980): 121–37.

Martinez, Suzanna M., Edward A. Frongillo, Cindy Leung, and Lorrene Ritchie. "No Food for Thought: Food Insecurity Is Related to Poor Mental Health and Lower Academic Performance among Students in California's Public University System." *Journal of Health Psychology* (June 1, 2018): 1359105318783028.

May, Emmeline, and Blue Seat Studios. "Tea Consent." YouTube video, 2:50. Posted by "Emmeline May and Blue Seat Studios," May 12, 2015. https://www.youtube.com/watch?v=oQbei5JGiT8.

Miller, Chanel. *Know My Name: A Memoir*. New York: Viking, 2019.

National Center for Education Statistics. *Digest of Education Statistics: 2018*. Washington, DC: U.S. Department of Education National Center for Education Statistics, 2019. https://nces.ed.gov/programs/digest/d19/tables/dt19_302.20.asp?current=yes.

Onesick mind. "I Remove the Condom Without Them Knowing During 'Stealth' Sex." June 24, 2012. https://perma.cc/453V-PPQJ.

Orenstein, Peggy. *Girls & Sex: Navigating the Complicated New Landscape*. New York: HarperCollins, 2016.

Orso, Anna. "N.J. Judge Cited Good Grades and Eagle Scout Status of Teen Accused of Sexual Assault." *Philadelphia Inquirer*, July 3, 2019. https://www.inquirer.com/news/new-jersey-judge-accused-teenager-sexual-assault-eagle-scout-good-grades-good-family-juvenile-court-20190703.html.

Paquette, Danielle. "Why Frat Bros Can Throw Parties but Sorority Sisters Aren't Allowed To." *Washington Post*, January 22, 2016. https://www.washingtonpost.com/news/wonk/wp/2016/01/22/why-frats-can-throw-parties-but-sororities-cant/.

Pierce-Baker, Charlotte. *Surviving the Silence: Black Women's Stories of Rape.* New York: Norton, 2004.

Plsek, P. "Why Won't the NHS Do as It's Told." Plenary address, NHS Conference, July 2001.

Redford, Jeremy, and Kathleen Mulvaney Hoyer. *First-Generation and Continuing-Generation College Students: A Comparison of High School and Postsecondary Experiences.* U.S. Department of Education: Stats in Brief, September 2017 NCES 2018–009. https://nces.ed.gov/pubs2018/2018009.pdf.

Rodger, Elliot. "My Twisted World: The Story of Elliot Rodger." News Documents, "The Manifesto of Elliot Rodger." *New York Times*, May 25, 2014. https://www.nytimes.com/interactive/2014/05/25/us/shooting-document.html.

Rose, Stephanie F., and Michael W. Firmin. "African-American Students on a Predominantly White University Campus: Qualitative Research Findings." *Psychological Studies* 58, no. 1 (2013): 58–65.

Russell, Diana E. "The Prevalence and Incidence of Forcible Rape of Females." *Victimology* 7 (1983): 81–93.

Selye, Hans. *The Stress of Life.* New York: McGraw-Hill, 1956.

Sexual Assault Support Center. "The History of Rape Laws." https://prezi.com/fo9lruzwgovn/the-history-of-rape-laws/.

Shapiro, T. Rees. "Expelled for Sex Assault, Young Men Are Filing More Lawsuits to Clear Their Names." *Washington Post*, April 28, 2017. https://www.washingtonpost.com/local/education/expelled-for-sex-assault-young-men-are-filing-more-lawsuits-to-clear-their-names/2017/04/27/c2cfb1d2-0d89-11e7-9b0d-d27c98455440_story.html?tid=ss_tw&utm_term=.a90429a-6ba3b.

Shor, Eran, and Kimberly Seida. "'Harder and Harder'? Is Mainstream Pornography Becoming Increasingly Violent and Do Viewers Prefer Violent Content?" *Journal of Sex Research* 56 (2019): 16–28.

Simon, Thomas R., Alan C. Swann, Kenneth E. Powell, Lloyd B. Potter, Marcie-jo Kresnow, and Patrick W. O'Carroll. "Characteristics of Impulsive Suicide Attempts and Attempters." *Suicide and Life-Threatening Behavior* 32, no. 1 (Suppl.) (2001): 49–59.

Smith, Carly P., and Jennifer J. Freyd. "Institutional Betrayal." *American Psychologist* 69, no. 6 (2014): 575–87.

Smith, Sharon G., and Sarah L. Cook. "Disclosing Sexual Assault to Parents: The Influence of Parental Messages About Sex." *Violence Against Women* 14, no. 11 (2008): 1326–48.

Solnit, Rebecca. "Younger Feminists Have Shifted My Understanding." *The Guardian*, February 29, 2020. https://www.theguardian.com/world/2020/feb/29/rebecca-solnit-younger-feminists-shift-understanding-give-new-tools.

Sommers, Marilyn S., Yadira Regueira, Deborah A. Tiller, Janine S. Everett, Kathleen Brown, Emily Brignone, and Jamison D. Fargo. "Understanding Rates of Genital-Anal Injury: Role of Skin Color and Skin Biomechanics." *Journal of Forensic and Legal Medicine* 66 (August 2019): 120–28.

Sorenson, Susan B., Manisha Joshi, and Elizabeth Sivitz. "Knowing a Sexual Assault Victim or Perpetrator: A Stratified Random Sample of Undergraduates at One University." *Journal of Interpersonal Violence* 29 (2014): 394–416.

Sorenson, Susan B., Judith A. Stein, Judith M. Siegel, Jacqueline M. Golding, and M. Audrey Burnam. "The Prevalence of Adult Sexual Assault: The Los Angeles Epidemiologic Catchment Area Project." *American Journal of Epidemiology* 126, no. 6 (December 1987): 1154–64.

Spinelli, Dan. "Flyers Cover Campus with Suggestive Email, Saying, 'This Is What Rape Culture Looks Like.'" *Daily Pennsylvanian* (Philadelphia, PA), September 6, 2016. https://www.thedp.com/article/2016/09/rape-culture-flyers.

Stratford, Michael. "AAU Pushes Climate Surveys." *Inside Higher Ed*, November 19, 2014.

Substance Abuse and Mental Health Services Administration (SAMHSA). *2015 National Survey on Drug Use and Health (NSDUH): Detailed Tables.* Rockville, MD: Substance Abuse and Mental Health Services Administration Center for Behavioral Health Statistics and Quality, September 8, 2016. https://www.samhsa.gov/data/sites/default/files/NSDUH-DetTabs-2015/NSDUH-DetTabs-2015/NSDUH-DetTabs-2015.pdf.

Swartout, Kevin M., Mary P. Koss, Jacquelyn W. White, Martie P. Thompson, Antonia Abbey, and Alexandra L. Bellis. "Trajectory Analysis of the Campus Serial Rapist Assumption." *JAMA Pediatrics* 169, no. 12 (2015): 1148–54.

Thomson-DeVeaux, Amelia. "A New Form of Justice for Rape Survivors." *National Journal*, May 2, 2015. http://www.nationaljournal.com/magazine/sexualassaultcollegecampuses20150501 2/12.

Traister, Rebecca. *Good and Mad: The Revolutionary Power of Women's Anger.* New York: Simon and Schuster, 2018.

Trends in College Pricing 2019. College Board, Trends in Higher Education, 2019. https://research.collegeboard.org/pdf/trends-college-pricing-2019-full-report.pdf.

U.S. Department of Education, Family Educational Rights and Privacy Act (FERPA). https://www2.ed.gov/policy/gen/guid/fpco/ferpa/index.html.

U.S. Department of Education, Office for Civil Rights. "Nondiscrimination on the Basis of Sex in Education Programs or Activities Receiving Federal Financial Assistance." *Federal Register* 83, no. 230 (November 29, 2018): 61462–61499, 61462.

———. *Pending Cases Currently Under Investigation at Elementary-Secondary and Post-Secondary Schools as of July 31, 2020 7:30am Search*. https://www2.ed.gov/about/offices/list/ocr/docs/investigations/open-investigations/tix.html.

van der Kolk, Bessel. *The Body Keeps the Score: Brain, Mind and Body in the Healing of Trauma*. New York: Viking, 2014.

Wade, Lisa. *American Hookup: The New Culture of Sex on Campus*. New York: Norton, 2017.

Warshaw, Robin. *I Never Called It Rape: The Ms. Report on Recognizing, Fighting, and Surviving Date and Acquaintance Rape*. New York: HarperCollins, 1988.

———. *I Never Called It Rape—Updated Edition: The Ms. Report on Recognizing, Fighting, and Surviving Date and Acquaintance Rape*. New York: HarperCollins, 2019.

Winfield, Idee, Linda K. George, Marvin Swartz, and Dan G. Blazer. "Sexual Assault and Psychiatric Disorders among a Community Sample of Women." *American Journal of Psychiatry* 147, no. 3 (1990): 335–41.

Wright, Paul J., Robert S. Tokunaga, and Ashley Kraus. "A Meta-Analysis of Pornography Consumption and Actual Acts of Sexual Aggression in General Population Studies." *Journal of Communication* 66, no. 1 (2016): 183–205.

Zahn, Harry. "Brock Turner Released from Jail After Serving Half His Sentence." *PBS NewsHour*, September 2, 2016. https://www.pbs.org/newshour/nation/brock-turner-released-jail-serving-half-sentence.

Index

About the Author

Susan B. Sorenson, PhD, professor at the University of Pennsylvania, is a public health researcher and clinical psychologist. Her research, teaching, community work, advisory service, and legislative testimony focus on understanding and preventing violence.

9 781538 117729